THE VOICE OF SILENCE
THE STORY OF THE JEWISH UNDERGROUND IN THE USSR

Jews of Russia & Eastern Europe and Their Legacy

Series Editor
   Maxim D. Shrayer (Boston College)

Editorial Board
   Karel Berkhoff (NIOD Institute for War, Holocaust, and Genocide Studies)
   Jeremy Hicks (Queen Mary University of London)
   Brian Horowitz (Tulane University)
   Luba Jurgenson (Universite ParisIV—Sorbonne)
   Roman Katsman (Bar-Ilan University)
   Dov-Ber Kerler (Indiana University)
   Vladimir Khazan (Hebrew University of Jerusalem)
   Alice Nakhimovsky (Colgate University)
   Antony Polonsky (Brandeis University)
   Jonathan D. Sarna (Brandeis University)
   David Shneer (University of Colorado at Boulder)
   Anna Shternshis (University of Toronto)
   Leona Toker (Hebrew University of Jerusalem)
   Mark Tolts (Hebrew University of Jerusalem)

THE VOICE OF SILENCE
THE STORY OF THE JEWISH UNDERGROUND IN THE USSR

Ephraim (Alexander) Kholmyansky

BOSTON
2021

Library of Congress Cataloging-in-Publication Data

Names: Kholmyansky, Ephraim, 1950- author.
Title: The voice of silence : the story of the Jewish underground in the
   USSR / Ephraim (Alexander) Kholmyansky.
Description: Boston : Academic Studies Press, 2021. | Series: Jews
   of Russia & Eastern Europe and their legacy
Identifiers: LCCN 2021016568 (print) | LCCN 2021016569 (ebook) |
   ISBN 9781644695913 (paperback) | ISBN 9781644696811 (adobe pdf) |
   ISBN 9781644695937 (epub)
Subjects: LCSH: Kholmyansky, Ephraim, 1950- | Jews—Soviet
   Union—Biography. | Refuseniks—Biography. | Political prisoners—Soviet
   Union—Biography. | Israel—Emigration and immigration—Biography.
Classification: LCC DS134.93.K45 A3 2021 (print) | LCC DS134.93.K45
   (ebook) | DDC 365/.45092 [B]—dc23
LC record available at https://lccn.loc.gov/2021016568
LC ebook record available at https://lccn.loc.gov/2021016569

Copyright © 2014, 2021 Ephraim Kholmyansky
Edited by: Marie Cochran, Judy Lash Balint, Esther Frumkin

All rights reserved. No part of this book may be reproduced or transmitted by any means, whether electronic, mechanical, photocopying or otherwise, without the prior written permission of the copyright holder. Permission requests should be sent to the address below.

For permissions contact: Ephraim Kholmyansky
http://www.jewish-freedom.net/en

ISBN 9781644695913 (paperback)
ISBN 9781644696811 (adobe pdf)
ISBN 9781644695937 (epub)

Book design by Tatiana Vernikov
Cover design by Ivan Grave

Published by Academic Studies Press
1577 Beacon Street
Brookline, MA 02446, USA
www.academicstudiespress.com

Dedicated to my parents,

Rosa Chaya and Grigory Kholmyansky,

of blessed memory

Contents

Acknowledgments   8

Introduction   12

PART ONE

Chapter 1   20
Chapter 2   38
Chapter 3   61
Chapter 4   91
Chapter 5   121

PART TWO

Chapter 6   144
Chapter 7   177
Chapter 8   203
Chapter 9   228
Chapter 10   251

List of Figures   276

Index   281

Acknowledgments

This book is not intended to be an exhaustive account of the struggle of the Jewish national movement in the Soviet Union. The ultimate success of the movement was a work of many hands. If I have not given equal space to some of the Jewish activists or our allies abroad, it is solely in order to keep the book down to a manageable size; all these courageous, talented, and generous people are forever in my heart.

My most sincere thanks go to all those who helped the cause of the Soviet Jewry, *refuseniks*, and Prisoners of Zion generally and my own case in particular. I am grateful to them for their tireless advocacy, compassion, and encouragement:

* George Shultz, US Secretary of State[1; 2]

* Lawrence Eagleburger, US Undersecretary of State for Political Affairs[2]

Lionel H. Olmer, Undersecretary for International Trade, US Department of Commerce

* S. Bruce Smart, Undersecretary for International Trade, US Department of Commerce

* Richard Schifter, US Representative to the UN Commission on Human Rights, later Assistant US Secretary of State

* Edward Kennedy, US Senator

---

[1] Each individual is listed under the title he or she held during the relevant period (1984–1988).

[2] An asterisk indicates that the individual is deceased.

Rudy Boschwitz, US Senator

Carl Levin, US Senator

* Russell B. Long, US Senator

* Dante Fascell, US Congressman

Pat Williams, US Congressman, and Mrs. Carol Williams

* Stephen J. Solarz, US Congressman

Barney Frank, US Congressman

Edward Markey, US Congressman

* Stewart B. McKinney, US Congressman

Constance A. Morella, US Congresswoman

Esteban E. Torres, US Congressman

* Tom Lantos, US Congressman

* Dean A. Gallo, US Congressman

Michael R. Steed, National Director, US Democratic Party

Hon. John F. White, Jr., Councilman, City of Philadelphia, USA

* Margaret Thatcher, Prime Minister, UK

* Beatrice Seear (Baroness Seear), Leader of the Liberal Party in the House of Lords, UK

* Rt. Hon. Roy Mayson, MP, UK

Sir Ivan Lawrence, MP, UK

* Sir Martin Gilbert, historian and writer, UK

Rita Eker, 35s groups, UK

* Robert Hawke, Prime Minister, Australia

William C. Attewell, MP, Canada

* Howard D. McCurdy, MP, Canada

Jerry Goodman, National Conference on Soviet Jewry (NCSJ), USA

* Lynn Singer, Executive Director of the Long Island Committee for Soviet Jewry, President of Union of Councils for Soviet Jews, USA

Pamela Cohen, Union of Councils for Soviet Jews, USA

* Micah Naftalin, Union of Councils for Soviet Jews, USA

Glenn Richter, Student Struggle for Soviet Jewry, USA

* Stuart Wurtman, past president of Union of Councils for Soviet Jewry, USA/Israel

Enid Wurtman, USA/Israel

* Sam Mirkin, USA

Lois Fox, USA

Rabbi Haskel Lookstein, USA

Rabbi David Goldstein and Mrs. Shannie Goldstein, USA

Irving Kagan, Senior VP and General Counsel, the Hertz Corporation, USA

* Melvin Stein, USA

Binyamin Netanyahu, Israel's representative at the UN

Rabbi Chaim Druckman, MK, Israel

Dan Meridor, MK, Israel

Rabbi Menachem Hacohen, MK, Israel

Rabbi Michael Melchior, Israel

* Ora Namir, MK, Israel

Chaim Chesler, head of the Israel Public Council for the Soviet Jewry

Dorrit Hoffer, who worked wonders in the struggle for my liberation

My dear Israeli friends who turned half of Israel upside down to help me: Rivka and Yoav Barzilai, Arie and Geula Landa, Shmulik Drori, and others from Kibbutz Rosh Tzurim who adopted me

* Sara Hammel, Kibbutz Saad.

Aryeh and Ora Ruthenberg, Alon Shvut

Ichy Fuchs, Kibbutz Tirat Zvi

Dr. Hasya Boshvits

Prof. Yeshayahu Gafni

Rabbi Joseph Mendelevich and * Yuri Stern, heads of the Information Center on Soviet Jewry

Minna Fenton and the Emunah Movement

Felix (Rabbi Asher) Kushnir

The Reichel family

My colleagues from the former Soviet Union

My brother Michael and his wife * Oksana (Ilana)

My wife Anna

I am profoundly grateful to all of you and to many other ardent champions of the cause of Soviet Jewry. Your help, your activism on our behalf, your love and prayers were invaluable; without them, our struggle might not have succeeded!

My special gratitude to * Mr. Isi Leibler for his generous financial support of this book at its inception and to Stefani Hoffman who translated a significant portion of chapter 6.

To all of you, now and forevermore: Thank you!

Introduction

Imagine a life where learning and teaching your own language could land you in prison. Where the act of passing on your heritage was deemed a threat to the public order.

Such was the life my fellow Soviet Jews and I lived during our two-decade struggle against the Communist regime for our right to learn and teach the Hebrew language and culture in the Soviet Union: two decades filled with risk, violence, arrest, and imprisonment. That I am now able to share this story with you is a testament to our victory.

* * *

In the decades preceding the 1917 Bolshevik Revolution, some 2 million Jews left Russia to resettle in the West and in Palestine. They were leaving behind a life marked by anti-Semitic persecution, violent attacks on their lives and property (*pogroms*), outrageous accusations known as "blood libels," and oppressive legal restrictions, such as those forbidding them to live outside a specified region in the western part of the Russian empire known as the Pale of Settlement.

The February Revolution of 1917 brought a temporary reprieve for the three million Jews remaining in Russia, including the abolition of the Pale of Settlement. The reprieve was short-lived: the Bolshevik takeover six months later, followed by a devastating civil war. During the Civil War there were widespread atrocities against Jews, particularly in Ukraine. As many as 150,000 Jews were massacred in *pogroms*. If most Jews supported the Bolsheviks, who emerged victorious in the 1920s, it was in large part because the establishment of the Communist rule put an end to the *pogroms*.

The Pale of Settlement, a region in the Western part of the Russian Empire (outside Russia proper), that was the only area where Jews were permitted to live prior to 1917

The nation-building effort that followed the end of the civil war opened many doors for Jews in an unprecedented way. The new Soviet government promised to build a society based on justice, the best and fairest society in the world. Attracted by this promise and encouraged by the lifting of the old discriminatory restrictions on residency and occupation, many Jews jumped at the opportunity to take part in building the new society, viewing it as part of the Jewish mission of *tikkun olam* (transformation, perfection of the world). There were exceptions: the Zionists, who saw no future for Jews outside Israel; the Labor Bund movement, which opposed Zionism, seeking to build a Jewish future on the basis of secular Yiddish culture; and religiously observant Jews, who emphasized the traditional Jewish lifestyle and discouraged excessive engagement with the secular society.

All such attempts to map out a distinctively Jewish path drew fierce opposition from the regime. Ideologically committed to a future where all distinctions of class, nation or culture must cease, the Communists pressured Jews to assimilate, branding anything that might delay or hinder this process as reactionary. Because Jews of the Diaspora owned no contiguous territory, having settled only where they were allowed to do so, Stalin denied them recognition as a distinct ethnic group or nationality and, in consequence, denied any legitimacy to the Hebrew language, the language of Zionism and the Jewish religion.

The Hebrew language was officially banned, becoming the province of a small group of academics. In contrast, Yiddish, the language of Jewish Diaspora that had become associated with secular proletarian culture, was—for the time being—tolerated and even encouraged.

Faced with relentless pressure to assimilate, the destruction of the Jewish communal frameworks and Stalin's escalating reign of terror, the Jews adapted more and more to Russian culture. Over time, their identity as Jews became blurred; most Jews became secular and began to see themselves as an integral part of the Soviet (first of all, Russian) people, while continuing to work enthusiastically for the benefit of their country. Many of them contributed prominently to Soviet advances in science and technology, which transformed the Soviet Union into a world power by the 1940s.

When Hitler invaded the Soviet Union in 1941, the Jewish population of the USSR, including the territories it had annexed, numbered more than four million.[3] Jews joined the war effort

---

[3] See Yitzhak Arad, The Holocaust in the Soviet Union (Comprehensive History of the Holocaust) (Lincoln: University of Nebraska Press, 2009), https://digitalcommons.unl.edu/unpresssamples/7/. As Arad writes about his work, "This book covers the borders of the Soviet Union as they were on June 22, 1941, the day on which Germany attacked the USSR. These areas include the Soviet Republics: Belorussia, Ukraine, and parts of the Federative Republic of Russia occupied by the German army, which up until September 17, 1939, were part of the Soviet Union and the territories annexed by the USSR during 1939–1940, the Baltic states—Lithuania, Latvia, and Estonia; parts of former Poland—west Belorussia and west Ukraine; and Bessarabia

en masse. As many as half a million Jews fought in the Red Army, with courage and distinction, and at least 140,000 of them gave their lives for the Soviet military victory. Many Jews also fought the Nazis as part of the guerilla partisan movement.

Yet, antisemitism continued to fester. Antisemites spawned slanderous rumors about Jewish cowardice and desertion. Ugly incidents erupted, especially in areas captured by the Nazis, where seeds of poisonous Nazi propaganda fell on fertile ground. Surviving Jewish evacuees who returned home after the war often found their houses looted or taken over by squatters.

The Holocaust and the rising antisemitism produced a negative shift in Jewish self-awareness. Still striving to fit in as part of the Soviet Russian society, many Jews nevertheless began to feel like second-class citizens, their Jewishness a source of stigma rather than pride. This was reinforced by an official effort to rewrite the history of World War II: the government refused to acknowledge the heroic deeds of Jewish soldiers and partisans, omitted all mention of Nazi massacres of Jews, destroyed the evidence of the local populations' participation in the massacres, and refused permission to Jews to hold memorial events at the sites of the mass killings.

In response, Soviet Jews redoubled their efforts to survive and succeed in every area of endeavor, pursuing excellence as a way of overcoming discrimination. Graduate and professional education was seen as the path to success, producing a highly motivated professional workforce.

In 1947, Stalin supported the United Nations vote to establish the state of Israel, as a geopolitical move intended to weaken Britain and turn Israel into a Soviet protectorate—a plan that ultimately proved unsuccessful. When Golda Meir, Israel's first ambassador to the Soviet Union, came to Moscow later that year with a diplomatic visit, the massive, spontaneous outpouring of support and solidarity from the Jews of Moscow took Stalin by surprise, showing that the thirty-year government effort to suppress the Jewish identity had

---

and northern Bukovina, which were formerly a part of Romania. Until the German occupation, these territories were home to between 4.1 and 4.2 million Jews—half of them in the old territories and half in the annexed territories."

failed. Incensed, Stalin unleashed a new and unprecedented anti-Semitic campaign.

Now came the turn of the Yiddish language and those remaining forms of Jewish self-expression that had been allowed to survive, including the Jewish Anti-Fascist Committee that had been established with Stalin's approval to help generate international support for the Soviet war effort: its chairman, Solomon Mikhoels, was murdered on Stalin's orders. In 1952, the best Yiddish poets and writers were imprisoned, tortured, and executed. Anti-Jewish sentiment permeated the public discourse; newspapers openly accused Jews of "rootless cosmopolitanism"—a code word for disloyalty.

The witch hunt reached its peak with the 1953 "doctors' plot," in which prominent Jewish doctors were arrested and charged of plotting to poison Communist Party leaders under the guise of medical treatment—a modern-day blood libel. This malicious fabrication sparked a wave of antisemitic hysteria: ordinary people all over the country stopped going to Jewish doctors. Stalin's death in March 1953, on the Jewish holiday of Purim, put an end to these plans: a month later, the charges against the doctors were dropped, and they were released from prison.[4]

In 1956, Stalin's successor, Nikita Khrushchev, began a program of de-Stalinization and relative political liberalization, releasing most political prisoners from labor camps and reining in the worst of KGB terror. Some tentative civil liberties began to emerge, and literature and journalism experienced a powerful resurgence. Uncensored and still officially banned, these materials were duplicated on manual typewriters and circulated by hand, at great personal risk, in a process that came to be known as *samizdat*—the original self-publishing.

For Jews, however, little had changed. Khrushchev's secret speech to the Twentieth Party Congress denouncing Stalin's crimes (smuggled out to the West for publication with the help of Israeli

---

[4] See Joshua Rubenstein, *The Last Days of Stalin* (New Haven: Yale University Press, 2016).

intelligence) made no mention of Stalin's anti-Semitic campaigns. Official antisemitic and anti-Zionist propaganda continued in full force, and the bans on emigration and on Jewish self-expression remained unchanged. So, too, was the Jewish response: Jews continued to strive for excellence. In many cases, they rose to the upper echelons of Soviet society. Eventually, the Communist establishment came to view the educated Soviet Jews as a kind of strategic national resource.

When the renowned Jewish writer Elie Wiesel visited the USSR in 1965, he saw a Jewish population that was isolated, dispirited, largely cut off from its Jewish identity, and seemingly destined to vanish entirely through assimilation. He published an account of that trip under a telling title: *The Jews of Silence,* acknowledging that the voice of Soviet Jewry was not being heard and might never be heard again.

And yet, the cultural and political ferment of the 1960s struck an answering chord in Soviet Jewish hearts. There began to emerge a new and different feeling—a yearning for new beginnings, a search for identity, a spirit of renewal. Jewish self-expression that had seemed almost extinct experienced a resurgence. Yiddish singers such as Nechama Lifshitz gained prominence. Readings of stories by the Yiddish writer Sholom Aleichem, given by artists like Emanuel Kaminka, filled Moscow concert halls to capacity. Books by the German-Jewish writer Leon Feuchtwanger were translated into Russian and widely read across the country, adding further impetus to the newly developing Jewish spirit.

On the eve of the 1967 Arab-Israeli war known as the Six-Day War, the Jewish population of the USSR numbered about two million people—similar to the total Jewish population of Israel at that time! It was as though a parallel Israel languished behind the Iron Curtain, trapped and consigned to total assimilation and disappearance.

Israel's dramatic victory in the Six-Day War literally changed the course of history. It galvanized Jewish opinion worldwide, shaking the Soviet Jews out of their despondency and dramatically changing their self-image. Soviet Jews began to associate themselves with the larger Jewish people, with Jewish culture and the Jewish state. Jewish identity, dormant for so long, was back.

Now began a new struggle for the lives of two million Jews, a dynamic, highly educated group that included prominent scientists, intellectuals, artists, and a multitude of professionals. Imbued with a new sense of purpose, they challenged the Soviet regime, seeking to reclaim their language, their culture, and their national homeland, Israel.

In their struggle against the mighty superpower, Soviet Jews were joined by Jews of the West and Israel, along with other Western freedom activists. And they won! Their efforts culminated in an unprecedented victory, eventually forcing then-Soviet leader, Mikhail Gorbachev, to open the gates to a mass emigration of Jews from the USSR. Though many went to the United States and elsewhere, this modern-day Exodus also brought more than one million Jews to Israel, causing far-reaching geopolitical changes in the Middle East.

This book is the story of the part I've been privileged to play in this momentous struggle.

Part One

Chapter 1

My first life began in 1950, when I was born in Moscow to the close-knit Kholmyansky family. Like most Soviet Jewish urban intellectual families of the time, my parents, Rosa and Grigory (Grisha), socialized primarily with other Jews but kept no Jewish traditions and gave my older brother and myself standard Russian names: my brother was named Michael (Misha), and I was named Alexander (Sasha).

With parents and older brother

In an effort to shield us from the surrounding antisemitic society and give us a happy childhood, our parents never mentioned our Jewishness. As a young child, I was totally unaware of my Jewish identity. I had heard from neighbor kids that Jews existed, that they were mysteriously evil, sinister, greedy creatures; I saw a kid in my kindergarten ostracized and treated like a leper once it came out that he was Jewish; I heard kids say to each other:

"Don't act like a greedy Jew!" But I gave it no thought, living in blissful ignorance until the day a government census taker rang our doorbell.

I hung around while the lady asked a litany of questions: the number of people in the household, marital status, and so forth. Then, suddenly:

"Nationality?" she asked.

"Jewish."

I remember the hesitant, even sympathetic look the lady gave my mother at the sight of my utterly shocked little face. I remember my indignation after she left: "Jewish? Who's Jewish? Surely not me!"—giving way to tears of grief and despair: "You can be whatever you want, but what about me? What did *I* do to deserve being a Jew?" Refusing to be comforted, I shut myself in another room, clutching at straws with my childish mind: what if we were all crossing a big river . . . and there was this bridge that broke, or one of those big drawbridges that opened, and I was separated from the rest of the family . . . would I still be a Jew?

I felt low, despicable, damaged. How would I defend myself now in a playground spat when the kids started calling names? I began to scan their faces for signs of awareness: *did they know?* Was my secret out? Oh, to be like everyone else!

My secret was still apparently safe when I started first grade, but now a new danger loomed. The Soviet regime, the best and fairest in the world, where all class and ethnic distinctions must cease, insisted on labeling everyone by their ethnic origin—including in our class roster, where each student's ethnicity was listed on the last page. For the next couple of years, I lived in fear that the class monitor, the student tasked with putting the roster on the teacher's desk during recess, might go leafing through the pages and discover that last page.

My fear had receded by the time I started fifth grade; in fact, I began to quite enjoy not being like everyone else. There was something romantic, charmingly mysterious and elusive about this. And in seventh grade, I began to make lists of Jews who were prominent in science and the arts, gradually becoming aware and proud of their achievements.

One day, while cleaning my brother Misha's room, my mother opened a drawer in his desk. I came in to get a book and happened to glance at the open drawer, where I saw a strange object: a small, tattered booklet with Hebrew letters. I had seen Hebrew letters before—in an old prayer book left by my deceased grandfather. Furtively I snatched the booklet, resolving to apologize to Misha later when he came home from work.

It was a calendar in very small print, in Hebrew and Russian . . . oh, my God: it was from Israel! I pounced on it, pored over it hungrily, savoring every phrase, every word. And what unusual words they were: *yishuv*,[5] *haganah*, *kibbutz*. Or this phrase: "the Jewish state." Was this what Soviet newspapers called "the Zionist entity" and branded as "bourgeois" or "reactionary"?

Here was another word: *aliyah*. What a beautiful word! It describes Jews moving to Israel because they want to live with other Jews. There had apparently been a First and a Second Aliyah.[6]

Carefully I closed the calendar. What a treasure . . . and yet so alien and remote, like something out of a fairy tale!

In eighth grade, my parents hired a math tutor for me. By the end of the school year, I had made enough progress that my tutor thought I might try taking the entrance exam to one of the best math schools in town, School no. 2, which was normally very competitive but just then happened to have an open slot. To my great surprise, I got in! I was elated, looking forward to being with the best and the brightest and the most highly motivated kids, but also anxious: could I keep up? And yet, it was sure to be a fascinating experience.

It was—in more ways than I could have known. My class was more than half-filled with Jewish students, kids who looked like

---

[5] The *yishuv* is the Hebrew word for the body of Jewish settlers in the land of Israel prior to the establishment of the State of Israel. *Haganah* was a paramilitary force serving the *yishuv* that later became the core of the Israel Defense Force (IDF). A *kibbutz* is a rural community in Israel with a collective economy, typically based on farming or small industry.

[6] The reference is to two major waves of immigration to the Land of Israel, in 1882–1903 and 1904–1914, respectively.

me, talked like me. This in itself was a new experience. I had never before felt this sense of belonging, because the Soviet Union had no functioning Jewish communities, neighborhoods, schools that could have allowed me to interact freely with my Jewish peers. It was intoxicating! For the first time, I felt a tightly coiled spring inside me begin to release.

School no. 2 fostered a wonderfully open, intellectually stimulating environment. The teachers were friendly and encouraging. The kids talked about everything, including both what the newspapers said and what we were able to read between the lines. I began to take part in these discussions, reveling in the exquisite play of the mind, the diversity of talents and interests. My classmates spent recess talking about intellectual matters: mathematics, history, music, literature . . .

Inevitably, the Jewish question kept coming up. We talked about Jews who were active in revolutionary movements around the world, from Soviet Communists to the protests and uprisings in France and Latin America. We talked about our unique history of persecution. And one day I felt the first stirrings of an idea, a fleeting dream: Oh, if only I could go away . . . go to a free country, where people don't live in fear of house searches, where they are free to say or write whatever they want! Imagining myself there, abroad, on the other side of the Iron Curtain, I felt a sweet sense of liberation. Somehow, a decision had been made; now it lived inside me like a piece of new and secret knowledge.

But where would I go? The daily barrage of anti-Zionist invective in the newspapers finally led me to pick up a map. The Soviet atlas showed Israel within its 1948 borders: a tiny speck of land! Good Lord, the entire country must be within range of a stray Arab bullet. How did people live there? What courage they must have!

Should I go to America, where I have relatives? No . . . Here it was on the map: Israel, a tiny country—but a Jewish country. There, and only there, were Jews masters of their own destiny. Israel was the only true home for Jews, and therefore, for me.

The Six-Day War of 1967 was six weeks away, and the Soviet media were in full cry. Their anti-Israel venom began to weigh on us; though final exams and graduation were upon us, we now found ourselves arguing less about Jewish issues in general than about Israel specifically. And finally, unable to contain myself any longer, I quietly told my closest friends about my desire to emigrate to Israel.

Alas, they didn't seem to understand: so impenetrably did the Iron Curtain loom that the very concept of leaving the country seemed unreal. They looked at me skeptically. They asked questions I had already asked myself: why Israel and not America?

Because (I said) I wanted to walk down the street every day and see faces that looked like one of theirs! Because for me, it was about the meaning and purpose of life. I wanted to use my talents and my efforts to help build the Jewish state: not this unjust, antisemitic regime, and not Uncle Sam's country, which—for all its peace and comfort—wasn't my own.

No, I couldn't convince my friends. Then, on the verge of the Six-Day War, none of us could imagine that in just a few short years the families of our fellow students would be among the pioneers of a new wave of *aliyah* to Israel, bringing official displeasure down on the entire school, which would be branded a hotbed of Zionism and purged of its Jewish staff.

In the meantime, our final exams began: a month of feverish cramming, summing up our entire school career. The only bright spot in the entire month of June was my birthday on the 5th— the day I turned seventeen, passing from a child to a youth. Was seventeen too old for birthday presents?

Evidently not, for I did indeed get a present, albeit a very unusual one. First thing in the morning, the radio began to scream about "Israel's barbaric aggression," "a treacherous attack" upon its peaceful Arab neighbors. The Israeli aggressor suffers heavy casualties! All progressive mankind condemns Israel! Dozens of Israeli aircraft destroyed!

Intrigued by the mounting hysteria, I tried to catch some foreign news in Russian but heard nothing but an annoying roar: the authorities were jamming the broadcast. Annoying—and suspicious: why were they so desperate to prevent us from hearing the other side? Were things perhaps not quite so dire?

In the evening, armed with a special receiver, we finally managed to tune the noise out and hear a Voice of Israel broadcast in Russian. Oh, what joy, what an incredible birthday present! The Israelis—I found myself thinking of them as "us"—has destroyed all of the enemy aircraft in an amazing lightning strike. Yes, they took some casualties, but not many. This was an utter, unprecedented aerial victory for the Jewish state! Sleep was out of the question for the rest of the night. Oh, if only I were there, with them!

And finally, five short days later—*victory*, a complete, stunning victory! The territory of the ancient Jewish kingdoms, the city of Jerusalem, all of it back in our hands. That I should live to see such a miracle!

The media yelped about aggression: as though it wasn't Egypt who had violated international law by sending troops into Gaza, as though it wasn't Syria who had committed an act of aggression by shelling our territory. And what about the Egyptian blockade of the Straits of Tiran and our port of Eilat? After all, what would England do if an adversary blockaded the port of Liverpool? What if it had been France and the port of Marseilles, or Russia and the port of Novorossiysk? Surely, they would use force to repel the aggressor. Thank God, we had lived to see the time when Jews were strong enough to defend themselves!

* * *

If the shock of Israel's victory astonished the entire Jewish world, it literally turned Soviet Jewry upside down. Suddenly Soviet Jews began to see themselves and each other differently. Jews who had been estranged from Israel and their Jewish heritage, used to being despised and insulted, suddenly made a quantum leap to a new reality. Almost overnight, they regained their sense of national identity. They realized that they, too, had a country—their own country, Israel, a tiny powerhouse that had just won an unprecedented victory, had made history! For the first time, they felt that being Jewish was a *good* thing.

***

After graduation, I tried to get into a top physics university but did not succeed, due to the highly competitive entrance exams combined with overtly anti-Jewish admissions quotas. I ended up enrolling in a program called the Faculty of Electronics and Computing, which trained specialists for the Soviet space program. Obsessed with secrecy, the Soviet establishment hid this program within the Timber Technology Institute located near the Space Center just outside of Moscow.

I felt that computer engineering was a useful profession that would help me later in Israel. Alas, this was the only good thing about my college experience. I quickly discovered that the student body was very different from the gifted and intellectually curious students at my high school. Nor were there many Jews. With no one to talk to, I sought my outlet in celebrating Jewish holidays.

The Soviets had closed down all of Moscow's many synagogues except for the one in the center of Moscow, on Arkhipova Street, which (together with a smaller one at the other end of town) now served the city's entire Jewish population of half a million or so. I knew it well: a nondescript, narrow street some 500 yards long, going up a steep hill to which it owed its popular name: "the Hill."

Now, in October 1967, on Simchat Torah, the first Jewish holiday since the Six-Day War, I stepped out of the metro to find rivers of Jewish faces flowing toward Arkhipova Street from all directions. The street itself was a sight: densely packed with people, from the foot of the hill it looked like a solid mass, a sea of people, in the tens of thousands, and most of them young adults—playing guitar, singing, having fun. It was impossible to get up close to the synagogue. I saw a stream of people slowly entering the synagogue and another stream slowly pouring back out into the street. These were Jews, coming to celebrate their national holiday—less as a religious festival than an outpouring of national feeling. Fifty years of Soviet rule had not erased our sense of belonging to our own people. The Six-Day War had shaken us, rejuvenated us, and here we were to make our statement!

In between the Jewish holidays, I sank back into my gray, monotonous existence, focusing on my studies while Israel and

Jewish issues receded to the back of my mind—not forgotten but hidden away, a secret dream to be treasured and protected from unbelievers and the hectic futility of daily life.

Three years passed in this way. The summer of 1970 brought explosive news: a group of young Jews had attempted to hijack a plane and flee abroad, to protest against the ban on emigration to Israel! They were caught, and two of them were sentenced to death. Once again, the Soviet media went on the attack, thrusting leading Jewish cultural figures in front of TV cameras to denounce the hijackers. In response, there arose an unprecedented worldwide solidarity campaign, and international pressure on the USSR mounted. We followed the story anxiously, wondering if these brave young people would really be executed, if there was any force strong enough to stop the Soviets.

And then, a miracle: Spain's General Franco pardoned a group of Basque terrorists that had been sentenced to death. Unwilling to appear more bloodthirsty than Franco, the Soviets followed suit; the hijackers Were saved. Victory! But there was more to come: suddenly, thousands of Soviet Jews were flooding visa offices all over the country—in the Baltic states, in Moldova, in Western Ukraine, in Georgia—demanding to emigrate to Israel. And the heavy gates of the Soviet Union began to open, letting first a trickle and then a growing stream of Jewish families leave for Israel—a sea change in a country that had imbued the very idea of emigration with shades of treason and moral failure.

What about me, my own dream of emigration?

Unfortunately, my family faced a number of obstacles blocking our ability to make *aliyah*. The worst of them had to do with security clearances. Obsessed with secrecy, the KGB had declared a whole range of fields classified, not only those related to defense but also those related to the space and high-tech industries. Ostensibly designed to protect domestic industries from American competition, in practice this policy gave the KGB immense power over ordinary people. Anyone working on a classified project was ineligible to emigrate. Anyone putting his signature to a classified document felt himself sinking deeper into the clutches of the KGB. In fact, many people who had no access to actual classified information were nonetheless made to obtain security clearances if they worked in a classified facility, giving the KGB an excuse to block them arbitrarily should they later decide to emigrate. Such was the situation of my mother and father, who had no access to any classified information yet still held security clearances, placing them at the mercy of the KGB.

My brother Misha, for his part, was happy working for a prestigious research institute alongside prominent scientists: could Israel offer him an equivalent job? And then there were his in-laws, who didn't even want to emigrate.

Where did that leave me? Should I go alone, leaving them all behind, not knowing if I would ever see them again? Besides, who knew if I would manage to make friends in Israel, or how soon. The locals likely had a different mentality, a different upbringing, their own set of problems that I might not relate to. And they, for their part, might not relate to my own problems. Of course, Israel as a whole supported *aliyah*, but would I find support from individual Israelis in my own day-to-day life there?

The solution was to come to Israel well-prepared: become skilled in my field; learn English thoroughly; earn a doctorate, perhaps; and get married. All of this would take time. I must be patient.

* * *

Another year and a half passed. I graduated from my program and got a job at what was probably the least classified facility in my field: an R&D enterprise called the Institute of Computer Peripherals. I worked hard, striving to become skilled and competent, to gain expertise that would help me later when I moved to Israel.

I did well in my job and began to be included in important meetings with the top management, even though my Jewish origins prevented any meaningful advancement. At the same time, I became aware that a man in my department, one Andrey Nagorny, a former army colonel, was likely a KGB informer. He certainly seemed to put a lot of effort into trying to trip people up in conversation, get them to say things that would get them in trouble. He might begin with neutral topics and then, out of the blue, turn to politics: about the decaying Western world, and how life over there was so awful, and yet some *renegades* and *traitors* were clamoring to emigrate there . . . He would say these things while scanning our faces for a reaction, the slightest glimpse of protest in our eyes. I realized that I must be on guard at all times, as the smallest twitch could get me reported to the KGB as "unreliable."

As harmless as my Institute of Computer Peripherals was, security clearance issues eventually caught up with me there; after all, computer developer jobs were classified pretty much everywhere. I had signed up for the lowest level of security clearance, the third level, which was really like a glorified building pass. Now, three years in, they started to pressure me to sign up for the second level, saying that they couldn't make full use of me without it because I couldn't travel for work, I couldn't access secret documents, and if so, why had they promoted me to senior engineer? The HR drone came right out and asked why I was holding out when everyone else had signed. The subtext was clear: was I, a Jew, planning to emigrate?

Work was becoming unbearable.

At night, I listened to any foreign news broadcast in English I could find: the BBC, Voice of Israel, Voice of America, and others. Unlike the Russian programs aired by the same radio stations, which we affectionately called simply "the voices," these broadcasts were never jammed, and I learned a lot from them. Apparently, there were Jewish activists in Moscow and Leningrad who got together and did things, including actual Hebrew classes! I felt it was time to move forward with the plan I had made back in 1967. I had my profession; I had learned English; now it was time to begin learning Hebrew and join the larger Jewish community.

Which was easier said than done. Naturally, the Voice of Israel did not disclose the identities of the teachers of Hebrew. Going to the synagogue to ask about Hebrew lessons under the watchful eye of the KGB was not an option. I began making discreet inquiries among my friends, but six months would pass before I finally found a Hebrew teacher. It turned out to be Lev Ulanovsky, an old friend and schoolmate.

I was struck by the change in him since we last saw each other. For a man who was under constant KGB surveillance, Lev was remarkably relaxed. There was a new dignity to him, and none of the tense, hunted demeanor of a Soviet Jew. So that's what these guys were like!

From the fall of 1977 on, Hebrew lessons became the highlight of my week: three or four hours once a week, with only a short break for tea. I paid close attention to Lev's teaching methods, not because I wanted to become a teacher but because the learning and teaching process had always fascinated me. My Hebrew studies cast a new light on my whole life: I had a sense of finally doing what I ought, of belonging. No longer did I feel out of place, as though a piece was missing: I myself was the missing piece, and I had finally snapped into place. Learning was both a joy and a revelation. I felt the joy of learning new words, yet these words didn't feel entirely new. I sometimes had an odd sense of having heard them before, back in the mystical, distant past, somewhere in prior generations. Their sounds resonated within my soul, enveloping it with a new serenity, like a touch of something eternal.

Infected with my excitement, the rest of my family—my parents, my brother, and his wife Oksana—began to study Hebrew.

By spring 1978, I began to suspect that people at work knew I was studying Hebrew. A dude from Security, who had never noticed me before, now shot me a venomous look in the hallway. Something was in the air. The head of another department also became aloof and unfriendly, and finally, the head of my own department, Tarasevich, told me to come see him after hours the next day. Clearly, there were rumors going around; I had to stop the rumors.

In the morning, I chatted up the biggest gossip in our department and let it slip that I was studying . . . Japanese! Money was tight, said I, and there was money to be made by taking in free-lance translation from the Japanese. Don't tell anyone, said I. I gave the same line to Tarasevich when I met with him that evening. Two days later, people I barely knew began stopping me in the hallway to ask how my Japanese was going. This put Tarasevich off the scent: evidently, Security never told him which foreign language I was studying.

***

I began to wonder how Modern Hebrew got started in Moscow. It seemed like a miracle, almost on par with the revival of spoken Hebrew in Palestine in the days of Eliezer Ben-Yehuda, or the restoration of Jewish sovereignty in Israel in 1948. It had the same sense of rebirth about it: after sixty years of Soviet efforts to suppress not only Hebrew but virtually all forms of authentic Jewish life, suddenly there was an entire community of young people speaking fluent Hebrew!

I asked Lev, who told me the name of his own teacher: Ze'ev (Vladimir) Shakhnovsky. But who taught Ze'ev Shakhnovsky? Who was the one that started it all?

Lev gave me that name, too: Moshe Palchan. He had long since made *aliyah,* and few people knew about him. Eleven years later, in Israel, my brother and I were fortunate to meet him and hear his story.

Moshe Palchan remembers

My parents were both born in the Ukraine. Their families left for Palestine to escape the pogroms while my parents were still little. At the time, Communist ideas were very popular here in the Land of Israel, and they had a strong influence on my parents. But the British who ruled the country at that time didn't think much of Communism (or Zionism, for that matter). And anyone who aroused the suspicion of the British security services was simply shipped back to his country of origin. So my parents were sent to the Soviet Union, along with many others.

What happened to these deportees in the USSR is well known: very few of them survived. The same was true of the many idealistic Jewish Communists who came to the USSR from various countries to build a bright future. We can only guess why my parents were not arrested: perhaps it was because they were little when they went to Palestine, and children were occasionally spared; or perhaps, and more importantly, it was because they kept in touch with the rest of the family in Israel. While most Jews who came to the USSR broke off all contacts with foreign countries, believing (with good reason) that such contacts were dangerous, my parents kept up their contacts with Israel, which meant that if anything happened to them, God forbid, the word would have gotten out.

Eventually, my parents moved to Moscow, where my brother and I were born. Besides the correspondence with Israel, there was nothing Jewish about our way of life. In my childhood and youth, I never heard a word in Hebrew—maybe an occasional word in Yiddish. We grew up among Communist ideas, which, of course, came to shape our identities. In 1956, three years after Stalin's death, when the liberalization of the Khrushchev era began, my mother requested permission to visit the family in Israel, which, surprisingly, was granted, making her the first official tourist from the Soviet Union to Israel.

She came back a different person, transformed by the experience of witnessing the Jewish statehood, something that had not existed when she left the country. She saw Jews rebuilding their own state and, in the process, remaking themselves. She was filled with enthusiasm and conviction that our place was there. But I, for my part, remained unchanged. The thought of leaving the USSR in order to emigrate to a bourgeois country seemed treasonous.

The only thing that I liked were the LP records of Hebrew songs, lots and lots of them, that my mother brought back from Israel. I listened to them over and over. These songs seemed to touch some secret string in my heart, awakening ancient melodies. Listening to these records became one of my little pleasures, something personal, intimate. I started asking the meaning of the most commonly occurring words, and gradually this remarkable language conquered my heart.

In 1963, I began to learn Hebrew in a more-or-less systematic fashion. At that time, there were several others in town who knew Ashkenazi Hebrew, besides my parents: some elderly people from areas that had not been under Soviet occupation before World War II, as well as a few linguists. This was before the authorities came to see Hebrew as a threat, and Hebrew textbooks were available at public libraries, where one could even make copies. I collected them all, but it was hard to learn without a teacher; and even people who spoke Hebrew didn't really know how to teach it. So I had two problems to solve: mastering the language thoroughly and developing a method of instruction. It was slow going for a while, gathering information bit by bit.

After the Six-Day War, when there was a sudden revival of Jewish identity and interest in Hebrew, there emerged in Moscow whole groups of young people who wanted to learn Hebrew. I began to teach in 1968 and continued until April 1971, when we left for Israel; in the last six months, after I quit my job, I spent all my time teaching Hebrew.

I wasn't the only teacher, there were others, but I was probably the only one who left behind students who themselves became teachers. This was due to the teaching method I had put together, which included an intensive classroom component combined with large amounts of homework and enabled the student to advance quickly. The course consisted of only thirteen lessons, to be learned over six months. By the end of the course, the student was expected to be able to hold simple conversations, understand the news and, of course, teach others. Of my five best students, four soon left for Israel but Ze'ev Shakhnovsky continued to teach in the USSR for many years, raising up a whole generation of teachers. So, Modern Hebrew in Moscow actually came from him.

In the meantime, I continued to study with Lev Ulanovsky. In spring 1978, Lev told us that the holiday of Purim was coming up in two weeks, and that it was customary to read the book of Esther during Purim. He handed out copies of the Biblical text and Jewish skullcaps (*kippot*) to put on our heads. We began, one by one, trying to read, struggling our way through the complicated text while Lev explained the new words. Soon, I found the text becoming less difficult. I found myself getting drawn in, feeling more and more affection for the text, feeling a sense of satisfaction and even power: for the first time in my life, I was doing what my ancestors had done, and their ancestors before them ... The Jewish holiday took on new meaning for me, a sense of continuity with the generations that came before, connecting us across time, making us into a people. No longer merely a "person of Jewish descent," I had taken my place as part of that people.

"Have you already been to see the *purimspiel*[7]?" someone asked me. "They're giving it again next Sunday." I didn't dare confess that I didn't know what a *purimspiel* was.

The apartment I was directed to on Sunday was packed to overflowing. My Lord, so many people! They stood on the stairs outside, they filled the entryway and hallway and the outer room, they packed the inner room with hardly any space left for the performers. Finally, the performers made their way through the crowd, and the play began: Queen Esther, Mordechai, King Ahasuerus, and, of course, the evil Haman—recounting the Biblical story of Purim in words layered with double meaning that, on another level, were clearly about *us*, the Soviet Jews of today, our joys and sorrows, mocking the regime with great wit, eloquence, and excellent literary taste. The whole room shouted with laughter, rang with applause. The short dialogues in Russian were interspersed with songs in Hebrew and Yiddish, followed by a cascade of jokes. What a delight!

This, too, was a change; here were Jews who were no longer afraid to gather in great numbers, to put on a Jewish performance or to attend one, despite the obvious risks: I learned that the director of this play, Igor Gurvich, had been summoned to the KGB, and the name of the writer was kept a secret. I felt a change in myself: now that I had reclaimed my own identity, my own culture and language, the prevailing antisemitism and the insults heard on the street somehow lost their power to touch me.

Eventually I got my letter of invitation from Israel, the first step toward emigration. Since the Soviet Union did not recognize people's right to move countries, anyone applying for permission to leave the country permanently had to produce a formal invitation

---

[7] A play reenacting the events of the Book of Esther.

from a family member in Israel, whether real or (more often) fake. Now it was time to start collecting all the other required documents, including the most problematic of all: a release from my workplace, confirming that I was not in possession of any equipment or other materials that must be returned. Which meant finally telling them of my plans to emigrate, the plans their snitch, Nagorny, had tried so hard to discover and I had worked so hard to conceal.

The director of the Institute, Comrade Sulim, read my request for release over several times, as though unable to process the words. Not a muscle moved in his impassive face. Finally, he jerked his head up, looking away, and spat out: "We'll get you your release. Go see Smirnov, my deputy."

I walked out with a sense of great relief. No more pretending to be someone I wasn't! I felt reborn, liberated from slavery. The hardest step had been taken; though now I should brace myself: they were sure to give me a hard time.

The next day I was summoned to see Smirnov.

"We have received your application, Kholmyansky. Are you aware that working in a classified facility, as you have done for the past six years, makes you ineligible to emigrate?"

"It's my understanding that these restrictions require actual possession of classified information. As I'm sure you know, I only signed up for the third and lowest level of clearance and never actually used it in my work. In my entire career here, I've never checked out or written a secret document, never went on a single business trip."

"But you are a senior engineer, one of our leading developers. A man with your experience might glean classified information simply by overhearing his colleagues chatting in the hallway. We can't give you a release."

Within hours, the entire Institute knew. Kholmyansky wants to emigrate to Israel! What a sensation! People in my own department still spoke to me (though some, reluctantly and others, without meeting my eye), while people from other departments refused to shake my hand, or looked straight through me as if I were invisible, or jumped and stared at the wall when they saw me pass. "Hang on," I told myself. "This is just the beginning!"

Two or three days later I found myself a pariah in my workplace. They reassigned me to a different lab as punishment. They held a staff meeting in my department to publicly condemn me and strip me of all prior awards and honors. The psychological pressure mounted by the day; I caught frequent glances of hatred, anger, contempt.

I persevered in my quest for the release, which was my key to emigration: without that document, my application was incomplete. I contacted all possible authorities, including the regional prosecutor's office, trying to get them to make my employer give me the required release, but got a bureaucratic run-around everywhere. Three and a half months of nerve-wracking efforts failed to produce the wretched piece of paper; I was beginning to feel trapped. My last resort was to mail my application directly to the Supreme Council of the USSR, the top Government authority, with a letter explaining the omission, and let them forward it to the visa office. I had heard that this irregular, and little-known, method of filing usually worked but was frowned upon by the authorities. Although it did not increase the chances of success, at least it offered a way— for me, the only way—of getting my application into the system.

I still remember going to the central post office of Moscow on November 23, 1978. A piercing wind flings wet snow in my face as though trying to stop me, to tell me: "Don't go, don't do it!" At the post office, I stuff all the documents into a large envelope with trembling hands: all these papers, three and a half months of struggle. I slide the envelope under the glass partition toward the clerk. There, I've done it! I have applied to emigrate. I wish it were easier, like it is for the rest of those applying to emigrate, whose applications are complete and who therefore are able to use the regular visa office. At least they know that their applications have been received. I won't know if mine has reached its destination or, God forbid, has gotten lost ...

But I do, in fact, get an indirect confirmation that my application has gotten there. A month later, the bus I'm taking home from work changes lanes to avoid a blockage, bringing the Institute of Computer Peripherals into view. I see the director's office window, brightly lit, and the director himself standing with his back to the window, facing some other people, with his arms spread wide in a theatrical gesture filled with amazement, rage, and helplessness. As the bus begins to move, I am suddenly sure that this meeting is about me, that my application has reached its destination and annoyed some big boss, and now Sulim is in trouble! A joyous sense of victory, sweet and hot, envelops me.

Chapter 2

The stress and strife of submitting my application to emigrate had pushed my Hebrew studies aside entirely, and no wonder. But once the tension subsided, I pounced again on my notes and textbooks and tapes, losing myself for hours in Hebrew words and idioms, reveling in the mysterious, timeless continuity. My studies were a daily relief from the oppressive environment at work. I made up all the ground I'd lost and surged ahead, making my teacher proud—at least, judging from his rare smiles and the glow in his eyes, for he was sparing with his praise.

One day, toward the end of one of our lessons, a trio of actual Hebrew professors from a college in New York paid us a visit. They were an odd group indeed: a professional-looking black man, a Catholic who looked Irish to me, and a Jewish man who seemed to glow with excitement. The professors laid a pile of papers out on the table and said they would like to test our Hebrew proficiency. We were a little taken aback but decided to give it a try, and all of us, including Lev, our teacher, passed the multiple-choice test and received a certificate of completion of a college-level Hebrew class.

Then came a day when a friend of mine asked me to take on a private student, a young woman who had gotten sick and fallen far behind her Hebrew group and now wanted to catch up. The offer caught me by surprise:

"It's way too soon for me," I said. "I don't have a method of instruction ready, and I'd hate to do it when I don't know what I'm doing."

"Come on," my friend insisted. "Your level is plenty advanced enough for her."

Me, a Hebrew teacher? At first, I had trouble imagining myself in such a role. Hebrew teachers were special people, they were honored and respected in the Jewish movement—as much for their hard-won knowledge of Hebrew and their ability to connect us with the larger Jewish civilization as for their courage in facing KGB harassment.

And yet, here was an opportunity to make my contribution to the Jewish community. I was uncomfortably aware that up until now, I had been a mere consumer, enjoying what others had created: Hebrew study groups, *purimspiels*, theatrical performances, and seminars. This way, I could start with one student and try out my improvements upon Lev's teaching methods on her before taking on an actual class.

I told the woman honestly that she would be my guinea pig, since I was a novice teacher. She agreed, and we began. My student knew how to learn languages, having mastered two other foreign languages, and became an avid participant in my teaching experiments, often giving valuable feedback and showing me how I could improve my methods. We started in March 1979 and worked intensively for two months. Then came the final exams at her university, and then she got married and dropped out of sight, but these two months had given me enough confidence to think about taking on a class in September, if I could spend the next three months preparing.

Lev Ulanovsky, however, had other ideas for me. At our next Hebrew class, he asked me if I would like to conduct a *dibbur* that summer. This was a Hebrew conversation group, led by another teacher, Yuli Kosharovsky, who would be unavailable in the summer. While our regular Hebrew classes allowed for some Russian conversation, for example, to explain certain nuances, the *dibbur* was an immersive experience where only Hebrew was spoken. I demurred, unsure that I had sufficient command of the language, but Lev insisted that this was both an honor and a service, since there was just one *dibbur* serving all of Moscow. Moreover, it would greatly improve my own Hebrew.

We spread the word that the *dibbur* would continue through the summer but only a few people showed up for my first session, which Lev later told me was normal in the summer. I cracked several prepared jokes in slow, easy Hebrew; everyone laughed;

the atmosphere became more relaxed, and people left happy and excited.

I decided to accelerate the *dibbur*, changing from biweekly to weekly meetings. Time flew; I used every spare moment to prepare. Making the meetings flow in a natural and spontaneous fashion required careful advance planning. After a few sessions, I began to run out of steam, to run low on ideas that would keep my students fired up each week. And there were more people now, from beginners with some listening comprehension to advanced speakers. It was a challenge to keep everyone equally interested and to keep it going all summer.

One day I arrived to find an unexpected guest, a Jewish girl visiting from France, whom our hostess, Natasha Rosen, had met "on the Hill"—at the synagogue on Arkhipova street. We asked our visitor to tell us about Jewish life in her country. Although she wasn't very advanced in Hebrew, together we managed a decent presentation. This added a welcome variety to our session and gave us an idea: now Natasha and others began to trawl the Hill for visiting Hebrew-speaking foreigners, who were relatively plentiful, since summer was a tourist season in Moscow.

Another idea suggested itself one day on the metro, where I found myself standing next to a man immersed in an Agatha Christie story in English. I had the same book at home and decided to translate the stories into Hebrew and present them at the *dibbur*. Problem solved!

My *dibbur* became popular, and some of the participants approached me about teaching a regular Hebrew class. By September 1979, with people returning from summer vacation, I found myself teaching as many as three groups at a time.

Nevertheless, when Lev received his permission to emigrate, I felt bereft and even a little nervous, like a baby bird being pushed out of its nest to fly on its own. Lev had given me my entrance into the Jewish life, had taught me the written and unwritten rules of dealing with the KGB and the police. A veteran *refusenik*,[8] a friend

---

[8] A person whose application to emigrate was denied, that is, one who received an *otkaz* (literally, a "refusal" to grant permission to leave), became a *refusenik*.

of Anatoly Sharansky,[9] he also handled most of our contacts with foreign journalists visiting, or stationed in Moscow. His loss would be keenly felt.

Soon after that I received an invitation to meet with Vladimir Prestin, another veteran *refusenik* and former Hebrew teacher, who was now mostly known as a leader of the "culture-first" movement. These people, representing one side in an ongoing debate about the future of Soviet Jewry, emphasized reconnecting people with their heritage, both as a means of helping them toward eventually making *aliyah* and of offering a more meaningful Jewish life to those who remained in the USSR. And the closer people felt to their Jewish heritage, the more likely they were to go to Israel, which needed them, rather than to the United States. Therefore, they said, it was essential to keep our activities scrupulously lawful, focusing on culture and avoiding the slightest whiff of political dissidence.

Their opponents held that culture solved nothing because Russia held no future for Jews, whether conscious of their Jewish heritage or assimilated. For one thing, Russia was always a dangerous place for Jews: in any geopolitical conflict, Russia would be sure to use its Jews as scapegoats. Secondly, how many Jews could we hope to reach with our language classes and cultural activities? These hundreds or even thousands were a drop in the bucket in a country where Jews were rapidly disappearing through mixed marriage and assimilation. Therefore, we should emphasize emigration and work with the international community to bring political pressure to bear on the Soviets to let the Jews out. Emigration was permanent, while the pursuit of cultural activities was a gift of the government. It could be permitted one day and banned the next. Splitting our efforts to pursue both emigration and the right to practice our culture could leave us without either one in the end.

"You are now in the spotlight," Vladimir cautioned me. We were walking outside to avoid government eavesdropping. "Your

---

[9] Anatoly (Natan) Sharansky is a Soviet-born Israeli politician who spent nine years in Soviet prisons and labor camps as a dissident, civil rights activist, and *refusenik*.

students are watching you, and so are other young teachers. A great deal now depends on your actions and how you express yourself. Please refrain from criticizing the regime and avoid anything that could be interpreted as anti-Soviet activity. Don't make the KGB's job easy by doing something they can use against you. And keep clear of the dissidents who are trying to reform the Soviet system. We appreciate what they're trying to do, but our own mission is different."

I told him I was committed to teaching Hebrew and wasn't planning to engage with the dissidents. I also told him that I ultimately saw no conflict between teaching Hebrew and emigration.

Before we parted, Vladimir took out a package.

"I have here twenty photocopies of a Russian-language brochure about the Jewish holidays. Do you want them?"

I nearly jumped for joy.

"You may give them out to people, for example, to your students, but on one condition: keep them moving among Jews, don't let them lie around gathering dust."

The photocopies were literally photographs. Xerox copiers were not available to ordinary Soviet citizens, and even in offices and factories, copy machines were under the vigilant eye of the KGB; using them without permission was very risky. Therefore, most of the materials produced by the Jewish movement were either typed out laboriously on a manual typewriter or photographed with a camera, developed, and printed on thick photo paper in home darkrooms, mostly in people's bathtubs. People passed them around in secret and read them avidly. Readership numbered a few thousand, about one percent of the entire Jewish population of Moscow.

Gradually I earned the trust of the people producing this literature. Secret doors opened before me, leading into the underground world of the Jewish *samizdat*. The *samizdat* publishers did not only produce standard materials for Hebrew teachers: they also accepted custom orders to meet the needs of particular students. The variety of their subject matter was truly impressive. Most were articles on Jewish culture, Jewish history, and stories about significant historical events, translated into Russian from English or Hebrew. Much of it was devoted to our Jewish heritage, especially the Jewish holidays and their spiritual significance.

Besides these, the *samizdat* movement published several magazines. How thrilled I was when I first held one of those in my hands, typed on a manual typewriter on onion skin paper interleaved with carbon paper to make several copies at once. My copy was almost unreadable, with blurry type and letters bleeding through from the other side. Over the next few years, I saw many different magazines, some 200 pages thick, others much more modest in size, varying in style and subject matter, but all of them had one remarkable thing in common: the names and addresses of the editors, printed in black and white on the title page. What courage these people had to declare themselves in this way, unafraid of the KGB! Their courage was inspiring, contagious, making me less nervous to keep the magazine at home or circulate it among my friends and acquaintances.

Here was a whole collection of articles written by *aliyah* activists, discussing developments in the Jewish world, the activists' personal journey towards Judaism, the role of the Hebrew language. Many articles dealt with the revival of the Hebrew language. There were articles about other Jewish languages such as Yiddish or Ladino, their mutual influences, the history of Hebrew names, and the history of Jews in Russia. All in all, a real Open University!

Meanwhile, over a year had passed since I submitted my application to emigrate, but I had heard nothing back—no response, no confirmation of receipt. The relentless persecution at work had finally led me to quit my job. I continued to take advanced Hebrew lessons and to teach, and also became a part of the teachers' *dibbur*— a meeting of other teachers where we practiced our Hebrew and discussed organizational matters.

One day, I received an unusual visitor: an American Jew named Jim Bellman,[10] who talked to me about *neshirah*, the issue of Soviet

---

[10] Not his real name.

Jews emigrating to the United States instead of Israel, something I had already thought about myself. He said:

"I've been trying to convince the American Jewish community that Israel needs these people more than America does, but we must hear directly from Jewish leaders in the Soviet Union: their opinion will have much more weight than our own. American Jews tend to focus more on getting Jews *out* of the Soviet Union, and after that, they feel that everyone has the right to choose where to go, especially since their own families chose America when they left Russia. But if we had taped interviews with activists here calling for Soviet Jews to go to Israel, no one could ignore your opinion. I can copy the tapes and send them to Jewish communities across the United States and tell them: 'Look, here's what Soviet Jewish activists themselves think.'"

"How are you going to get the tape across the border?" I asked.

"That shouldn't be a problem. Why should the KGB care, this is a purely internal Jewish issue."

"Maybe, but I'd rather not let the KGB get their hands on this material, even if it seems innocent."

"I have a way to smuggle it out, I'll use that if you insist."

Jim turned on his tape recorder. A skilled journalist, he asked precise, logical questions designed to clarify my position. At the end of the interview, he said: "And now I will introduce you to our listeners: Alexander Kholmyansky, one of the leaders of the Hebrew teaching movement in the Soviet Union." Me, a leader? I snorted at the word, he left with the tape, and I forgot all about this episode.

* * *

I asked my teacher a question, which had been troubling me for some time.

"Lev, I've saved up some money and would like to put it to good use. Can you find a way to get it to a *refusenik* family in need? I've heard that there are many families who are in dire straits. I would be happy to help out even a little!"

"How much are we talking about?" Lev asked.

"Not a whole lot, about half of a monthly salary."

"Tell you what. That won't do much for a family, but I have a better idea. You can travel to another city to teach Hebrew there, say, for a month: that would be a much more efficient use of the money. You buy the tickets, and the people there will be happy to put you up. There are almost no teachers in the provincial cities across the USSR, but there are potential students—not many, perhaps, but they do exist. Anyone wanting to make *aliyah* will need Hebrew. The problem, of course, is that the KGB monitors all contacts between activists in Moscow and Jews in other cities. They prefer to see us all isolated, each sitting frightened in his own corner."

Lev's words made a big impression on me. We here in Moscow had been so wrapped up in our own problems that we tended to forget that seventy-five percent of all Soviet Jews actually lived outside the two metropolises of Moscow and Leningrad. As hard as it was for us here—never enough teachers, textbooks, time—how much harder it must be for the Jews in other cities! It was time for one of us to make this his priority. We could relieve him of all his other obligations so he could focus on planning, teaching, training teachers, coordinating, and supplying teaching materials to the provinces. This was an enormous project, one that would change the picture for all of Soviet Jewry.

The issue of reaching Jews in the provincial cities began to consume me. I felt their situation keenly. Unlike other countries, where Jews could build functioning communities with their own relief agencies, places of worship, and schools, where they and their children could socialize with their peers, the Soviet Union kept its Jews mostly isolated. We were seeing some beginnings of a Jewish life in Moscow and Leningrad, but fully three-quarters of our Jewish population, a million and a half people, went unserved. If it took me six months to find a Hebrew teacher here in Moscow, what would have happened if I were living in the provinces?

Yes, it was time to make the Jews in the provinces our top priority. We must create a small group of dedicated individuals to bring the teaching of Hebrew to the provinces, and to do it professionally, systematically, and wholeheartedly, not to mention discreetly. I felt that language studies were the right place to start, both because Hebrew really was the key to Jewish cultural revival, the backbone

Map of the Western part of the USSR in the 1980s

of the Jewish national movement, and because the Soviet authorities would look truly ridiculous in the eyes of international public opinion if they tried to crack down on grassroots efforts to teach a language.

When, not *if*. The KGB would surely do everything in their power to try and prevent the spread of Jewish national sentiment across the USSR. They probably cared less about our Jewish activities in Moscow and Leningrad, which gave their Jewish department its reason for being. But to allow the dangerous contagion of Jewish nationalism to spread across the entire country—the KGB would never stand for it. Undoubtedly, there was danger in joining the kind of group I was proposing.

And then there were the logistical problems. This was uncharted territory: no one knew how to operate in the provincial cities, how to locate potential students, how to teach, where to get enough training materials for everyone.

I broached the issue with Yuli Kosharovsky on Chanukkah, in December 1979, while we were walking back from a teachers' *dibbur*. "Yuli," I whispered, taking him aside, "there's something I've been meaning to talk to you about. The other cities: we haven't been thinking about them enough. Do you know what I'm saying?"

Yuli jumped and grabbed me by the arm. "Awesome, I've been thinking about this myself! Great idea! Let's get together and talk soon."

We met a few days later at his place to talk—or what went by that name in our crazy environment. Yuli's apartment, like those of many other activists, was bugged; there was little doubt that the KGB would hear every word we said. Therefore, the only things uttered out loud were meaningless grunts or trivialities; everything important was written down on a child's erasable drawing tablet. It wasn't terribly convenient, but the tablet could be wiped clean with a sweep of the hand in case the KGB came knocking on the door. All of us got so used to using these tablets that to sit down to talk without one came to feel like sitting down to eat without a fork or a spoon.

Yuli Kosharovsky with his wife and son

We agreed that our goal was to replicate in the provinces everything Jews in Moscow and Leningrad already enjoyed: cultural life, the Jewish *samizdat*, religious activities, Jewish holidays celebrated together, and visits by Jews from other countries. But the core, the backbone of all this activity was the teaching of Hebrew. It paved the way to Israel, to Jewish heritage, to Jewish self-awareness. It was harder for the Soviet authorities to twist language study into anti-Soviet activity. What's more, when people studied together, they had a reason to get together every week, they could share common problems, they acquired common goals. Hebrew classes were a way to bring people closer together and eventually form the kernel of a community.

Strict secrecy was essential. We must make contact with Jews in the provincial cities, get lists of names, find out what they had going on in the way of Jewish life. Yuli and I agreed to invite two others to join our project: my brother Misha and Yuli Edelstein, a talented young activist who had already started a second *dibbur* in Moscow. We scheduled our first meeting to take place in two weeks.

However, before the meeting could take place, Soviet troops invaded Afghanistan, triggering a major international crisis. The arms control talks between the United States and the Soviet Union known as SALT II were suspended. In a blink of an eye, the era of *détente* came to a close. As always, Israel and the Soviet Jews would feel the impact. The KGB would be unleashed. Not a great time to start a large clandestine project!

Our meeting was postponed until February. At last, we found a meeting place that wasn't bugged, where we could speak freely. We agreed not to have a leader but to divide the roles as follows:

- Yuli Kosharovsky would coordinate our activities with Israel and the Jewish communities abroad and would be in charge of funding and the supply of educational materials from abroad.
- Misha would take charge of Leningrad and the Baltic republics. His job in Leningrad included training new teachers, but also improving their teaching methods and promoting the use of modern audiovisual aids.
- Yuli Edelstein would take two key cities, Minsk in Belarus and Kharkov in the Ukraine, and eventually the whole of Belarus.
- For my part, I would take on the biggest chunk of territory, the entire South of the USSR: Moldova, southern Ukraine (including Odessa), and the Caucasus and Central Asia.

Each of us further agreed to keep up the pace of our current activities in Moscow: Misha, his IT support work on everyone's audiovisual equipment, plus his work on curriculum development; Yuli Edelstein and myself, the running of the regular *dibburs*; Yuli

Kosharovsky, the teachers' *dibbur* and all the rest of his diverse workload. This way, our KGB watchers might not suspect that we had initiated a major new project.

Yuli Edelstein

In April, Misha, Edelstein, and I left on our first exploratory visits to the provinces. I went to Tbilisi, Georgia. I was only gone two weeks, but when I returned to Moscow, I felt a distinct change. The United States had declined to participate in the upcoming Olympic Games in Moscow in protest against the Soviet invasion of Afghanistan. Tensions between the two superpowers were increasing, and the KGB had stepped up their harassment of Jewish activists, calling them in for "chats" and telling them openly not to be in town during the Olympics . . . or else. The "chats" had been going on for a while, but now we noticed a marked change in the KGB's behavior. They were cockier, more arrogant; they must have received additional authority and instructions to get all Jewish activists out of Moscow and prevent their making contact with any of the foreign visitors that would be in town. It looked like Moscow would be virtually empty of any Jewish activists during the Olympics. Only a handful had been spared a summons to the KGB, and I was among the lucky few.

Misha Kholmyansky with wife Oksana and son Maxim

In this tense, dark atmosphere, small private joys tended to become especially precious. My thirtieth birthday was coming up on June 5. Surely, the KGB couldn't ruin a birthday. Or so I thought.

Early in the morning on the 5th, I was awakened by an unexpected phone call. Annoyed, I pick up the phone: silence. Hmm, that's strange. Barely five minutes later, the doorbell rings. I open the door and see a man in civilian clothes. He pulls out a KGB identity card.

"My name is Ivanov. I am with the KGB. We have serious issues with you, Alexander. A car is waiting downstairs. Get dressed, you're coming with us."

The car arrives at the district branch of the KGB, and I am ushered into an office. A middle-aged man sits behind a desk, radiating malevolent authority: he must be the boss. Ivanov takes a seat beside him.

"So, tell us, Alexander," asks the boss, seething, "what's this organization of which you claim to be a leader?"

I am speechless. Of all the stupid things! We've all had it drilled into us to never, ever do anything that might look remotely like an *organization*. This is their favorite charge to pin on political prisoners: membership in an anti-Soviet organization. And me, a leader! This is all so absurd that I give an involuntary giggle.

Both KGB men look taken aback; the sound of laughter is not something that's often heard inside these walls. There is a subtle change in their eyes; some doubt is creeping into their minds.

"I see no reason for levity, Alexander: we have it on tape. I hope you recognize your own voice?"

He pops a tape into a player . . .

Oh God, it's my interview with Jim Bellman! I had forgotten all about it. Oh, Jim, Jim, you goose, what have you done! Did I not warn you? But you ignored me, you took the tape straight to the airport, so stupidly, so recklessly. What did I even say in that interview? Ah, here's where he introduced me: "One of the leaders of the Hebrew teaching movement in the Soviet Union." And, let's see, what did I say in response? Nothing. I said nothing,

I just snorted derisively. Well, that's some relief, at least: the word "organization" is not mentioned.

The boss glances down nervously at a piece of paper on the desk. "Well, Alexander, what do you say now?"

Then it hits me: that's a Russian translation of the interview! This guy has no English, he can't tell what was actually said. I feel a tiny bit better.

"What do I say? Nothing. This says nothing about any organization. He said 'movement,' and a movement is not an organization! Besides, that's Bellman talking, not me. I didn't say anything when he used that word, I just snorted, you heard me."

"Now, Alexander, you say in this interview that there are about 50 teachers and 500 students of Hebrew in Moscow. Where are these numbers coming from? I've never heard them before. Who gave you this data?

"That's not data, it's just a rough estimate. An average teacher has about ten students. There are several dozen teachers. That's not a secret. We all know each other, that's all."

"But even so, there must be some among you that are more prominent while others are less so. For example, some teachers have more students, and others, not as many. I'm sure this creates certain networks, certain hierarchies. What do you know about that?"

"There is nothing formal about the relationships among the teachers. There is no structure, nothing that resembles an organization. There are no bosses or subordinates, only colleagues."

"OK, Alexander, let's talk about something else: who authorized you to teach Hebrew? Do you have a teaching license, a diploma?

"Yes, I have a diploma from a college in New York. I took an exam administered by a panel of examiners that visited Moscow, and I passed. As regards licenses, you know perfectly well that there is no agency anywhere in the country that will issue such a license."

"Why, Alexander, several of our universities offer Hebrew classes!"

"The classes are tiny, and they don't admit Jews at all. And anyway, we're not talking about learning Hebrew but teaching it!"

"Alexander, let's be honest. We've got enough evidence against you to support some serious charges. You've been teaching Hebrew without a license, using that as cover for promoting nationalism and emigration."

"Are you saying that it's illegal to teach Hebrew?"

"Not illegal per se: didn't we just talk about the universities?"

"Let me ask *you*: why don't you let municipal governments offer Hebrew classes to the general public? There are municipal English classes, and no one suggests that teaching English will encourage people to emigrate to the United States. Why not Hebrew? What is this—discrimination? Plus, it would be easier for you to watch both the students and the teachers: this way you can be sure it's not *used as cover* for anything nefarious."

The boss jumps out from behind the table, and Ivanov turns beet-red.

"Alexander," splutters the boss, "you're conducting anti-Soviet agitation and propaganda! Slandering the Soviet system, falsely claiming that it oppresses Jewish culture! Spreading your corrupting influence among the youth—yes, we know all about that, too! And now we learn from this interview, which Jim Bellman—a well-known Zionist agent!—tried to smuggle abroad, that you're working to ensure that all Jews who emigrate go to Israel. In other words, you're trying to strengthen the military and economic power of the Zionist aggressor—that outpost of world imperialism, a country we don't even have diplomatic relations with! We've been watching you for over a year, waiting for you to stop, to come to your senses. Yet your impudence knows no limit! But our patience does. You've set yourself on the same dead-end course as Sharansky, and you will end up in the same place he did. Don't think we didn't warn him! Come on, Alexander, it's not too late to stop . . . yet."

"Is that a threat?"

"Of course not. It's a warning. It's really in your best interests to stop. Do you really think you can fight *us*, beat *us*? I know what you're thinking: your application to emigrate is still pending, maybe you'll get to leave soon. Make no mistake, Alexander, your application will be rejected, you're going to hear from the visa office. You're going to be here with us for a long, long time, and

I urge you to read the Criminal Code closely, especially articles 64, 70, and 190.[11] Give it some serious thought."

Something catches in my throat; I can barely breathe.

"I . . . will take all of this under advisement."

"Is that all you have to say to us?"

"Yes."

The meeting was over. I stepped out into the street, my heart pounding, my head heavy. No bus for me; I needed to walk, to cool off. I felt like a boxer who had received a heavy blow to the head. I needed to review the meeting, what was said, and how it was said, and how I behaved. This certainly wasn't one of their ordinary "chats": this was a planned, serious attempt to break me down. Now they would watch me to see how I behaved under stress, whether I was easily rattled. They would watch—which really meant that they would listen. Our apartment would be bugged, if it wasn't already. From now on, we must watch our words at all times, never let anything significant slip; we must live as though a KGB officer had moved in with us!

It was also time to give serious thought to the best way to conduct myself during interrogations. There were two main schools of thought on this issue. One, ascribed to Vladimir Albrekht, a prominent dissident, was to treat these informal (but still unavoidable) "chats" like regular interrogations and try to stay strictly within the topic declared by the KGB, ignoring all their attempts to fish for other information by talking about other, seemingly innocent things. Albrekht had published a seminal *samizdat* brochure entitled *How to Be a Witness*. I had read it and found it encouraging; it was good to be reminded that an interrogation was not the end of the world, that it was possible, indeed, necessary to keep one's head and put up a resistance.

The other, developed by Gennady (Gena) and Natasha Khasin, was to talk as little as possible during a "chat." This meant keeping silent, giving random, non-responsive replies, or repeating the

---

[11] The reference is to the Soviet Criminal Code: Article 64, treason; Article 70, anti-Soviet agitation and propaganda; and Article 190, knowingly slandering the Soviet system of government.

same words or phrases over and over, ignoring the logic of the conversation. The point was to show the KGB that they would get nothing out of you so they would give up and perhaps not summon you again. It was thought that this was easier for ordinary people to do, since it relieved them of the need to fight KGB's interrogators—many of whom were consummate professionals—on their own turf.

After my "chat," my family and I decided that I should do something to show the KGB that I had heeded their warning. I should change my activity slightly, give up something of secondary importance, while retaining the most important thing: the Cities Project. In that regard, I would go forward with my planned summer-long trip to survey my assigned territory, which would have the additional benefit of getting me out of Moscow during the Olympics.

On June 20, I left for Dushanbe, Tajikistan. It started well enough; within two weeks, I was teaching two full groups, holding classes almost daily and filling the rest of my time with meetings, talks, slide shows. Unfortunately, progress was slow, and none of my students seemed inclined to become teachers.

I found the pace of life in Dushanbe to be markedly different from Moscow. Time passed slowly; no one was in a hurry. Also, the Jews in this ancient Bukharan community were steeped in Jewish tradition, unlike their assimilated peers in Moscow.

With a new friend from Dushanbe, I took an exploratory trip to Samarkand, Uzbekistan, known since the Middle Ages as one of the world centers of Islam. Its magnificent architecture attracted tourists from all over the world, and wherever there were foreigners, there was also the KGB—which was additionally drawn to Samarkand because of its separate Jewish quarter (a rarity in the USSR) known as the Makhala.

The Bukharan Jews of the Makhala, numbering some 20,000, were more religious than those of Dushanbe. To them, Hebrew was a holy language to be used only in Torah study. The idea of studying it like any other foreign language seemed alien to them, and nationalist considerations that resonated in Moscow and Dushanbe carried no weight here.

I flew to Tashkent, Uzbekistan, with a heavy heart. In Tashkent, we already had a Hebrew teacher—Nehemiah Rosenhaus, who had traveled to Moscow for his training—but no students. Some 80,000 Jews lived in Tashkent, about the same percentage of the total population as in Moscow, many of them educated people and intellectuals, but there was no Jewish life at all; everything must be built from scratch. Nehemiah set up meetings for me with local Jews. All week, I moved from one group to another, arguing, cajoling, showing slides of Israel, to no immediate effect. Perhaps someday my efforts would bear fruit.

At the end of the week, I took the long flight to Odessa, Ukraine.

Odessa is a unique city, with its own distinctive lore and a storied past, including a Zionist tradition that predates the Soviet Union; a city that's as famous for the plethora of artists and writers it has produced as for its thieves and thugs. I approached it with some trepidation: what would my welcome be in Odessa?

They had another Moscow-trained teacher, who had done a bit of teaching among the youth and now introduced me to them. One of the girls, Edda (Yehudit) Nepomnyashchy, literally bombarded me with questions about Hebrew, about Israel, about life in Moscow.

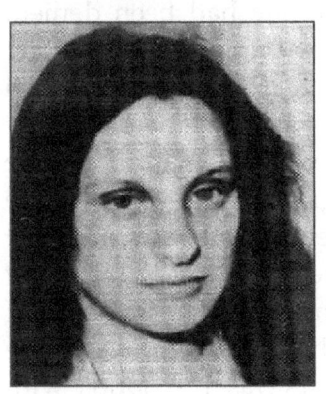

Edda (Yehudit) Nepomnyashchy

Her enthusiasm was infectious; for the first time in recent months, I began to feel joy.

Through Edda, I met her parents, Meir (Mark) and Chana (Zhanna), and their friends: Shay Gisser, a young man slightly older than Edda, and his mother, Ella. I felt that these two families could form the core of a major group. I told them a little about the Cities Project. From now on, they would have a regular channel to Moscow, to the Center. They would get access to a supply of Hebrew learning materials, literature on Jewish holidays, history, everything that was in short supply in Odessa. They received the news with such enthusiasm that I had to try to cool their ardor.

However, I had trouble convincing them of the need for secrecy. They told me that there were only a handful of *refusenik* families and Jewish activists here who were all known to the KGB, and that Odessa was a place where neighbors gossiped, so they didn't think they could keep our activities hidden from the KGB, not even their ties to me.

This put me in a difficult situation, since I couldn't tell them everything—only their own small piece of the picture. If our contacts in other cities felt the same way, it could jeopardize the entire Cities Project. Yet I could not make demands: I could only make suggestions and hope they would come around to seeing things my way.

While I was away, Yuli Kosharovsky held a summer seminar in Koktebel, a resort town in the Crimea, for teachers and advanced students of Hebrew from all across the country. Despite my warnings, little effort was made to keep the plan secret, and the KGB found a way to sabotage the seminar and detain Kosharovsky for thirteen days on the standard fabricated charge of "petty hooliganism."

Back in Moscow, the autumn of 1980 promised to be busy, as usual. On the eve of my trip, just as the KGB had promised, I had learned that my application to emigrate had been denied: I was now a *refusenik*. It was now imperative to find a job, to get on an official payroll somewhere, since unemployment (the official term was "parasitism") was a literal crime that carried a penalty of imprisonment; the KGB were known to be more lenient to people who lost or quit their jobs while their emigration applications were pending, but they were merciless to unemployed *refuseniks*. Yet no agency in my field of work would hire a *refusenik*. Like many of my fellow *refuseniks*, I ended up taking a menial job, that of a groundskeeper at a kindergarten, which shielded me from a charge of parasitism. The Soviet Union in those years was the country with the most highly educated janitors, groundskeepers, and security guards in the world.

Meanwhile, Moscow's Jewish season had begun. One of the highlights of the season was the amateur Jewish song festival known as Ovrazhki (the Ravines), which took place in a clearing in the woods outside Moscow and took its name from the nearby train station. They said that the tradition of Jews getting together on weekends in a forest clearing had been born back in the mid-1970s. For a couple of years, it was held in a place called Luntz's Meadow. This new place was harder to get to, so it never became very popular, and eventually, the festival stopped for a few years. In the late 1970s, Jewish activists Michael Noudler and Ari Volvovsky decided to revive the tradition. They approached a friend, Anatoly Schwartzman, who was an avid hiker and camper and knew the countryside around Moscow very well. It was he who found this large comfortable clearing in a forest, not far from the Ovrazhki train station.

Ari Volvovsky

The first Ovrazhki festival was held in the autumn of 1978; I attended for the first time in spring of 1979, on Israel's Independence Day. Some sixty people gathered there. A beaming Ari Volvovsky placed some logs for people to sit on and gave an inspiring speech about the holiday. After the song contest—the main purpose of the festival—was over, everyone broke up into small groups to socialize, play badminton, walk around.

I went there for the second time on the holiday of Lag B'Omer in May 1979. This time, about 150 people had showed up. So, too, did the KGB. Walking to the forest from the train station, we passed three unmarked cars and several groups of plain-clothes men. The whole clearing was surrounded by them, several sporting armbands of the volunteer forest warden brigade as camouflage. Some of them tried to mingle with us; the fellow who approached my group, clearly an experienced provocateur, tried to provoke and insult us ... and, indeed, one of our young guys began to talk back. How to stop him, how to calm him down before he got himself arrested for "hooliganism"?

Just then, Volvovsky emerged from the crowd. He listened for a moment with his head bowed, before dropping a single sentence: "We don't talk to strangers." And just like that, the danger passed.

Jewish song festival in Ovrazhki

The young hothead ceased to react and paid no more attention to the provocateur than if he were a light pole.

Ovrazhki quickly gained popularity. People began to come from other cities; now attendance was in the hundreds. The KGB hit back. On one occasion, we arrived to find a loudly idling tractor parked in the clearing. KGB men surrounded the tractor, grinning, not letting our Jewish men get close enough to turn it off. Tension mounted. The noise was too loud to talk over, let alone hold a song contest, but if we turned tail and left, Ovrazhki would be finished: next time they would bring ten tractors.

Suddenly, a little girl, the daughter of a fellow Jew, Boris Chernobylsky, broke away from him with a cry and ran toward the tractor. Before the KGB men could react, Boris ran after her: a split second, and he was in the cab. He switched off the tractor, took the keys and, holding his child, jumped down. Coming to their senses, the infuriated KGB men tried to seize him, but the Jews surrounded him with a human shield. Apparently, the KGB had no instructions to arrest people that day, so Boris was safe. (Not for long, unfortunately; they got him later, at the end of 1981, when he was arrested, sentenced to a year in prison, and sent to Siberia.)

The next song contest that I attended in the fall of 1980, after my summer trip to other cities, drew as many as two thousand Jews. For many of them, it was their first time seeing Jewish activists and hearing these issues discussed. This was an unprecedented show of strength that would stay in people's memories, keeping our spirits high for months to come, especially now that the authorities were slowly turning off the spigot of emigration.

But the next time the train from Moscow carrying Jews to Ovrazhki simply did not stop at the station. Nor did it stop at the next station, where soldiers were lined up at the platform right up to the edge, leaving no room at all to step off the train. The few intrepid souls that tried to get off at the next stop after that and make their way back to the forest were turned back by another solid line of soldiers. The KGB had finally succeeded in killing the Ovrazhki gatherings.

A new wave of KGB persecution broke out in Odessa. They hauled every single Jewish activist in for questioning; they searched the homes of the Nepomnyashchy, Gisser, Kofman, and Mesh families. Odessa was quickly becoming the capital of KGB harassment and intimidation. In desperation, our friends from Odessa began to call me directly at home, throwing precautions to the wind. A frantic Edda Nepomnyashchy called me just as the KGB were pounding on her door, threatening to break it down. I shuddered each time I heard the distinctive ring of a long-distance phone call: someone was in trouble!

A few days later, Edda called again to say that Shay Gisser had been arrested and given fifteen days of administrative detention. "They're forcing him to carry heavy buckets of cement, and he's got a back problem!"

"Beasts, they are torturing the boy!" I said to myself, grabbed a taxi and rushed to see the Khasins, a prominent *refusenik* couple and the authors of a guide to conducting oneself at a KGB interrogation. Gena Khasin was also one of the most respected Hebrew teachers in Moscow, and his wife Natasha was head of a group providing support to Jewish activists who had been arrested, known as "Prisoners of Zion." Her group provided them with clothes, medicines, and other necessities and kept our friends abroad updated about their condition. Gena and Natasha always had good advice to share whenever one of us was in trouble. Natasha reassured me that they would get the word of Shay's arrest out to the foreign media, and Gena contacted Professor Alexander Lerner, a prominent scientist who had acquired many contacts in the Western media during Natan Sharansky's trial and imprisonment. Our combined efforts were partially successful: Shay was not released, but he was no longer forced to carry cement.

Chapter 3

Once Yuli Kosharovsky had recovered from his detention, the quartet in charge of the Cities Project met to hold a post-mortem of his summer seminar in Koktebel. We all felt that, in disrupting the seminar, the authorities had clearly signaled that they would not tolerate the spread of Hebrew to other cities. Two conclusions followed. First, maximum secrecy was the way forward: no more open summer events, and no support for new cities whose Jewish activists, like those in Odessa, insisted on openly flaunting their activities. Second, we had to make the authorities think that Kosharovsky had been the only one reaching out to other cities, and that he had gotten the message and had given up on the whole thing.

Accordingly, although his loss was keenly felt, we relieved him of any further duties related to the Cities Project. The only role he kept was that of coordinating with the Liaison Bureau, an Israeli agency that had agreed to support the Cities Project with funding, equipment, and teaching materials.

Our main challenge now was recruitment. Finding the right people was key. They should be reliable, tight-lipped, courageous, and not known to the KGB. They also should be at least partially interchangeable in case one of them should receive permission to emigrate or, God forbid, should have something less pleasant happen to them. The best place to look was among our Hebrew students. We saw them often enough to form an impression of their personality and suitability, and the logistics were already in place: we could easily stay after class, either to talk then and there or to set up another meeting without using the telephone (which was undoubtedly tapped). Accordingly, we decided that I would only admit new students to my Moscow Hebrew classes if they seemed suitable for the Cities Project. I began to invite visitors from out of town to attend my classes in order to assess them, if only briefly. In this way, I signed up Bella Rabinovich, a psychiatrist from Ufa in the Povolzhye region in south-central Russia.

At almost the same time, Nehemiah Rosenhaus, our contact in Tashkent, came to town and attended my class. During the lesson, someone suggested going to visit the home of a religious Jewish family, who were holding a traditional Shabbat observance, the *Kabbalat Shabbat*. This was another facet of the post-1967 Jewish revival: some families were returning to Judaism and integrating religious observance into their daily lives. Our own movement at that time emphasized the Hebrew language and Jewish culture rather than religious aspects, and most of us had been raised atheist, but this sounded like an interesting thing to see. Why not? Jewish religion was an integral part of our culture; besides, this would give our guests a chance to witness something they had never seen before. So the three of us—Nehemiah, Bella, and I—went together to the religious family's apartment. We were pleasantly surprised by the relaxed, intimate atmosphere; we found our hearts responding to the traditional Jewish melodies chanted by the host. Long afterwards, my thoughts kept bringing me back to that Kabbalat Shabbat, with its peculiar, quiet charm.

In the meantime, the ever-vigilant KGB also redoubled its pressure on the Jewish *samizdat*. Though *samizdat* writers always practiced strict self-censorship, avoiding any criticism of the Soviet regime, the very existence of a free Jewish press was intolerable to the regime. To us, however, it was a great psychological boost. Persecution had eased off in the aftermath of Khrushchev's "thaw," and although *détente* had ended with the Soviet invasion of Afghanistan, so long as the magazines were circulating, we felt that perhaps a new "ice age" was not yet upon us.

Now, however, the KGB came down hard on the most popular magazine, *Tarbut* ("culture" in Hebrew), which had been created by Vladimir Prestin several years ago and featured articles by many prominent Jewish activists. Understanding that a magazine of this size required a pool of professional typists, the KGB redoubled its search for them. Finally, the pressure grew so heavy that the publication of *Tarbut* ceased. Two other Moscow-based attempts at publishing a *samizdat* magazine—*Our Hebrew*, devoted exclusively to the Hebrew language, linguistics, and teaching methods, and *Magid* ("storyteller" in Hebrew)—fared no better; their founder received an official warning from the state prosecutor. A Leningrad-based *Leningrad Jewish Almanac* (abbreviated *LEA*) lasted much longer, but eventually it, too, was closed down.

* * *

As though someone had looked into my heart and decided that I needed encouragement, I began to receive letters from Israel, from total strangers. Among others, a young woman named Rivka Barzilai from Kibbutz Rosh Tzurim began to write to me. A mother with two small children, somehow she found time to help me, to encourage me: how wonderfully uplifting! Deciphering hand-written Hebrew was also a new challenge. But how could I respond to her? I couldn't write a single word to her about the work I was living and breathing, my clandestine project, especially since the KGB were undoubtedly reading all mail to and from foreign countries. Besides, I was a big-city man while she lived on a tiny kibbutz: what did I know about agriculture?

But Rivka persisted, and soon I began to feel bad about not answering. I sent back a few lines—nothing substantive, just mere politeness. She responded immediately, writing with enthusiasm and joy. Over time, to my surprise, I found myself becoming interested in her letters, the developments in the Barzilai family

Rivka Barzilai

and her kibbutz, the agricultural cycle. These people were not just ordinary farmers—they were farming *our* land, the same land from which we had been expelled two thousand years ago and where we had only recently returned! Farming this land was a mission, a matter of national survival.

* * *

The failure of the Koktebel seminar did not turn us off to the idea of a summer Hebrew-language camp for the cities. Of course, it must be held in secret. Thorough advance preparation was key: another failure could foreclose this avenue for many years to come. The camp should be small, eight to ten participants at most; only key people—teachers and local Jewish leaders—should be invited, and only those who could be trusted not to divulge the actual location of the camp. We had to find a way to thoroughly brief everyone in advance, both to tell them when and where the camp would be held and to lay down some precautions: for example, everyone should assume they were watched and be sure to make it look as though they were leaving town to go on vacation. But finding a way to brief everyone was a challenge, since the authorities eavesdropped on our phone conversations and read our mail (and the Internet, of course, was decades in the future.) One of us could meet with some of the potential candidates during their visits to Moscow; as for the rest, someone would have to travel to their cities to brief them in person. Despite the effort, expense, and uncertainty involved (what if the person was away when the traveler arrived?), this way was the safest because at the time, railroads were not checking or keeping track of travelers' identities.

Our next two recruits were Golda Akhiyezer, a young teacher of Hebrew with a mop of fiery-red hair who was planning to move to Tbilisi, and Reuven Ben-Shalom, a young man whose courage and dedication I had noticed in class. Reuven was invited to join after he agreed to store our cache of educational materials for the Cities Project when the man who was keeping them for us began to fear a house search. Reuven took over the storage of materials, including searching for new storage locations.

Golda Akhiyezer

Reuven Ben-Shalom

* * *

By the end of December 1980, the KGB offensive in Odessa had abated somewhat, and I decided to take another trip there to assess the damage first-hand. It was a risky proposition for me personally after all those desperate telephone calls our friends in Odessa had made to me during the KGB onslaught, requesting assistance, and my own attempts to get them help. I had to keep my trip completely secret: if the local KGB knew about my visit in advance, they might set up an ambush to get me arrested.

But what if . . . Yes: what if I were to travel on December 31, the New Year's Eve, when the whole country would be preparing for the traditional all-night celebration, with lavish feasts and copious libations, and virtually no one else would be traveling? The next day, January 1, was a national holiday. Since Soviet Jews celebrated the New Year like everyone else, most KGB staff would be at home, and the ones on duty would be tired from their revels and would have a hangover.

It worked! I left for Odessa without telling anyone and arrived at Edda's home early on New Year's morning. The streets were empty; a few solitary drunks or groups of revelers stumbling around but no KGB. For the first time, we were able to talk openly and without interference. I told them more about the project and about the planned summer camp. I returned to Moscow without incident.

* * *

I was having trouble finding new contacts in most of my assigned territory, except for the city of Baku, Azerbaijan. At the same time, new potential contacts were emerging, but they were from Kiev, Sverdlovsk, Novosibirsk—cities that were outside the scope laid out by our leadership quartet. We had no one to assign to them— but didn't we have a moral obligation to them, too? How could we ignore these contacts that might lead us to new students? After all, the number of Jews living in Kiev was comparable to that of Leningrad! No, there was no way around it: one of us must take on these gigantic additional regions. Which of the three of us could do it? My brother Misha had Leningrad and the Baltics, a very active area. At the same time, he was still working his regular job and teaching Hebrew in Moscow. He also maintained all our equipment in working order and produced our training materials. Yuli Edelstein had recently married our Hebrew teacher in Kharkov in the Ukraine and lost his permanent residence in Moscow. Already, he was struggling to keep up his Hebrew classes in Moscow.

Which left me.

For a while, I was afraid to volunteer. Taking on the remaining areas—most of the Ukraine, the Urals, and Siberia—would make me directly responsible for 90% of the territory of this vast country and for 80% of its Jewish population! The workload and the risk seemed overwhelming. I sat in my room paralyzed with indecision, staring at my scraps of paper with names and addresses of potential contacts from unreached cities . . . until one day I felt as though something had shifted in my heart. "All right, I'll do it," I said to myself—and was filled with an immediate sense of rightness.

* * *

In March 1980, as the Jewish holiday of Purim drew near, the KGB turned their attention to the people who put on annual *purimspiel* shows, hauling everyone in for "chats." Coming on the heels of their suppression of the Ovrazhki song festival and the *samizdat* publishing industry, the attack on *purimspiels* continued their strategy of crushing all activities aimed at the mass Jewish audience. While the KGB had never completely stopped harassing people, the pressure was relatively mild for a while; now, however, it gave way to crude, brazen intimidation. However, neither Igor Gurvich nor any other member of his ensemble yielded to the pressure. The *purimspiels* took place that year as usual.

A massive wave of intimidation broke out in Kharkov. The first to fall was the informal Jewish University under the direction of Dr. Alexander Paritsky. Then all the other kinds of local Jewish activity were suppressed, leaving this major hub of Soviet Jewish life effectively paralyzed and taking half of Yuli Edelstein's territory offline.

I was beginning to realize that the coordination between the three remaining active members of our quartet needed to be rethought. Because my area was so much larger in size and in scope of activities, I had to operate differently from the others. What Michael and Yuli did directly, I had to do by means of organized teams, by means of an infrastructure. My activities were qualitatively different from theirs. In fact, I realized that an infrastructure that served 80% of the population could serve all 100% just as easily. Our current arrangement led to inefficiency and a duplication of functions.

For example, I needed a traveling teacher who could go to a city and give a crash course. I needed a system of communication with the cities. I also needed an organized group to take care of people coming to Moscow for a crash course. Someone had to arrange lodgings for the visiting students, find space for their lessons, and coordinate with the specially trained Moscow teachers assigned to teaching visiting students. Needless to say, all this required utter and complete secrecy. Once it was set up, it could easily serve Misha's and Yuli's needs as well as mine. This infrastructure would make their work much more efficient and would give the whole project a better chance of survival if, God forbid, something should happen to one of us.

It looked as though I had unwittingly assumed responsibility for the entire Cities Project, in fact if not in name. Should I offer to the quartet to formally take over the leadership of the project? It might be better for the project... but immeasurably more dangerous for me. The KGB loved titles: to them, there was a huge difference between informal responsibility and a formal title. Once again,

I was gripped by fear and indecision. "No, I can't do it," I said to myself; but my words had a false, off-key ring to them. It truly was time to fish or cut bait. If I didn't do it, it would not get done. As simple as that. I couldn't let the project fail. It was my calling, my purpose in life.

We convened the quartet and decided that I would lead the entire project. The others would take over all my other activities in Moscow, except for my three Hebrew classes that I would continue to teach. Kosharovsky would continue working with the Israeli Liaison Bureau and with the Jewish communities in the West and overseeing the flow of funds from abroad to finance the project. Edelstein would stop all work in Kharkov for the time being but would continue to work in Minsk and even try to expand his activities in Belarus. He would also continue to conduct his summer hiking camps.

In my new capacity, I began to meet separately with Yuli Edelstein and Misha. We made each meeting look accidental, burying important discussions among streams of random small talk. We decided to merge all our contact lists into one master list that each of us could access and each of us would help keep updated. Each of us would organize a summer camp: Misha in the Baltic states, I in the south, and Yuli would set up a hiking or boating trip. This format allowed us to create a true immersion experience, where all communication would be in Hebrew. Accordingly, we would invite only those of our students who already were able to communicate in Hebrew.

After much hesitation, I picked Sukhumi, Georgia for my camp location. A popular vacation destination on the Black Sea, it attracted a diverse tourist population among whom our Jewish faces would be less conspicuous. I sent a new project member, Alex Bayevsky from one of my Moscow classes, to Sukhumi to rent space for the camp.

Another piece of my project infrastructure fell into place when I recruited a Moscow-based teacher for visiting students from the provinces, Eugene Gurevich, an old friend who had taken Hebrew classes with me under Lev Ulanovsky. Eugene had recently married, and his wife was expecting a baby, but still he agreed to help and to be trained in teaching crash courses in Hebrew. This was no small thing: it required him to be always available, ready to drop everything on short notice in order to sequester himself with a visiting student and try to pack as much knowledge as possible into the student's head over a week or two of intensive study that would leave the student with both language proficiency and teaching skills.

In April, I went to Kiev to assess the situation. I found Kiev to be a tough environment, and not only because of the KGB. The local activists were divided, mistrusted one another, and didn't work well together. I had three contacts, all of whom I had previously met in Moscow: Joseph Berenstein, Lev Elbert, and the Ute family.

Clara Schwartzman

Joseph Berenstein

Elbert was known to the authorities as a Hebrew teacher and, although he kept his class very small, the KGB watched him closely. Berenstein and Ute were known primarily as activists for *aliyah*. The KGB were apparently still unaware of the Berenstein family's interest in Hebrew, so I decided to start with them. Cautiously, I told them a little about the Cities Project, and the daughter of the family, Chaya, enthusiastically joined the project.

Upon my return to Moscow, I made another recruit: Clara Schwartzman, who was visiting from Kishinev in Moldova. Born in Kishinev, Clara had done her university studies in Moscow, where she got in touch with Jewish circles and took Hebrew classes from

Ze'ev Shakhnovsky's wife, returning to Kishinev after graduation. Here was someone who was virtually ready to be a teacher, and in a key city, too: a valuable asset and a prime candidate for my summer camp.

Clara came up with a secure method for communicating and sending packages, using an old friend of hers in Moscow, Anya Yerukhimovich, who kept in touch with Clara and even traveled occasionally to Kishinev to see her.

* * *

My summer camp in Sukhumi was scheduled for August 1981, the peak of the holiday season. The greatest difficulty lay in finding a way to leave town without the KGB noticing. I took a month's leave from work, since my kindergarten was closed for the summer, and told everyone I was going to the Baltic Sea on vacation, to throw off KGB eavesdroppers. In fact, I used half of my time to make a tour of several cities in the Ukraine and Moldova to promote the study of Hebrew to Jewish groups there, before making my way to Sukhumi via a circuitous route, traveling by train, plane, boat, and hitchhiking. Each of my students faced the same problem in their hometown. Thankfully, everything went smoothly enough, and finally we all gathered in Sukhumi. How glad I was to see them!

Our rented apartment proved clearly unsuitable for holding classes: the walls were thin, and the landlord or his family would hear everything. The space was only good for sleeping. But some of my students had already explored the area and found two high hills nearby with some bushes and trees, even a small grove, such that no one could see or hear us. Great! There was room enough there for two groups, so we wouldn't get in each other's way but could still keep an eye on each other just in case. I decided to hold the academic segment in strict seclusion but allow people to practice their Hebrew in ordinary conversations outside class, even in our apartment, thinking that in Sukhumi's multilingual environment they would stand out less. After all, the whole point of this was to let people talk!

I taught the more advanced group, and Golda Akhiyezer taught the beginners, but I gave grammar lessons to both groups. We aimed at giving them both the Hebrew and some teaching skills, since all our students were to become teachers. I used the conversation prompts I had tested in my advanced group in Moscow to stimulate discussion; so passionate did our students become about the topics that they forgot they were in class!

Very soon, to my great satisfaction, I began to see changes in our students. Not only were they speaking more fluently with their teacher, and even with one another, but their demeanor, their gaze, their gait also changed. Already there was in each of them something of a free, proud person who knew that he (or she) was doing a good thing. And doing it well! We felt the first taste of success, especially since we saw no sign of any surveillance or KGB attempts at entrapment. I also was enjoying myself, but the anxiety never left me: the KGB might not show themselves until the very last minute, like they had done in Koktebel.

In fact, as the end of our stay drew near, our landlords grew increasingly nosy. Apparently, we stood out even in the incredible diversity of Sukhumi—not by our speech but by our conduct. We were too quiet: no loud music, no dancing, no drunken antics, no flirting, none of the typical behavior of a group of young people vacationing together. The landlord's family invited us over for a cup of tea—an invitation we couldn't refuse without giving offense to their Georgian hospitality. After a lengthy introduction they began to question us.

"And who might you be? Are you scientists, students . . . ?"

We tried to laugh it off, but it soon began to look like an interrogation.

"We're just a group of friends on vacation."

"And what's that language you're speaking all the time?"

"It's our Jewish language. You Georgians speak your language, and we speak our language."

"But we know a lot of Jews, and they don't have a language: they all speak Russian, or Georgian, if they are Georgian Jews. There's something fishy here."

"That's right, many Jews don't know their own language, but we do. Imagine a Georgian who was born and raised in Moscow—would he know the Georgian language? And anyway, why should you care?"

"No, you're hiding something. You better tell us what it is, or we'll call the authorities!"

What should we do? Ignore their threats? They would report us to the KGB. Should we offer them more money? That would mean admitting that we were, in fact, doing something wrong. They might take the money and still report us to the KGB—and even say that we had tried to bribe them! Neither option was looking good. In the end, we let them raise the rent a little if they would leave us alone.

The camp ended; one by one, our participants left—satisfied, even elated. Success! I, too, headed back home, anxious to know how the other two camps went. As soon as I got home, I called my brother Misha; the real question could not be asked openly over our tapped phone, but the tone of his voice reassured me. When we met, Misha told me that he and his wife, Oksana, had taught a successful camp at a Baltic Sea resort. And Yuli Edelstein had led a kayaking trip, and Bella Rabinovich had participated in it. Three camps—three successes!

* * *

Fall came, and a new school year started. Jewish Moscow awoke; new Hebrew classes were formed, and existing classes resumed work. The KGB, too, seemed to have kicked off a new season: a new wave of persecution broke out in Odessa. Once again, I started getting desperate calls: more house searches, interrogations, threats. A year ago, they had targeted leaders and activists, but now they were harassing beginners, anyone and everyone they knew of: a carpet-bombing approach. They were becoming brazen, like frenzied sharks scenting blood.

Something must be done in response; we owed it to our people. Together with Misha and several other activists, I wrote several letters of protest and mailed them to various authorities: to the Prosecutor General, to the Central Committee of the Communist Party. We got the word out to Jewish organizations abroad. Would our protests accomplish anything?

This put me in a quandary. It had always been clear that our clandestine activities in the cities must be kept completely separate from our efforts to protect our people from harassment, since protest activity by its very nature must be open and public. Ideally, there should be a separate system, an infrastructure for organizing international support campaigns, or even domestic protests. But we had no such thing—only a few brave people willing to pass information on to foreign visitors or reporters at great personal risk to themselves. As a result, the network we were building was completely exposed. We had nothing to say to the local Hebrew teachers and activists when they asked what to do when the KGB came knocking (as it inevitably would), or whom they should call for help. I was painfully aware that I was involving people in dangerous activities without being able to help them in their time of need.

I tried to line up people who had established connections abroad and put them in charge of those cities where the KGB were most active. But what about me? If I got personally involved, I could put the entire project at risk! And yet, how could I abandon our friends in a time of danger? As a result, every teacher in every city knew that in case of emergency, if no other help was available, he or she could call me as a last resort.

* * *

That same fall 1981, the biennial International Book Fair in Moscow opened. It was probably the only place where a Soviet Jew could say the word "Israel" without fear, could see Israelis, communicate with them, socialize with them. Naturally, Jews were enormously interested in the Israeli exhibit. So, too, was the KGB.

Thousands of people flocked to the exhibition from all over the country—a unique opportunity to meet potential activists from other cities. I scanned the crowd constantly, trying to identify possible recruits for the Cities Project.

In the end, the right person found me: at an after-hours meet-and-greet with the Israelis, Kosharovsky introduced me to a laconic young man named Felix Kushnir, from Moldova.

Felix seemed both motivated and mature: a rare combination! His quest for his own identity had led him to Jewish values, and then, all on his own, he came to the idea of making *aliyah*. He had heard that Hebrew teachers in Moscow met on Saturdays near the synagogue. So he went there, addressed the person standing next to him, and told him he wanted to learn Hebrew. Five minutes later he was taken to meet Kosharovsky, who then brought him to me. As simple as that.

Did the KGB goons, always lurking in the crowd around the synagogue, see him being introduced to Kosharovsky? I checked to see whether he had a KGB "tail," but he seemed clean.

Felix Kushnir

I watched him the rest of that week while the book fair was on, arranging to run into him at meetings, striking up conversations, observing his reactions, asking loaded questions. Yes, he seemed like a great candidate for the still-vacant role of traveling teacher, a key part of the framework I was building. The traveling teacher would have visibility into the whole structure. Did I dare tell him everything? That might put the entire project at risk. But if I didn't, I might lose him. This was a one-time opportunity!

Finally, I took him for a walk down a deserted street and haltingly, with trepidation, told him my secret. Felix listened intently, clearly shaken to the core. He took his time responding, but in the end he agreed to take it on and to come to Moscow in a few months' time for a crash course in Hebrew.

* * *

At the end of September, after the High Holidays, when the KGB were focusing their attention on Jewish activists and Hebrew teachers in Moscow, I thought it was a good time for me to disappear for a few days. I went to Tbilisi, ostensibly to attend Golda's birthday party.

Golda had wasted no time in attracting Jewish students and starting a class. She became the talk of Jewish Tbilisi, all the more remarkable because the local culture frowned upon women in positions of authority—such as a teacher—over men.

Unfortunately, trouble wasn't slow in coming: Golda's success didn't sit well with the authorities.

Golda Akhiyezer remembers

I moved to Tbilisi because at that time it was one of the few places in the USSR where one could still apply to emigrate to Israel. I found students soon enough, but these young people didn't understand the dangers of studying Hebrew and tended to shrug off my calls for caution. They said that Georgia wasn't Russia, that antisemitism was not a thing here, never had been, never would be.

I got two groups going. I told them about Jewish tradition, history, and holidays, and everyone started attending the synagogue. We met at the home of one of the students. We all became good friends. This idyllic interlude lasted about six months, and then trouble started.

First, all my students were summoned to the KGB and threatened with expulsion from the university. Some of them immediately dropped my class; others stayed on in spite of everything. Then the authorities began to put pressure on me.

I had brought a lot of Jewish literature from Moscow for distribution: photocopies of Hebrew books, dictionaries, books, samizdat on Jewish history and traditions, etc. I stored it in my rented apartment because there was nowhere else to keep it, and I didn't want to endanger my students. For my part, I lived in fear of a house search, since they would certainly charge me with storage and distribution of anti-Soviet literature, a criminal offense, even though there was nothing anti-Soviet in it.

One evening, when I came home, the landlords told me that a policeman had come by to talk to me, that they didn't want trouble with the authorities and therefore wanted me to vacate the apartment immediately.

The KGB started watching me openly; they had a "tail" on me wherever I went. It was unnerving to always have people following me and not know if they were just street thugs or actual KGB agents.

I rented a new apartment. One evening, when I got off the bus near my building, I saw a light in my window; it went off again immediately. When I entered my room, I found all the electrical wiring cut and all my money stolen. At first, I thought this was a common burglary, but when I saw that all my Hebrew teaching materials were also gone, I knew who had done it—and I knew I had to leave immediately. I spent the evening packing my belongings by candlelight. At 1 a.m. came a knock on the door. I opened the door and saw two men; one identified himself as a policeman and said he wanted to search the place because they had heard that a murder had been committed there. It was all very strange. The men poked around a bit and left, dropping heavy hints that it wasn't safe for me to sit alone in the dark.

I rented another apartment, and at first, everything was fine. But one day the landlady told me: "A strange thing happened this morning: a policeman came by and told me that you are a thief, you robbed your husband, and now they are investigating you. He said I must not keep you in my house."

This story repeated itself several times. Finally, I ran out of patience and decided to go to the visa office to check the status of my application. When I entered, I was greeted by a KGB official rather than the visa office clerk I expected to see. A different breed from the faceless goons in Moscow, he was neither inarticulate nor uneducated. He told me openly that if I wanted to emigrate, I should give them information about all the people who took my classes, and in general, become an informant, otherwise I would never get my visa.

"I guess I'll never get my visa, then," I said mechanically.

"Since you don't want to work with us, you should keep in mind that Tbilisi is not a safe city. There are bad people out there, anything might happen—you might get killed, raped, robbed . . . "

"Oh, I know," I said, "I've already had some experience. Where is my money and tapes and things that were taken from my apartment?"

"I don't know what you're talking about."

After that, he started asking me all kinds of questions, which I refused to answer. I had no prior experience of being interrogated, but I had heard that it was advisable to talk as little as possible. I said that I didn't think we had anything to discuss, since I was there about my visa application. The man changed tactics: "You should bear in mind that if you refuse to work with us, your parents in Moscow will lose their jobs and get into serious trouble."

That hit close to home. My parents were in fact afraid of losing their jobs because of my activities, even if they didn't know their full extent. I don't know what gave me the idea—probably some sort of intuition honed by a long struggle for survival; at any rate, I said: "I don't care. I'm estranged from my parents. If they are willing to continue to live in a country that mistreats their own daughter and makes a mockery of the basic rights of its citizens, I can't help them. Do whatever you want."

A blatant lie, but an inspired one, because it worked: he dropped the subject. Instead, he said I was free to leave and offered me a ride so we could "discuss a couple of questions along the way."

I don't know why I agreed; I wasn't thinking clearly from stress and fatigue. He drove me out of town, into the woods, and stopped the car.

"Now you won't get away until you sign a paper saying that you are willing to collaborate with us."

"I guess we'll just sit here, then."

"I told you, Tbilisi is a dangerous city, and if you are killed or raped, no one will be surprised."

"Then you shouldn't be surprised, either, if it gets all over the foreign news that my body was found in the woods, beaten and raped—everyone will know who did it!"

We sat in silence for a long time. I sensed him beginning to falter: he had achieved nothing and didn't know what else to say or do.

He asked if I wanted to hear some music, but I stopped him and asked him to take me back to the city. And, strangely enough, he gave in. He drove me back and dropped me off in the center of the city. I never saw him again.

Still, the KGB continued their efforts to get me evicted from any and every rental apartment, and I realized that it was too dangerous to continue living in Tbilisi.

Then, during a brief visit to Moscow in 1982, a friend from Yerevan offered to let me stay with them and even find me students if I moved there to teach Hebrew. I became Yerevan's first teacher of Hebrew and taught there for a year. On my very first evening there, my hosts gathered enough Jews to form several groups. Surprisingly, the local KGB did nothing to hinder me; the Armenians weren't antisemitic, and they hated their Soviet overlords too much to bother harassing me."

* * *

That fall, it became clear that the KGB had decided to sideline Yuli Edelstein from all Jewish activity. They harassed him relentlessly, trying to draft him into the army, forcing him to go into hiding for long periods. Yuli valiantly tried to find ways to continue his work in Moscow and in the cities, but eventually the moment came when we realized that Yuli was effectively off the Cities Project. All we could hope for from now on was that he would continue his remarkable travel summer camps.

* * *

In those years, we saw a near-constant stream of foreign visitors, which became an integral part of life for Jewish activists in many cities, especially in Moscow. Most, though not all, were sent by the Israeli Liaison Bureau. They included people from all walks of life: speakers who came to give a public talk; scientists who came to meet with their *refusenik* counterparts; rabbis who came to teach; university students. These people brought updates on new developments in the international struggle for freedom of emigration from the USSR. They smuggled in books and training materials for Hebrew instruction and information about Israel, as well as those related to religion and religious observance. They brought items that were hard or impossible to find in the USSR, which families of *refuseniks* in financial distress could use or sell, and medicines for *refuseniks* with medical conditions that a designated team of activists distributed to those who needed them.

The work of these foreign emissaries was not easy, because of the KGB's constant surveillance of *aliyah* activists, but it was vitally important. They gathered information on the plight of Soviet Jews to fuel international political campaigns and clandestine relief efforts, but no less importantly, they came to encourage, to lift the spirits of the people held captive for years behind the Iron Curtain.

We are forever grateful to the thousands of these volunteers who donated their time to travel to a hostile country at significant personal risk, having no prior experience in dealing with the KGB, and to the staff of the Israeli Liaison Bureau for finding such people, briefing and instructing them, tracking every visit, and rejoicing over the safe return of each emissary.

Dorrit Hoffer

One of the emissaries was Dorrit Hoffer, an Israeli with Swiss citizenship. In the fall of 1982, she traveled to Central Asia and, beyond all expectation, managed to smuggle back to us her report on the state of affairs there, a report that was of great help to me in planning our outreach in that territory. Many years later, I learned that Dorrit was also one of those Israelis who began writing encouraging letters to me in the fall of 1980.

* * *

As the Cities Project grew, a new problem became apparent: that of information storage and retrieval. New contacts kept emerging, both in our core cities and in those cities that were still unreached.

The names of activists numbered in the dozens, but those of general contacts, in the hundreds. For each person, we had to know their address and telephone number, what work they were already doing in the Jewish movement, as well as what tasks they might like to take on: teaching, promoting Hebrew studies or *aliyah* to newcomers, storage or transportation of literature, organizing a local summer camp, and so forth.

Beyond that, we had to know which of our contacts had taken our training in how to behave under KGB questioning. We had to keep track of which training materials had been sent to each particular city, and what else the students and teachers there might like to get. And, of course, we needed to know which of our contacts would be the local Hebrew teachers, which ones should be invited to take a crash course in Moscow, which ones would participate in the upcoming summer camps; we needed to keep track of specific requests, minutes of meetings…

All this could not be kept in my head. Oh, a computer would be so welcome! But personal computers were a rarity in the USSR of 1981. Besides, its presence might tip off the KGB that something big was going on, and since all of us lived under constant threat of a house search, if the KGB were to confiscate the computer, it would be a mortal blow to the project. Alas, we had to rely on old-fashioned pen and paper.

Our information system must reconcile the need for rapid access to information with the need for maximum security. There was nothing more valuable than the addresses and other details of our contacts in the cities. This was the heart of the entire project! Let the KGB confiscate our tapes and players, our slide projectors and books—but the information on our contacts must be protected at all costs. Otherwise, we put defenseless people in jeopardy.

On the other hand, if it took too long to access the data or to receive, store, and update it, the system would also fail. It had to be fast, because people from the cities were arriving in Moscow in an ever-growing stream. Without a secure means of communication to allow us to make arrangements in advance, people often showed up without warning, leaving us even less time to access information.

Sometimes several people from different cities might arrive on the same day. Each of them carried information that must be properly received and safely stored. Many needed information from us: a new contact in their town, or a list of books that had been sent to their city and to whom they had been sent. Very few people were aware of the sheer scale of our project, and therefore most didn't understand that, while for them a trip to the capital was a significant event requiring individual attention, we, for our part, were increasingly dealing with a problem of large numbers that created its own unique demands on our time and resources.

I concluded that the information storage system must have three tiers. The first tier should provide the fastest access to the smallest amount of data; the third tier could sacrifice the speed of access in favor of a large volume of data and maximum security; and the second tier would be a compromise between the two.

No sooner said than done. For the third and most comprehensive tier, I chose several families whom I had known for a very long time, even before I got involved in Jewish activities, and I knew they could keep their mouths shut. These families were considering making *aliyah* at some point in the future but had not yet taken any practical steps in that direction, had not participated in Jewish activities, and therefore had probably not attracted the KGB's interest.

I wrote down our entire database in tiny handwriting and left it with the first person on my third-tier list in a large sealed envelope. I told the person to store it securely for about a month, after which I would remove it. At the first sign of a house search, or if something suddenly happened to me, the envelope should be destroyed.

I began transferring the envelope from place to place once a month, choosing each next address randomly so the KGB could not predict where the envelope would be kept next. I got the idea of this "mobile storage system" from media reports on the storage of US strategic missiles. According to these reports, the missiles were not kept in fixed locations, but rather moved randomly via a system of underground passages to increase the chances of their survival in case of Soviet attack.

I also prepared an emergency back-up copy, to be stored in the safest place I could come up with. I dropped by there occasionally, as if by chance, no more than once every few months, to replace the envelope with one containing updated data.

The first tier contained the absolute essentials—carefully selected data which I thought likely to be needed in the near future. It was a small piece of very thin paper, written in a kind of code. I brought this piece of paper with me to all meetings with visitors from other cities and updated it there in real time. At home, I kept it between the pages of a book in a large bookcase, hoping that the KGB might miss that one small piece of paper among almost a thousand books if they came to search our apartment. We sewed a secret pocket in my clothing, undetectable even in a body search, to allow me to carry it outside the house. If all else failed, I hoped I would have enough time to swallow it.

Second-tier storage was an expanded version of the first, containing more information on a selected number of contacts. This I also wrote out in tiny handwriting on thin paper so that everything would fit on several small sheets. My mother volunteered to manage this system. She kept the data in a hidden place where she could retrieve it on two hours' notice, bring it to me for correction and updating, and return it as soon as possible. My mother's courage and resourcefulness were amazing; parents of activists, even those who were much younger than my parents, rarely got involved in their children's activities, to say nothing of taking on a major responsibility. The KGB paid scant attention to my mother, allowing her to come and go undetected for a long time.

It took me several weeks to deploy this system while maintaining ongoing operations, but once I realized that the system was live, I felt immense relief.

* * *

Our next challenge was to scale up the production, storage, and distribution of literature. We tried to provide every visitor with literature about Israel and Jewish life, culture, and religion, as well as Hebrew training materials. Now that we had many visitors arriving at unpredictable times, we needed a place to store sets of books, ready to be accessed on short notice. We kept everything in Reuven's apartment, which was literally turning into a warehouse.

A house search might come any day, and when it did, the KGB would find a vast amount of materials and comprehend the massive scale of the project we were carrying out under their noses. The project would be destroyed, to say nothing of Reuven's life.

Here, too, I created a two-level system: one for long-term storage and another for short-term storage and retrieval. Long-term storage should be distributed among several locations, the more the better: a distributed system was more difficult to detect, posed less risk to the custodians, and caused less damage in the event of a house search and confiscation of materials. But secure locations were hard to find; with great effort, we managed to come up with three new locations and to move everything out of Reuven's apartment, although he continued to manage the overall storage system.

Once the problem of storage had been solved, it was time to organize our own production of educational materials in Moscow. Until then, we had used existing materials that were not specific to the Cities Project. Our Hebrew teaching materials came from Igor Gurvich, the *purimspiel* director, who supplied all of Moscow's Hebrew teachers and was certainly known in this capacity to the KGB. Our Russian-language books about Israel and Judaism came from Victor Fulmakht's *samizdat* operation. Fulmakht, a known *refusenik*, had created a sociable and talkative public persona that helped him keep his publishing operation out of KGB's view. He found foreign-source materials and had a network of readers review them for suitability to the needs of our audience. In addition, he ran his own production line, entirely separate from Gurvich's and strictly secret: I was among the few who knew about it.

For the long term, however, we needed to begin producing literature dedicated specifically to the Cities Project. Aside from helping us minimize the risk of discovery, both for ourselves and for Gurvich and Fulmakht, this would enable us to plan our production several months in advance, thereby avoiding the delays that happened every fall when demand peaked at the beginning of the new academic year.

The first step was to find a photographer who was willing to set up a darkroom in his home and could be trusted to keep his mouth shut. We found such a person in Grigory Danovich, a physicist. He would work under Reuven, although for security reasons they must keep their direct interaction to a minimum. They would coordinate production with storage in order to ensure that the literature being produced was what we actually needed. Grigory, with an assistant, would bring his output to an intermediate storage location. Reuven and his team would remove it, making sure they were free of interference or surveillance, and transfer it to the long-term storage location.

The master copies and duplicate originals were made by my brother Misha, who was also responsible for storing them in special secure locations. He also made master copies of audio tapes: we had tapes of Hebrew instruction and tapes of Hebrew songs. A member of his team was in charge of duplicating the tapes for the cities. We now were able to make a standardized set of tapes that included Hebrew tutorials along with a "bonus"—music and educational literature on Israel, Jewish culture, and Judaism. These sets were produced, packaged, and stored in our short-term storage location, to be handed out to each newcomer upon arrival.

* * *

As I continued to meet with my fellow activists and students, I began to notice uninvited guests—seated on a nearby bench or passing by, seemingly by chance. I was developing surveillance detection skills. Before long, I was able to identify them at every meeting: those peculiar wooden faces, as though bearing the mark of Cain. "But what if these are just the ones you can see?" I said to myself. "What if the KGB have others who are so good that you're missing them?" Each encounter caused me to recoil in disgust, as though I had come upon a scorpion.

The one thing I could not do was let the KGB photograph and record my conversations with visitors from other cities using electronic surveillance equipment. I developed a system for protecting our venues: letting the KGB overhear me set a false meeting time on the phone but actually meeting an hour earlier, by previous agreement; taking my guests on a long zigzag course through side streets to an open area where the spies could not sneak up on us. But the KGB goons persisted: though we might succeed in shaking them off one time, they would pop up again next time.

One of my main challenges came from my visitors themselves. Many of our new contacts from other cities, especially if they had not yet had a direct encounter with the KGB, had trouble understanding my insistence on total secrecy. After all, what could be more innocent than learning a language? They didn't know that the KGB saw our Hebrew studies, quite rightly, as a major factor in Jewish national revival. Therefore, our visitors viewed my calls for secrecy as an exaggeration and would occasionally slip up and say something important out loud while talking to me on the phone or meeting with me in my bugged apartment, even with an erasable tablet in hand.

When Felix Kushnir arrived in Moscow for his two-week crash course with Eugene Gurevich, I discussed with him his new role of a traveling teacher and gave him his first assignment: to make contact with the potential activists whose names we had obtained from various sources. He would present himself sometimes as a messenger, sometimes as a supplier of educational materials, and sometimes as a visiting teacher for beginners. It was a big job: I had close to a hundred new contacts to check in more than fifteen cities! His task was to get to know these people and find out how serious their intentions were. In certain cases, Felix would even be given authority to bring new people into our network.

But first, we must establish a safe and secret way of arranging meetings in Moscow so that I could be briefed on his latest results, and he could receive new materials and instructions. We came up with a code. For example, he might call me on the phone:

F: "Hey, are you coming tomorrow night?"

E: "I think so."

F: "What time?"

E: "Oh, I don't know, maybe eight or nine—I'll have to see how it goes."

F: "Oh, I was going to be there earlier than that. Never mind, if I don't find you there, I'll see you next time, it's nothing urgent."

This meant we were to meet *today* at *5:00* (subtracting three hours from the time mentioned). We arranged several meeting places beforehand and assigned a number to each. If one of us mentioned one of the places, this meant that we would meet in a location corresponding to the *next* number.

***

Toward the end of January 1982, the authorities began a new campaign against me. I began receiving written notices in the mail summoning me to appear at my local police station to answer some unspecified questions. When I ignored them, they started sending them by messenger, and then police officers of increasing seniority began to appear at my door almost daily, bearing the summons and accompanied by plain-clothes civil guards. Clearly, this was not a police matter. It was common knowledge in activist and dissident circles that the KGB used these tactics to lure people to one of their "chats."

I began to stay away from home, leaving early and returning late, in order to prevent them from serving the summons, but one evening I came home to find my parents very anxious. The new summons said: "to appear as a witness in a criminal case." I felt an unpleasant chill of anxiety. To ignore this might be deemed a refusal to testify, a criminal offense. But a witness in a criminal case—what criminal case? I mentally reviewed all my acquaintances; no one I knew was involved in any criminal case.

However, like everyone involved in clandestine work, I had become conversant with the Soviet criminal code, and more importantly, with the code of criminal procedure, which dealt with many minute details of form and process. As I examined the summons more closely, I noticed that it did not list the name of the accused or the case number. This was not a real summons—it was a fake!

Still, according to my mother, it had been delivered by the highest-ranking policeman yet, a major; and moreover, it was signed by a Lieutenant Colonel Murashov. Things were clearly escalating.

The next day I show up at my local police station. Lieutenant Colonel Murashov turns out to be the chief of a department for the prevention of the crime of parasitism. Fixing me with a hate-filled antisemitic stare, he demands to know my current place of employment. I decline to answer, and he begins to shout. I half-listen, wondering if the KGB are waiting in the wings. It seems odd that they would chase me for two weeks, sending a police major, no less, and all that just to have me spar with Comrade Murashov about parasitism. Or is this a test? Are they listening, trying to see if I will waver so they can pounce, like sharks drawn to blood?

If so, then let us dust off our trusty criminal procedure. When Murashov comes up for air, I counter-attack:

"Has there been a court order to place me under police surveillance? Please tell me its number and effective date. Because that is the only situation where a citizen is legally required to disclose his place of employment."

Murashov jumps up and flushes, gasping for air. Bingo! I've found his weak spot. I press my advantage:

"In fact, I'll tell you *why* I'm not telling you my place of employment. You see, I'm not on the best of terms with the KGB just now."

Murashov even takes a step back in the face of such arrogance. So steeped are they in sacred awe of the KGB that to name it openly, without euphemism or circumlocution, sounds like an utter sacrilege.

"See, if I tell you, you'll tell the KGB, and then I will be fired. And jobs are not easy to find."

Murashov's voice is suddenly hoarse.

"What does the KGB have to do with it? Why should I pass this information on to the KGB?"

"Oh, come on, we're not children, are we? You are an officer, and the officer must follow orders. They'll order you to tell them, and tell them you will."

Murashov's face turns gray. I continue:

"Plus, I still don't understand why I'm even here. I received a summons to appear as a witness in a criminal case. What is the name of the accused, the charges against him and the case number?"

"The form of the summons is irrelevant! It's just a formality! We used the forms we had on hand."

"Ah, no, it's not a formality, it's a matter of principle. I was called as a witness in a criminal case and I am prepared to serve in that capacity, but I will not speak about any other topic."

"Enough of your tricks! Either you tell me where you work, right here and now, or . . . or I will immediately transfer your file to the State Prosecutor!"

Enraged, Murashov ran out of the office. I had won that round.

However, Murashov apparently made good on his threat, because I received one more procedurally deficient notice summoning me to the prosecutor's office. Instead of going, I sent a letter to the prosecutor asking to verify whether my original summons to the police department had complied with procedure. Since the prosecutor's office clearly knew that it had not, they did not pursue the matter further, beyond a half-hearted response to which I, in turn, replied that I had consulted an attorney, was advised that the summons had been invalid, and now considered the matter closed. In this way, I had succeeded in deflecting the issue from the dangerous matter of my employment to the trivial matter of procedure.

I heard nothing more from Murashov, and the barrage of summonses stopped. Their attempt to intimidate me had rebounded upon themselves.

At the end of spring 1982, they changed tactics. I began receiving anonymous phone calls. Heavy breathing in the receiver, vague threats: "So you want to play games with us? Just you wait. You'll get what's coming to you!" "I wouldn't stay out late if I were you . . . Anything might happen!" They would hang up and call back right away, several times in a row, alternating threats with the foulest curses. This went on for a solid three weeks.

Eventually, this onslaught of threats and harassment began to chip at my confidence and optimism, draining my mental energy. It was becoming harder to function normally.

One day my mother answered the phone. A woman, speaking good English with a barely perceptible Russian accent, asked for Mr. Kholmyansky: a KGB agent posing as a foreigner, no doubt. My mother found this new trick disturbing: "What if they sent someone in to you this way, an infiltrator, a plant?"

Yes, they might just do that. They assumed that I would be inclined to say more to a foreigner, so they might glean some valuable information. We must be prepared for this.

And yet, I was careful never to say anything to foreign visitors that was confidential or not already known to the KGB, except to the official messengers of the Israeli Liaison Office, but those were very rare, and I always knew about their arrival in advance. Moreover, in dealing with people from different parts of the country and the world, I had developed an ear for accents: it was unlikely that I would fail to discern traces of a Russian accent in English, however faint, especially if we exchanged more than a few words. More importantly, no English-speaking spy could feign the genuine understanding, compassion, and special warmth radiated by our guests, Jews from other countries.

***

Sometimes, the ever-increasing pace of work got to me. I sat at the very nerve center of the project's network, while people's troubles flowed to me like tributaries into a river: this one had been summoned to the KGB; that one had had a house search; one had lost her job; another had been threatened with arrest. The burden of compassion and responsibility for all these people was weighing heavily on me. I had my moments of weakness when I entertained a momentary thought of stepping down. But who would carry the project on if I quit? Everything would collapse, the KGB would rub their hands with glee, while the lives of my colleagues and students would be ruined. No, quitting was not an option.

***

In the meantime, the project was humming along like a huge machine, like an enormous flywheel turning at top speed, like a giant conveyor belt, carrying me with it inexorably. It was hard to believe that it had only been two years, but how much we had accomplished in that time! We had stirred up a real Jewish awakening. More and more people from the cities were getting involved in the project. Several new teachers from the cities had advanced to the point where they were ready to teach beyond their own cities. Now the central team need no longer consist only of Muscovites: someone like Bella Rabinovich from Ufa, for instance, could teach a summer camp.

In fact, I thought we might begin running multiple camps. To test that idea, I would hold one myself in the Crimea and have someone else teach another one in September, in the same location. By that time I would be back in Moscow, the KGB would see me and stop looking for the other camps, and we would sneak in more teaching under their very noses. A neat trick!

Chapter 4

Summer was approaching. The last preparations for our Hebrew summer camp were drawing to a close. Felix had worked hard and had managed to rent a quiet cottage in the resort town of Alupka in the Crimea on the Black Sea.

Map of the Crimea

Approaching the place, I noticed a hill in the distance with a sizeable grove on top that could accommodate both our study groups, out of each other's hearing but within sight. Climbing up there in the summer heat would be a chore, but on the other hand, it would keep unwanted guests away. Holding classes indoors was out of the question: we had learned that lesson last year in Sukhumi.

Classes started the very next day. I taught the advanced group, and Golda Akhiyezer taught the beginners. Counting Golda herself, we had eight cities represented: Felix (a town in Moldova),

Golda (Yerevan, Armenia), Clara Schwartzman (Kishinev, Moldova), Chaya Berenstein (Kiev, Ukraine), Esther Futoriansky (Kemerovo in Siberia, Russia), Shmulik[12] (Odessa, Ukraine), Alex Kogan (Kishinev, Moldova), Valery Stratiyevsky (Novosibirsk in Siberia, Russia), and Polina Green (Tiraspol, Moldova). A record number of cities!

This time I did not invite either Shaya or Edda from Odessa: less risk for them and for the camp as well, since they had had so much KGB exposure all year. Instead, I invited Shmulik from the group headed by Yan Mesh—the second Jewish activist group operating in Odessa. Yan's group worked with Natasha Khasin to provide practical aid to Prisoners of Zion nationwide: a noble mission. To them, however, Hebrew studies and related cultural activities seemed secondary and harmless, involving little risk; therefore, they had trouble taking my calls for caution seriously.

To my dismay, Shmulik began to flout my secrecy rules, and my leadership in general, as soon as he arrived. Given that the KGB in Odessa had everyone under surveillance, the danger was clear: had his carelessness revealed our camp to the KGB?

"Shmulik, did you take precautions when you left Odessa?"

"Do you want me to be afraid of my own shadow? The KGB doesn't give a damn about your Hebrew and your phony heroics."

"But we had an agreement with Yan: we decided to take you on condition that you would keep your mouth shut and take all possible precautions!"

"You know what I think? You've got delusions of grandeur with your Hebrew!"

What should I do now? Send him back home? He would immediately blab our location out, paint himself as a poor victim... and the relationship between Edda's group and Yan's, already strained, would suffer even more. Let him stay? That was also dangerous; discipline was essential to the security of the camp. Which was the lesser evil here?

In fact, because of his negligence, the KGB probably already knew our location. Should we kick him out and change locations?

---

[12] Not his real name.

There was little chance of finding another quiet, secluded place at the height of the summer season. But if we closed the camp and went home, there was every chance of being followed, since we would all have to travel together.

I decided to take the risk and proceed, and if there were any signs of danger after a day or two, we would close the camp and send everyone home.

Our studies got off to a good start. My advanced group pounced on the discussion prompts I had prepared like a fish swallowing bait, passionately debating in Hebrew whether a special school should be set up to train Israeli political leaders; what would have happened if the UN had not made a decision to establish a Jewish state in 1947; whether the Israeli education system needed changing; whether public transportation should operate on Shabbat . . . I stayed out of the discussion, only occasionally adding topics for debate or arguments in favor of each alternative, before retreating again. I listened and was happy to see my students becoming more fluent with every passing day.

Felix arrived a week after we started, bringing sausages (a rare commodity in the Crimea), a gift that won our landlord's heart. I asked Felix:

"Did you notice anything suspicious on your way?"

"That odd-looking van that's parked on the corner, with that small turret on the roof, has it been there all the time?"

"We first noticed it two or three days ago. It's only there during the day but at night it's gone."

"Have you ever seen anyone inside it or around it?"

"No, but I've heard crackling noises coming from it, as if someone's fiddling with a radio."

"Any signs of surveillance?"

"Nothing overt, but there have been suspicious characters around . . . my gut says they're KGB. The question is, are they after us? The worst thing is that they made us all register with the local police, everyone except me."

"Why did everyone have to register? Our agreement with the landlord was that we wouldn't have to!"

"I know, but he says everything's changed now, the police are prowling around looking for unregistered renters—it's against the law. They're coming again tomorrow morning."

That evening I came down with a high fever: a nasty virus laid me low at the worst possible time. Valery and Felix left at midnight so that the number of people registered would match the number of those sleeping at the house. I wrapped myself in a blanket and fell into a deep, feverish sleep.

The police came at 5:30 a.m. They took all our identity papers and counted heads; they checked every corner, peered under every bed, no doubt looking for an extra person. Finally, not finding what they sought, they left the house, taking our papers with them.

Then our landlord disappeared. An hour passed, two, three . . . The suspense was becoming difficult to bear. We couldn't leave the house without our IDs. Finally, the landlord returned, dragging himself along, pale as death. Felix ran to meet him. "What happened?" He did not answer, shaking his head. "But what happened?" The landlord looked around furtively and muttered: "Get inside, we have to talk." He locked all the doors with shaking hands and then blurted out:

"They summoned me to the KGB! They said: 'You're sheltering a bunch of Zionists, they're studying a secret language, you're in trouble, we're going to look into this house you built—to see if you got all the right permits, and where you got the money to pay for it . . .'" You all have to leave immediately!"

Felix jumped over to my bed to wake me up.

"Get up, this is an emergency! There's no time to be sick. The police may show up at any moment! Get up, we're going outside to talk, right now!"

With an effort I hauled myself up and followed Felix outside. We went out through the back gate and into a vacant lot overgrown with weeds and bushes in front of a nearby school, where Felix told me everything. Deep in discussion, we nevertheless noticed a middle-aged man with an umbrella stroll leisurely out of the school building. He took a few steps and suddenly turned off the path and began crashing through the bushes towards us: an eavesdropper?

Instantly, my illness vanished. In shock, Felix and I ran back to the apartment, where we called everyone together for a war council.

I: "We must close the camp immediately. That's not local police, it's the KGB."

Felix: "Let's tell the landlord we're leaving tomorrow morning, but actually leave at midnight tonight. That damned van only shows up during the day."

Golda: "I don't think this will help us. I think we should split up. You and Felix must disappear right away, because you're not registered. You should leave without your stuff, as if you're going to the beach, and then disappear. Without you, we're just a bunch of people on vacation; with you, we're a 'Zionist conspiracy.'"

I: "But how can I leave the group in time of danger, abandon everyone?"

Clara: "Listen, it's better for the rest of us this way, and it's certainly better for the Cities Project. You'll help no one by getting arrested now."

Esther: "If you leave, the KGB will be less interested in us."

Polina: "Sometimes it's wise to retreat if it will keep the army intact."

Shmulik: "But I thought the captain should be the last one to leave the sinking ship!"

Clara suggested putting the matter to a vote. Except for Shmulik, all voted in favor of my leaving. Felix concurred. We agreed that Felix and I would leave now, the rest of them would go in the morning, and we would all meet up in the nearby town of Simeiz at 10 a.m.

Without wasting any more precious time, Felix set off toward the beach. I followed half an hour later and made my way to Yalta. Once there, I was shocked to see the whole town crawling with KGB, black cars everywhere with revolving antennas on their roofs. I remembered hearing that one of the Party bigwigs kept a summer residence outside Yalta: perhaps that explained their presence. I met up with Felix, and together we boarded a bus for Alushta where we could take a local cruise boat to Simeiz—an-hour-and-a-half trip.

We were looking forward to a nice short coastal cruise, a time to calm down, unwind, breathe the fresh air. But no sooner did we get underway than thick black clouds covered the sky, and the merry little ripples of fifteen minutes ago turned into menacing storm waves fiercely battering the hull. We were barely making headway: at this rate, we would be late to meet the group! Who could have expected such a storm in the middle of the summer?

"We regret to announce," said the loudspeaker, "that due to severe weather conditions, the cruise will terminate at Alupka." Good Lord, they're taking us back—this was exactly what we wanted to avoid! We ran uphill from the quay to the highway to flag down a ride. This time we were lucky: twenty minutes later we were in Simeiz. There, we found our group . . . as well as two carloads of KGB and the familiar van with the turret on the roof. We desperately needed to talk and decide what to do before it was too late.

There was a small park nearby; perhaps we could talk there beyond the range of the electronic eavesdroppers? Alas, no such luck. As soon as we sat down on a bench, a guy in a jogging suit and a teenage boy plopped down on the next bench. We moved to another bench, once, twice: each time they followed us as though tied to us by an invisible string, even though almost all the other benches were empty. The guy was telling the boy something with a nasty smirk on his face.

Clearly, we were in serious trouble. And yet we must meet somehow and plan our next steps. In furtive whispers, we set our next meeting for 8 p.m. in Yalta and went our separate ways.

Shortly before 8 p.m., we were at the agreed place. The agreed hour came and went, but our friends were nowhere to be seen. KGB agents, however, were out in force; we could feel their hostile, watchful eyes on us from every side.

"Look, there he goes—so he *can* walk!" Felix exclaimed, agitated.

"Who?"

"That guy over there! I saw him at that corner half an hour ago, he was pretending to be a cripple, half-paralyzed, and begging alms."

Time passed: 8:30 . . . 9 p.m. . . . . When it got to 9:30 p.m., an hour and a half past the agreed time, Felix said we would only attract attention if we continued to stand there. We decided to return to Simeiz in case our friends had misheard us and were waiting there.

Felix set off immediately, heading toward the bus station. I followed him at a distance. We wandered through the bustling streets of the busy resort town in the gathering darkness, seeing many more pretend cripples and others who looked like KGB agents. It was rapidly getting dark. I began to walk faster, trying to get closer to Felix so as not to lose him, but just then, he crossed the street, and the light turned red. I stood there, helpless and frustrated, waiting for the green light with every fiber of my being.

As soon as the light changed, I leapt across the street. It was now completely dark; the streetlights had come on but they didn't help much. Desperately, I scanned the crowd but could not see Felix anywhere.

Had I lost him for good?

Shaking, as in a fever, I turned and began to walk at random, imagining the worst...

"Sasha!" I heard Felix's voice.

I ran to him . . . and just like that, the world around me changed from menacing to benign; my heart began to sing with joy.

We boarded the bus just in time and were back in Simeiz half an hour later. Alas, there was no one at the meeting place, nor any sign of them. Deeply frustrated, we returned to Yalta, wandering aimlessly around the city. We passed the place where we were supposed to meet three hours ago: an eternity! Where were our friends?

Suddenly, a fiery redhead stepped out of an underpass. "Golda!" I yelled. She turned to me, astonished.

It emerged that, in the confusion of dodging surveillance at Simeiz, we had gotten our wires crossed: while we waited for them at Yalta, they were indeed waiting in Simeiz, thinking that we had been arrested. It was a miracle that we all happened to come together at the same time in the same place in a strange city.

"What are the odds of such a meeting?" I wondered out loud.

"Even lower than you think: on our way back, Valery ran into an old friend, they started talking, and we missed the bus!"

I asked Golda what happened to them after Felix and I left.

"After you were gone, Alex Kogan and Shmulik also went out for some reason, leaving us girls alone. That's when it started, as if they were waiting for this opportunity. Out of the blue, the police and the Civil Guard showed up and busted through the door, yelling: 'This is a house search, you've got unregistered people living here!' But the girls kept their heads, blocked the entrance to the apartment and demanded to see the search warrant.

"Things were escalating, the police were working themselves up into a frenzy, yelling and cursing and waving their hands around: it looked like they were about to tear us to pieces. Esther saved us by screaming at the top of her lungs: 'Call the KGB, call the KGB right now!'

"The police paused, confused: why was she calling for the KGB when it was the KGB that sent them to search the house? But, apparently, they had no instructions for this scenario, so they left.

"Instead, a KGB man showed up and started questioning us. Dozens of questions, trying every which way to get at the same thing: who was the participant from Moscow, and who had rented the apartment? Finally, he realized that he wasn't going to get any answers from us, so he gave us back our IDs and left.

"We tried to slip away at dawn, but the KGB were everywhere. Then we decided to just take the bus openly. You wouldn't believe it: we had one KGB car driving in front of our bus and another one following, as if we were VIPs. When we arrived in Simeiz, the van with the turret was already parked there, waiting for us. Then you and Felix came, we had our meeting in the park, and we went to Yalta.

At the port of Yalta, a stranger came up to Polina and told her: 'You'd better get out of town right now!' We walked to town and went into a café.

As soon as we walked in, everyone sitting there turned around and stared at us. Then, as if on command, all these people who had been sitting quietly at their tables a moment ago suddenly jumped up, surrounded us, and began screaming, shouting threats and vile curses, making threatening gestures. 'Hitler died too soon! Put your yellow stars back on!'

"I had never experienced such a powerful psychological attack. It looked like a scene from a horror movie: dozens of seemingly ordinary people turned violent and insane in an instant. It's hard to imagine a more impressive show of power by the KGB.

We left the café. Everywhere we went, we saw these cripples sitting on every corner, hissing curses and insults at us. Then we would see them again, walking perfectly well! Towards evening we started looking for a place to stay overnight. Alex chatted up a local girl, and she got us into a youth hostel. We had barely stepped inside when we noticed the KGB cars outside the window and heard voices in the hallway announcing an ID check, and we had to climb out the window. The girl knew some KGB men and told us later: 'Guys, you don't know what kind of mess you've made here! The entire Crimean KGB is on the alert; they've had all their vacations cancelled. They've put every available agent on your case!'"

Despite these harrowing events, everyone made it back home safely. With the closure of our camp, the KGB calmed down and did not go looking for other Jewish summer camps. This allowed us to hold several other, smaller camps in September, led by the new teachers: Bella Rabinovich, Boris Dubrovsky, Golda, and Felix.

Although I felt the failure of the camp in Alupka keenly, I was not defeated. After only a few days in Moscow, I left on a reconnaissance trip to the Caucasus with Rashi Abayev. Rashi was a remarkable man who came from a dynasty of religiously observant Jews of the Caucasus, an ancient tribal group known as "Mountain Jews," believed to be the descendants of Persian Jews from Iran. He was a *mohel*[13] and a *shochet*[14] who had moved to Georgia, learned to speak Georgian, and lived there for some years before moving to Leningrad. He did well in Leningrad, too: he adjusted to the urban Ashkenazi lifestyle and even learnt Yiddish. I wanted to take

---

[13] A *mohel* is a Jew trained in the practice of *brit milah*, the "covenant of circumcision."

[14] A *shochet* is a Jew trained to kill cattle and poultry in the manner prescribed by the Jewish law.

advantage of his connections among the Georgian and Mountain Jews. This was my first foray into this region. We toured city after city, attending countless meetings, looking for prospects. For example, I had heard of a clandestine Jewish religious school, an actual *yeshiva*, very deeply hidden—so deeply that, unfortunately, we never did find it. But we did find, here and there, potential candidates for our project.

I parted with Rashi Abayev and went on to Baku, a city with a large Jewish population that included both Ashkenazi and Mountain Jews. I had contacts among the Ashkenazi community: I met with Professor Michael Farber and his younger brother Ze'ev, as well as with Michael Silberstein, a Hebrew teacher trained in our system and a rising star of our Cities Project. In the Mountain Jewish community I had one contact, coincidentally also named Rashi, on whom I counted to open doors for me. This Rashi took me to meet the city's rabbi.

"He is a real rabbi," Rashi whispered, "not appointed by the KGB, but he has to tread carefully so he will probably be leery of joining a dangerous project, especially one that's run from Moscow. But his daughter Miriam—you may want to talk to her."

Miriam and I had a cautious conversation, feeling each other out. This girl seemed to have something like second sight, because her reaction to my proposal was a little unexpected:

"You're doing important work, and I'm sorry that I can't take part in it. But you—I sense that you're working too much, wearing yourself out, both physically and spiritually. Someone has to tell you this. You've become so enslaved by your project that it's consuming your essence, your personality. But the Torah says that man was created in God's image. When you let your personality be consumed, you diminish the image of God imprinted in your soul!"

What an amazing thing to say—and so true! Yet I felt neither fear nor sorrow at her words. To be honest, I actually felt a sense of satisfaction and even pride. Yes, it was a steep price I was paying for my work, bordering on self-sacrifice, but I was doing it willingly. Human beings are a diverse lot, I thought. Many there are who enjoy fame, but there are those like me, who value secret knowledge more. Yes, I certainly am wearing myself out, expending my essence. But haven't Jews sacrificed far more than that for the sanctification of His Name?

* * *

In November 1982, Leonid Brezhnev, the head of the Communist Party, died. Who would be his successor? Behind the scenes, a battle for succession raged between two candidates, both elderly: Konstantin Chernenko, possibly a slightly lesser evil, and Yuri Andropov, the head of the KGB. Alas, Andropov won, marking the first time the KGB openly held the reins of power in the country. We were in for some dark times. Which manifested themselves quickly: the police began stopping people in the street in broad daylight to check why they weren't at work, tactics unknown even under Stalin, as far as I knew. What would the future bring?

In Kiev, the police came to search the Berenstein home. In Moscow, I was now under open police surveillance: no sooner did I set foot out of doors than a black KGB car, bristling with radio antennas, would follow me, dogging my steps, as if to remind me: "Your time will come, we're just waiting to pounce." Two weeks later, the car disappeared but I remained on high alert.

I thought I had become good at picking out the spies and even said so once out loud in my apartment. As if to prove me wrong, one day, two men and two women appeared right behind me, quite out of the blue. They tailed me blatantly, staying a mere ten or fifteen yards back, stopping when I stopped at a shop window, waiting outside when I stepped into a shop, never letting up. It was unnerving—not just the fact of the surveillance but their faces, oh, those faces: all with blank, dull, nondescript features—where *did* the KGB find such faces? Like human robots, radiating a low-key but unmistakable menace. The KGB must have gone through thousands of candidates to pick out two such couples; in fact—scary thought— they must have had thousands to choose from. This was, without a doubt, a top-notch, masterful psychological attack.

The weeks followed one another. One day, as I was walking down the street, two men suddenly stepped in front of me. They showed me police detective badges and pored over my ID for what seemed like forever, looking from my photograph to my face and back, as though trying to sniff out a secret. I waited patiently. Finally, the senior of the two men handed me back my ID, saying: "You have a close resemblance to a wanted criminal. You'll hear from us again."

A noted Jewish activist, Joseph Begun, was arrested—his third arrest. The authorities called Yuli Kosharovsky in as a witness in the case and sharply stepped up their harassment of Yuli. We all told Yuli: "You have to step down." So his role as the leader of the teachers' *dibbur* went to Lev Gorodetsky, while his role in the Cities Project, alas, fell to me. This included maintaining contact with the Israeli Liaison Bureau, which provided us with funding and sent us foreign visitors, who smuggled in teaching materials for us.

What a pity about Yuli—and what a loss to the project! This enormous additional responsibility for all the finances was just too much for me; the work was more than I could handle alone, and the risk to me personally had escalated beyond all reason. It was time to restructure the entire system and to bring in at least two more people at the top to replace Yuli Edelstein and Yuli Kosharovsky. We must distribute all the major functions among different people and build in redundancy everywhere; otherwise, God forbid, the whole project might collapse.

My first recruit was Ze'ev Geyzel, a new student in my Hebrew class. Ze'ev was a brilliant man and very visible: he was always the center of attention; he staged great *purimspiels*; he conducted excellent Passover Seders. Geyzel was everywhere. Very sociable, a little impulsive, he seemed like the least suitable candidate for clandestine work. A shame, really; Geyzel's dedication was beyond doubt, and his potential was huge. And yet . . . if he seemed unsuitable to me, he would probably also seem so to a KGB analyst. They might not suspect him, and he might be able

Ze'ev Geyzel

to come and go without surveillance. This meant he could take on some of the work associated with our project.

Geyzel agreed enthusiastically when I approached him. I was delighted: this allowed us to offload some functions from Reuven and lower the related risk. Geyzel's first task was to take over orders and delivery from the photographers who produced the literature and textbooks for the Cities Project.

Meanwhile, the authorities launched a new cycle of harassment. They summoned Misha's and Oksana's students to the KGB and made pointed threats aimed expressly at me and Misha.

For our part, we now had a foothold in Kuibyshev (former Samara). I had met Frieda Natura and her adult sons when they visited Moscow: excellent people all, very strongly motivated. Now I must get them trained and supply them with teaching materials. Frieda offered to make herself available to take on assignments nationwide. That was an interesting new model: older ladies, women in our mothers' age group, could travel without attracting KGB's attention. We would start with Frieda, and then we would redeploy the Odessa group to travel to other cities to teach, now that the KGB had brought our work in Odessa itself to a halt.

To Odessa, then, I went with my secret mission. After a little refresher course, Ella, Shaya Gisser's mother, went to Kiev to give a class, and Chana Nepomnyashchy headed to other cities in the Ukraine. Her daughter Edda went to Kiev to train local teachers.

We also had a new project headquarters: the Moscow apartment of my student Alla Sud and her husband, Lev, who were both away at the time. The Cities Project was going full speed ahead; I had an uneasy feeling that our time was running out.

My mother remembers

One day, our phone stopped working, and we called the state telephone company. The technician they sent to repair it did his job quickly enough, but I was suspicious and watched his hands very carefully as he poked around inside the device. But he didn't insert anything into the device itself, so apparently the wiretapping bugs were installed somewhere else. I did notice that he was missing one joint on the third or fourth finger of his right hand.

Then one day, when Sasha left on one of his trips, we found a bag he had forgotten to take. We knew we could still catch up with him and bring him the bag. We met him inside the metro station, handed over the bag, and he left. We sat on the platform for a while. Suddenly, I sensed the presence of a spy; I turned and noticed a man who stood right next to our bench, leaning against the wall. His tense face seemed familiar to me.

The train arrived, but we stayed seated, and he remained where he was. When the next train came, my husband, Grisha, said: "Maybe we should get on," and made to stand up. Our neighbor immediately headed toward the train, but I held Grisha back at the last moment. The man got on without us, the doors closed, and I saw his hand through the window—with a joint missing on one finger . . .

The KGB now watched our entire family. We were constantly followed by all sorts of people: men with flat, expressionless faces, stocky women with large shopping bags, girls with vulgar, loud make-up. We sensed them immediately. We often met with Misha in the metro, to discuss something, or to give him things, or just to spend a few minutes with him, as he was always so busy. All these meetings were arranged over the phone ahead of time, and pretty much every time there would be a nosy stranger loitering nearby and trying to sneak a peek into our bags to see what exactly I was giving to Misha.

They spared no effort watching us at home. A family of professional informers, a mother and a son, lived next door. The mother didn't trouble with subtlety: she would sit on a stool in front of her front door, which she kept ajar, and watch people coming to visit us. Her son, Valery, a PhD student at the Department of Geography of Moscow State University, stood for hours on the landing outside our door with a cigarette and a newspaper in his hands.

One day I figured out how they were able to send a spy after Sasha as soon as he left home. Each time Sasha left, I would watch him through the peephole in the door until he got into the elevator, and then I would go out onto the balcony and watch until he went down into the metro. Sometimes it was clear that he was being followed. But that day, as Sasha stepped out of our front door and walked to the elevator, Valery was standing at his post. Before the elevator door had fully closed, he bounded back into his apartment and then emerged slowly a few seconds later. He stood there for a few more minutes, in case Sasha might come back again, and then quietly went home. Evidently, he could just press a button to alert the spy waiting outside.

They spent big money on wiretapping equipment. They drilled the wall between us and Valery's apartment and the walls on the other side. Once, a whole team of men showed up and stomped up the stairs leading to the attic over our apartment; we happened to live on the top floor—how convenient for them! They made so much noise that I looked out and asked what had happened. "Nothing . . . yet," replied one of them insolently. They set up microphones or other kinds of devices above our ceiling, and especially near the air vents. In this way, we were surrounded by listening devices on all sides. They probably got to hear our voices in pretty good stereo sound.

* * *

At the beginning of 1980 the authorities halted the giant flywheel of Jewish emigration, trapping tens of thousands of people in *refusenik* limbo. They began to say quite openly to visa applicants that the previous policy of allowing some emigration had been a mistake that must be corrected, that it had caused a massive "brain drain," and why should our human capital, our chief asset, go to strengthen our imperialist adversaries?

Stirred up by the idea of emigration, people couldn't imagine that the gates of the Soviet Union would close so suddenly and abruptly. People who had quit their jobs, severed their social connections, taken their children out of school, some who had even moved out of their apartments, now found themselves behind closed doors again—for a very long time, if not forever. They were like fish washed up on shore, gasping from lack of oxygen. Some began to withdraw their applications, especially in the Ukraine, where the visa offices were becoming especially brazen. Masses of *refuseniks*, losing hope, began seeking ways to put down roots again, no longer looking for short-term odd jobs but trying to reclaim their place in society. Emigration? . . . Ah yes. It had been a nice dream while it lasted.

Among Jewish activists, however, the mood was quite different. Here, people strove to see the big picture. Perhaps it wasn't mere chance that had put a halt to emigration? Might there be a reason behind it, a higher meaning? Might it be that we yet had a job to do, things to learn and to understand? Many, especially the younger people, tried to find ways to fill the spiritual void that had gripped the country.

Jewish brains threw themselves into a search for answers. Groups studying Jewish history grew dramatically. People explored their national heritage, their Jewish identity. But the biggest change was in people's attitude toward Jewish religion. Religious groups, until recently a marginal phenomenon, experienced rapid growth. Some of my own students also began attending classes in Hebrew Scripture, the Torah, wondering if the reason we were being forced to remain in the USSR was to fulfill the Jewish religious duty of learning the Torah.

In each of my classes, I found myself fielding volleys of tough questions about the secret of Jewish survival, the role of religion in the Jewish state, the spiritual essence of Jewish holidays, about ways to prevent physical assimilation. There were also questions related to the Torah itself, many of which I didn't know how to answer. In order not to lose face, I got myself a *Chumash*[15] and tried to puzzle things out on my own. Alas, I was painfully aware that the answers I gave my students were shallow and unconvincing. I was out of my depth. It was time to take some Torah classes.

The Jewish religious scene in the USSR in the early 1980s included the Chabad movement as well as a new Orthodox religious

---

[15] The *Chumash* contains the five books of the Torah in book form, as opposed to the scroll form.

group led by Ilya Essas, one of the initiators of Jewish religious revival, which became an important force in Moscow. Many of my students began to study Torah there. The Orthodox were split on the issue of *aliyah*: not all of them favored engineering a return to the Land of Israel by human and political means (instead of waiting for the Messiah to do so upon his return). Those who did, led by Pinchas Polonsky, Ze'ev Dashevsky, Yakov Belenky, and Michael Kara-Ivanov, split off into a separate religious Zionist group, which in years to come would become known as the *Machanaim*. These people became my good friends.

I started to attend Pinchas Polonsky's Torah classes, while he came to my Hebrew classes. Now my tough questions were being answered. A whole new realm opened up before me, sending me on a long and intense spiritual journey that would eventually lead me toward faith.

* * *

One day a friend introduced me to Dov Kontorer.

I had heard about Dov: he traveled around the country on sensitive assignments sponsored by Chabad, on behalf of Simon Yantovsky, a remarkable older man who had made it his mission to describe and photograph synagogues destroyed by the Soviets throughout the country. Dov—young, mobile, and little-known to the KGB—was helping Yantovsky with this project.

Dov Kontorer

Dov Kontorer remembers

I met you in December 1982, prior to my last trip for Yantovsky. I didn't know then who you were or what you were doing, but you made an impression on me with your seriousness and absolute discretion. You gave me no contacts in the cities I was going to, but you asked me to find out whatever I could about Jewish activists.

After this trip, we met again in January 1983. You seemed pleased with my results, and that's when you told me about your great project for spreading Hebrew studies and Jewish literature all over the Soviet Union and invited me to join it.

At the time, other kinds of unofficial and unsanctioned Jewish activity in Moscow, like general Hebrew classes or religious groups, operated as a kind of open community: although they did not advertise themselves, there were certain places or people—access portals, so to speak—accessible to anyone not known to be a KGB plant. In contrast, the Cities Project operated in strict secrecy. Very few people knew of its existence at all, and those who did, knew very little. There were no access portals, since you (or later, Ze'ev Geyzel and I) personally selected the participants. Very few people in Moscow were directly involved, and they kept everything related to the project absolutely secret, even from their families or friends in the Jewish movement.

The scope of your proposal, when I finally understood it, came as a shock to me. There I was, barely nineteen years old and about to get involved in something massive, secret, dangerous: this was serious business. Thus began our intensive collaboration that lasted until the dramatic events of the summer of 1984. During these eighteen months, I traveled a lot: usually once a month, for a week at a time, and often twice a month.

Besides a strong commitment to Jewish issues, the key people involved in the Cities Project had to meet rigorous criteria: they had to be charismatic, know Hebrew, be able to teach it, be mobile and, of course, be able to keep their mouths shut.

The project became my main preoccupation. My activities consisted of three interrelated tasks: teaching, distributing literature, and carrying messages, in addition to other occasional tasks of a technical or emergency nature.

Some of my teaching was done one-on-one, whenever we found a relatively young, talented, energetic, and courageous person who showed enough potential as a local leader and Hebrew teacher to justify a trip. But our main emphasis was always on group classes, either given in a city or in our summer camps, where we invited activists from a number of different cities.

Gradually, by trial and error—none of us were trained as educators—we developed a special technique, used in our summer

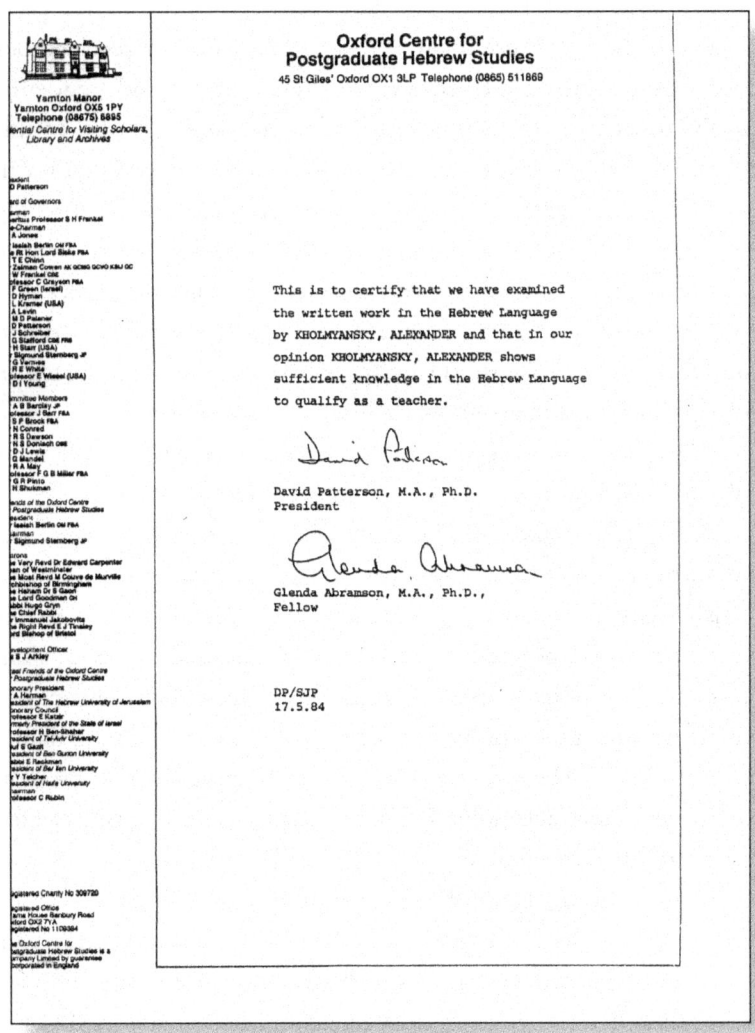

Teaching certificate issued to Alexander Kholmyansky by the Oxford Centre for Post-Graduate Hebrew Studies

camps and in one-on-one teaching, which allowed us to convey a massive amount of information in a very short time, no more than two or three weeks, letting the student to gradually master it on his or her own over the following year. We gave them both substantive material (a myriad of Hebrew verb root associations, a great many grammatical rules, and so forth) and clear directions on how to study and teach. The latter represented the unique value of this method, because it allowed a student who had received our crash course not only to progress in the language independently for the rest of the year but also to start teaching beginners. In this way, we seeded the cities with new teachers and equipped them with everything they needed to compensate for their lack of teaching experience or their isolation from a Hebrew-speaking environment. This was part of our strategy to turn Hebrew language studies into a self-replicating train-the-trainer system that could withstand and survive the inevitable assault by the KGB when it came. Later, in Israel, we realized that such front-loaded methods are not common in language instruction, but in our environment, with its unique risks and objectives, they proved uniquely effective.

Our newly trained teachers also became distributors of the literature we supplied: dozens of titles on ancient and modern Jewish history, the classics of Judaism, collections of essays, works of fiction, Israeli periodicals, and other educational materials, all in Russian translations, all photographed and printed on heavy photo paper. A standard set of books for each city fit into a large, tightly packed hiking backpack. How many of these backpacks we brought to different cities across the USSR no one can tell. I myself carried these bags dozens of times.

And finally, my third role was as a messenger. We didn't use the telephone, and therefore sending any message required taking a trip. For example, if we were going to hold a summer camp near city A, we had to travel to A at least once, and perhaps several times, in order to make arrangements with the local person in charge of camp logistics. We also had to travel to each of the cities where our camp participants lived, in order to invite them to attend. All these cities could be hundreds if not thousands of miles from A and from each other, because we chose students based on their level of Hebrew proficiency rather than their location.

Obviously, this method of communication was both costly and labor-intensive (and besides, the messenger never knew on setting out whether our local contact would be at home or even in town when he arrived), but it kept the risk of disclosure to a minimum. We saw indications that the KGB tracked some of my trips, but I'm convinced that they knew at most a tenth of what we were actually doing. Otherwise, you, the leader of the project, would never have remained at large for so long; Ze'ev Geyzel and I would never have avoided prison altogether; and the number of arrests in the provincial cities, where the authorities felt much freer to act than in Moscow, would have been much greater.

These trips gave the local people much more than information and books: they gave them a sense of connection, attention, a sense of a common destiny. Thanks to these visits, our friends in the Volga region, the Baltic republics, and the Ukraine were able to receive news of one another, to keep in touch and feel that they belonged to a community of like-minded people. The need for this was much higher in remote cities than in Moscow, which by the first half of the 1980s possessed a sizeable and self-aware Jewish community.

As for me, I loved to travel. I enjoyed being a stranger in a new place, experiencing the atmosphere of another city, exploring unfamiliar streets alive with their own life, so different from Moscow. But even so, my travel schedule in the years 1983 and 1984 was absolutely insane. Though I continued to travel until 1988, when I left for Israel, I would never again travel with such intensity.

Our policy of strict secrecy—even my own parents virtually never knew where I was going—allowed us to keep the bulk of our activities hidden, which not only kept us safe but also helped minimize the risk to our friends in other cities, where the authorities were much less tolerant than in Moscow.

* * *

In May 1983, my brother Misha left town for the May Day holidays with his wife Oksana and their son Maxim. A few days later, I got a call from Oksana: "Misha has been arrested, he got fifteen days' administrative detention!" Oh my God! Like a man possessed, I started calling everybody in Moscow who could give me advice; many *refuseniks* and dissidents had gone through this. Unfortunately, they were unanimous in their opinion: "It can't be helped. There's nothing to be done."

Natasha Khasin gave us the only piece of practical advice: to go to the Central Reception Office of the KGB.

"Central Reception is not just a bureaucratic kind of place, it's like their nerve center," she said. "They staff it with high-ranking people who know what's going on. In any case, they're not expecting you to come to them; that's a move that's way outside their rules of engagement. Plus, technically you'll be there to complain about the cops, and the KGB hate the cops. You should go; it can't hurt."

That was an original move, and my mother and I liked original moves. And so it was that we found ourselves standing in front of the heavy front door to the Central Reception Office of the KGB. Everything in there was calculated to instill fear and make the petitioner feel small and insignificant in the face of this all-powerful organization. The receptionist told us to wait on a couch. We made ourselves comfortable. Time passed: half an hour, an hour, but no one came to get us. A thought flashed through my mind: perhaps they were filming us with a hidden camera to see how we behaved under stress.

After months of sleep deprivation, an enormous overload, an inhuman pace, the sudden, enforced stillness took its toll. Soon, my surroundings began to feel unreal, irrelevant, I began to feel strangely relaxed—and drifted off into a deep sleep. I don't know how much time passed before my mother woke me up and the receptionist told us to go in.

We were received by an official whose high-handed manner suggested a high rank. He looked at me with genuine interest: the look of a man who knew many details about me and my brother, who knew what I wanted to tell him and maybe also what I wanted to hide. I also peered intently into his face: perhaps I would gain some new insight.

While my mother and I complained, protested, expressed our outrage, I noticed that he wasn't listening; instead, he continued to study my face, my manner of speech. And suddenly—perhaps from some slight change in his expression—I realized that this was a look of respect: in his own way he saw me as a worthy rival. The very fact that I fell asleep right there in their den, instead of sitting there shaking with fear, was a point in my favor. Natasha was right! We came home with a peculiar feeling of a game half-won.

Over the years I had thought a great deal about optimal behavior during interrogations. Gradually, I have developed my own technique, taking into account both Albrekht's and Khasin's approaches. Unlike Albrekht, I favored talking less, but like him, I strongly advised resisting any attempt by the interrogators to steer the conversation away from the declared subject of the interrogation onto other topics, a favorite tactic. Unlike the Khasins, though, I did not recommend total silence: I knew from experience that no one could remain silent during an interrogation.

My approach was to talk in blocks of words, preferably repeating them, not varying the subject and the words too much. The goal was neither consistency nor responsiveness; in fact, the more absurd and illogical, the better. For example, a woman under interrogation might exclaim: "Decent people don't talk to ladies in that tone!"

It was also a good idea to say: "I'm scared, I'm afraid of you—you are trying to intimidate me!" Hearing the words "I'm afraid" tended to annoy the investigators a great deal, because they knew perfectly well that a person who was truly frightened and about to lose self-control and "break" would never say these words because he would be unaware of what was happening to him. His fear resided in his subconscious. But anyone who recognized his fear enough to name it wasn't all that frightened or intimidated: he was self-aware, he was resisting, and therefore he wasn't "broken." Plus, threats and intimidation were prohibited by the code of criminal procedure, and even though the KGB acted as though they were above the law, they liked to pay lip service to it. Therefore, whenever the investigators heard a subject say: "You're trying to intimidate me!"—they began to deny and make excuses.

* * *

Michael Kholmyansky remembers

On May 1, 1983, I came to Odessa on vacation with my wife and son. We stayed at the apartment of Mark Nepomnyashchy, Edda's father. On May 4, we came back from a show at the Opera House to find a house search in progress, conducted by a Captain Gongalo and several people in civilian clothes who did not identify themselves. Among them was a known KGB operative by the name of Sergey Motsegorov.

When I entered the apartment, Gongalo shoved me roughly into the room and demanded to see my ID, without showing his own. He was annoyed at my own request to see his ID and produced it only after several requests. Then my wife and I showed him our identity papers. Gongalo addressed me in the following manner: "So, Kholmyansky, what do you do in life? Have you got a job, or are you a parasite?" I replied that I was employed; he asked where; the conversation began to resemble an interrogation, until I declined to answer any more questions and he threatened to continue the conversation "elsewhere."

When the search was over, around 1 a.m., Gongalo ordered me to follow him. I asked to know the legal basis for my arrest but got no explanation. I was taken to the district police station. At 2:30 a.m. I was called into a room where Gongalo, Motsegorov, and a man in civilian clothes, known as KGB Lieutenant Colonel Krasnov, were sitting.

Krasnov took the lead and started an hour-and-a-half "chat," in a style that ranged from the inappropriately familiar, for example, "my dear Michael," to unprintable abuse. He asked me many questions, but when I asked if this was an interrogation, he said it was just a friendly conversation; and yet, when I asked a question, I was told: "We are the ones asking questions here!" In addition to the questions, I had to listen to a lot of threats and insults. At the end of the "chat," around 4 a.m., they told me: "We're keeping your ID. You are under house arrest until tomorrow."

Later that day I was taken to the District Court. Neither my wife nor any of my friends were allowed to accompany me. I was ushered into a room where there was a man sitting at one table and three women at another. None of them introduced themselves or deigned to explain to me what was happening. The man began asking me questions about my personal information and place of employment. Only then did I realize that I must be talking to a judge.

To make sure, I asked the man if he was a judge, and he replied in the affirmative. Then he told me that a claim had been filed that I had caused a disturbance at the district police department, that I had shouted and cursed. He asked what I had to say to that. I replied that it was a false accusation. Then the judge said: "Well, here are your fifteen days," and the procedure was over.

It goes without saying that during my entire time at the district police department I had never raised my voice or used a harsh word. This hearing did not include even a semblance of legal procedure: no witnesses were questioned, no documents presented to me, and Motsegorov, who was not in the room during the hearing, already knew the verdict when I came out. Even the name of the judge was not disclosed; my wife learned it later, and then only with great effort.

From the court, Gongalo and Motsegorov drove me to the Odessa detention center, where I spent my fifteen days' detention. Interestingly, I was put to work only once, unlike ordinary detainees.

Forty-five minutes before the expiration of my detention term, Lt. Col. Krasnov and a police captain came for me. I was led out of the building and seated in a chauffeured government car. All this seemed like too much honor for a petty hooligan. The car sped through the streets of Odessa and stopped in front of the railway terminal just as the train to Moscow was pulling out.

Since we had missed the train, they drove me to the airport, where Krasnov went to book two seats on a plane for me and my wife, who had come there on her own. (Our son Maxim had left earlier.) Before leaving, Krasnov gave me back my ID and told us that we were free to walk inside the airport terminal and even go out to the square in front of it. But under no circumstances were we allowed to return to the city. "And don't you ever come to Odessa again," he added. When my wife asked how that comported with the freedom of movement guaranteed by the Soviet constitution, he replied: "All that crap's in Israel."

* * *

While Misha was still under arrest, Felix arrived in Moscow to say farewell. His application to emigrate had been approved, quite unexpectedly; he was going to make *aliyah*. Our parting was emotional. I was happy for him. He had done so much for our project. Dov would take over Felix's role. Felix was leaving . . . while we stayed behind—with the KGB, with the interrogations, the house searches, the arrests.

* * *

The struggle for the right of Jews to emigrate began to feature more and more prominently in the overall struggle against human rights violations in the Soviet Union. While the dissidents' hopes to change the very nature of the Soviet regime seemed utopian, the struggle for the freedom of emigration was universally believed to have a realistic chance of success. This cause was all the more important because it affected an entire, discrete population group—tens of thousands of people. The continuing official and unofficial persecution of Jews in the Soviet Union supplied the *aliyah* movement with an ongoing stream of information to provide to Western media, ensuring a favorable media coverage and attracting international public interest to our cause.

Public interest, in turn, encouraged political figures to take part in the struggle against the Soviet ban on emigration, which was perceived in the West as a violation of one of the most fundamental human rights. While the effort was framed as a struggle to get Jews *out of* the country, most of the work was done by the *aliyah* movement, which sought specifically to get them *into* Israel, their national home, since those seeking to emigrate to other Western countries such as the United States had never established their own movement.

Jewish organizations in the West, such as the US-based National Conference on Soviet Jewry, Union of Councils for Soviet Jews, and Student Struggle for Soviet Jewry, or the UK-based 35s groups, and others, managed to introduce the issue of emigration into the public discourse in the West. They sparked a wave of empathy across a whole spectrum of political groups and public organizations.

A rare moment of happiness (from left to right):
my Mom, I, Shannie Goldstein (New Orleans), Papa

As a result, more and more prominent political figures began contacting us and coming to Moscow to visit and interview us. They included US government officials, senators, and members of Congress, members of the UK Parliament, as well as an array of other prominent figures. Who could have imagined that our national struggle would become a kind of spearhead for the overall struggle for human rights? I sensed that we—a handful of Jewish activists—were causing significant pain to this monstrous creature known as the USSR.

* * *

In the meantime, I had begun seeing Anya Yerukhimovich. So much time had passed since we first met. We had gotten together occasionally before, but always as friends, no more. Now, somehow, everything changed: all of a sudden, I saw her in a new light.

The magic charm of these meetings . . . the subtle play of shadows, the rustle of the wind, the crunch of twigs under our feet in the quiet woods . . . so soothing. Struggle, anxiety, stress—everything faded away. I felt warm inside, descending into the veiled depths of my soul. Someone had touched the hidden strings, and unearthly music began to sound.

Long after each parting with Anya, a trace of the sublime, unearthly mood kept me warm. I imagined that these meetings had become important for both of us. Had I found what I had dreamed of for so long—the person who was meant for me, my soulmate, my missing half?

Oh God, what was I talking about? How could we indulge in such wishful thinking? Anya was not likely to make *aliyah*—her father worked in a highly classified enterprise. And I myself was walking along the edge of an abyss. Yet we couldn't help ourselves: we started seeing each other more and more often.

* * *

Meanwhile, the KGB were becoming increasingly menacing.

Dov Kontorer remembers

We intentionally gave this enormous project no name. Even though there was vigorous activity all across the country, in our conversations we simply called it "the Cities." Of course, just by being a movement, an unsanctioned collective effort of many people, it was a thorn in the KGB's side. Intolerant of any whiff of independent organized activity, the KGB were always quick to trot out the label of "anti-Soviet organization," even for things that were not at all subversive or critical of the regime. Naturally, like any bureaucracy, they couldn't move against something that had no name. Having lost hope of discovering one, the KGB tried to invent something plausible. They began to use the expression "the nationwide ulpan."[16] This expression popped up simultaneously in several places: for example, they used it on someone during an interrogation as an explicit threat.

By the spring of 1984, it became clear that you, the project leader, were under attack. More and more often, they asked about "the nationwide ulpan" during interrogations, and more and more often, they mentioned your name. Your arrest seemed imminent. I remember how you yourself called us together and gave us instructions and authority to act in your stead in case something should happen to you. By that time, Ze'ev Geyzel and I had accumulated considerable experience in the project. We all decided that the two of us would split your responsibilities between us.

Valentin (Benny) Lidsky

My main assistants became Valentin (Benny) Lidsky and Michael Volkov. Our technical needs were handled by Grisha Levitsky and Igor Mirovich. For a long time, the main manufacturers of our photographic literature were Grisha Danovich and Max Zakharin.

* * *

Once again, I am under surveillance—heavy, sticky, and relentless. Once again, the black KGB car, bristling with radio antennas, trails me as though tied to me by an invisible rope. Once again,

---

[16] *Ulpan* means Hebrew classes.

our students are called in for interrogations, but not to talk about "the nationwide ulpan": now, the interrogators repeat one simple message: "Kholmyansky is first on our list of future arrests. It's been over a year since the arrest of Joseph Begun; now it's Kholmyansky's turn; there will be a new show trial." The feeling of impending danger becomes acute.

Chapter 5

In May 1984, all my efforts to organize a summer Hebrew camp for the most promising potential new teachers fell flat. Everything that could go wrong, did; none of the people I invited were available; and the KGB watched me so closely I had the hardest time shaking them off to leave town. I was really disappointed, as I had looked forward to teaching. I also had a sense that this might be my last Hebrew camp, my swan song. But in the end, I managed to pull together a different group and took them to Estonia in early July.

Map of Estonia

A grueling journey by train and several buses brought us to the small town of Võru in the south-east of Estonia, and from there to a small holiday village called Ähijärve. A true wilderness: a vast lake surrounded by huge trees, a few wooden houses nearby, and nothing else. It would have been heavenly, were it not for the nasty autumn-like rain, especially unpleasant in the middle of July.

The bad weather had scared off other tourists. A middle-aged man checked in the next day, a group of truck drivers a couple of days later. The man, trim and reserved, did his morning exercises together with one of our girls on the grassy patch in front of our cottages. The truck drivers stayed more or less drunk the whole time but didn't give us too much trouble.

Classes began. I poured myself into my work, teaching with abandon. The summer camp format allowed the teacher almost no downtime: every spare moment was used in teaching, explaining, answering questions, giving individual attention that created that momentum, that sense of a joint effort, a hunger to learn more. A few days in, I could already feel the change: the students were absorbing the material, speaking more fluently and freely, and their eyes had acquired a special gleam.

On Friday night, July 19, I had an unusually vivid nightmare. I dreamed I was in Moscow, on my way to a meeting, when suddenly two policemen stepped in front of me. They began to rifle through my bag. With that sense of utter powerlessness that is peculiar to dreams, I saw them take out my notebook and begin to leaf through it, looking at me with revolting grins of sadistic pleasure. Even in a dream, I knew that there were no addresses from the cities in my notebook, and yet I was overcome with a sense of failure and irreparable loss. They had put their dirty paws on my most closely guarded secret, and now it was ruined. Defiled. All gone.

I woke up to a delightful early summer morning: the sun shining, birds chirping, a light breeze barely stirring the curtain, my friends sleeping peacefully all around me. But the dream was still with me in all its powerful emotional reality, an unrelenting anxiety gripping my heart. Was it a sign from above? What could it mean?

When my friends got up, I made everyone go through all their notes to make sure there was nothing incriminating in them, nothing remotely ideological or critical of the regime. Everything looked fine. We resumed our studies; the hours flew by. But on

Friday evening, I learned that one of our girls had written a letter home in violation of my instructions and dropped it into a mailbox at the entrance to the neighboring Estonian village.

This was a serious problem: the KGB could trace us here! We borrowed a screwdriver from the locals, and one of our guys neatly removed the side of the box and retrieved the letter. He replaced the side panel, leaving no visible trace of the break-in, but now the box would not lock back up. We returned the screwdriver and apologized to the director of the holiday village. We debated cancelling the camp and going home but in the end decided to stay.

Monday was a particularly productive day of study. It was nearly seven in the evening when I heard a frightened Chaya Berenstein shouting: "There's a police officer coming this way!" I looked out and saw a police officer, accompanied by two men in civilian clothes, hurrying toward our house.

They burst in and began rummaging through every book and piece of teaching material in the house. They had a search warrant written in Estonian, which, when translated into Russian by the policeman, turned out to contain an utterly surreal charge. Apparently, a large flowerbed in the neighboring town was regularly being vandalized. The flowers were arranged to spell out something like "Fortieth Anniversary of the Liberation of Estonia"—little wonder the locals wanted this reminder of the forcible annexation of independent Estonia by Soviet forces during World War II destroyed. Now, somehow, we were the main suspects, and the police had come looking for the flowers. The broken mailbox was also mentioned, albeit in passing.

The search went on for seven hours, well into the night. At one point, we stepped out on the lawn in front of our building and were surprised to find there our truck drivers, miraculously sober, standing around waiting to drive us to Võru.

We spent all next day at the police station being interrogated—by the same trim middle-aged man who had stayed with us at Ähijärve and had done his morning exercises outside. Evidently, every other guest at the vacation complex that week had been a plant: the KGB must have got wind of our plans, despite all our precautions, and had set this up in advance like a military operation.

One of our girls came out after talking with him, with an odd sparkle in her eye:

"The KGB sends its compliments," she said to me.

"??"

"Yep. He said he could see that we've been trained in what to do during an interrogation. He said he recognized Kholmyansky's method in us."

In the evening, they let us go, but we hadn't been home ten minutes before two figures appeared outside the door: a rather large police sergeant with a polite and guilty smile on his face and a gloomy-looking soldier.

The sergeant addressed me. "Alexander, please excuse us for bothering you at such a late hour, but they found some problems with your ID papers that need to be fixed. The chief sent us to ask you to come back right away. I know it's after hours but he's waiting there for you. Please come with us."

It was 8 p.m. by the time we got to Võru. A dull, weary indifference came over me. As soon as we entered the police station, my guides disappeared. The commander, of course, was long gone: they had tricked me. I waited in an inner room for a while; no one paid any attention to me. Then a burly sergeant came up to me and, putting his arm around me in an incongruously affectionate gesture, began dragging me bodily into the next room. I protested angrily, struggling to break away, when, in one quick, practiced movement, he yanked the belt out of my trousers. How little it takes to turn a free man into a prisoner: all they need to do is force him to hold up his own pants!

"Now give me your shoelaces!"

"This is an outrage! The chief himself asked me here!"

"What chief? It's half past eight! He'll be back tomorrow morning and he'll decide what to do with you, but tonight you're staying right here."

A heavy metal door was unlocked, and I was shoved out to the hallway. What a disgusting smell!

The policeman on duty asked:

"Where do I take him?"

"Take him to number one."

The door of the nearest cell swung open with a grating shriek of metal, and a moment later, I found myself inside. The door slammed shut. Stunned, I stood there in the dark, unable to understand where I was. Good God, the stench! This was a nightmare. I felt sick, unable to breathe. Suddenly, a wild rage seized me, and I began pounding furiously on the metal door, but to no avail.

Two other bodies lay on the floor beside me. I began to peer intently around the dark cell. One corner was filled with puddled urine, a pile of feces lay in another, and there were people on the floor a scant few feet away. No, not on the floor: on some sort of platform about a foot off the floor. How in the world could they just lie there in such filth?

Now I knew what this was: an administrative arrest. According to the code of criminal procedure, an administrative arrest could last up to fifteen days. Clearly they weren't going to let me go soon; once they had sunk their claws into someone, they held on to him as long as they could. I knew how they operated. They wanted me behind bars so they could pick the charge that would stick: the flowerbed, the mailbox . . . what else?

But two weeks in here? The thought froze the blood in my veins. This place was as close to hell as I could imagine. How was I going to last two weeks without going insane?

Calm down, I told myself. Pull yourself together. Remember that this is actually not as bad as what many Jewish activists had gone through. And besides, it was proof that the KGB took me seriously: time to act accordingly.

Which meant, first of all, getting through the night.

I tried to sleep standing up, leaning against the door, but eventually I found a spot on the floor, as far away from the puddle of urine as I could, and curled up so as to take up the least possible space. I dozed off, woke up with a stiff neck and drifted off again, I heard scratching, biting, chewing noises all around me. Eventually, there were steps on the other side of the door, the sounds of morning, but hours passed before the door opened.

I flew out into the hallway, savoring the cleaner air. I felt I had aged ten years. They took me back to the same room where they had taken my belt and shoelaces—and there were my friends, waiting anxiously, their faces haggard after a sleepless night. Thank God for true friends: they were uncowed, they were saying encouraging things, they had already complained about my illegal detention to all imaginable authorities in hopes of getting me released! And yet, my night behind bars had opened a chasm between us. It was as though I saw my friends receding into the distance before my eyes. We belonged to different worlds now. They were still in the free world, while I already felt the mark of the vast penal system upon me.

Quite literally, in fact. My whole body itched. I took off my jacket: my arms were covered with ugly black spots. Ugh! I wondered what kind of vermin I had picked up in that cell.

"No, guys, let's not imagine that you can get me out of here so quickly, even if they did trick me to get me in here," I said. "Once they get someone behind bars, he's not getting out just like that, it's like an unwritten law in this country. What this is, of course, is administrative detention. Well, I'm not the first to get administrative detention, and I won't be the last. We'll get through this."

From the police station I was transported to court for a two o'clock hearing before an Estonian judge who stared at me with hate-filled eyes and declared that I stood accused of resisting police and inciting my whole group to resist the authorities. My request to bring my friends in as witnesses was denied. In fact, to my astonishment, the judge actually yelled at me; I had heard of police and KGB yelling at people—but a judge in court? "In the name of the law," said the judge in the end, "I find you guilty on all charges and sentence you to ten days' imprisonment."

And there I was, back at the police station. The same double door with bars on it opened before me, leading into the reeking corridor; the foul stench intensified outside cell number one. But no, praise God, this time they led me right past it, to cell number five. Larger than the first and, thankfully, somewhat less foul, at least by comparison, it even had indoor plumbing of a sort, albeit operated by the guards from the outside, so that using it required much loud banging on the door to attract their attention. This was my home away from home for the next ten days. Of course, who could say whether they actually would release me when my time was up?

Chapter 5

Without books or newspapers, without paper and pen, I had ample leisure to contemplate the abrupt change in my life. From the furious pace of even two days ago—to this enforced stillness. From being at the center of things, being responsible for people, for important decisions—to utter powerlessness. My world had shrunk to the size of a prison cell.

Time passed slowly. It felt so different from the passage of time on the outside. Here, time became a strange, viscous substance, flowing aimlessly and carrying me with it in a state of half-dazed, semi-conscious detachment.

Only sounds from the outside sometimes roused me: the only evidence that there was still a world out there, that life went on. I had become like a man who had lost all his senses except hearing. How varied the sounds were—an entire realm of sound I had never noticed before. Most were ordinary sounds: an exclamation, a cry, a shout, a muffled sentence, the rumbling of a car engine. There were also other sounds that I couldn't identify: hostile, hysterical, and unsettling.

With every passing day, the tension inside me grew inexorably. What made it worse was the uncertainty, the sense of a looming great evil. True, they had only given me ten days instead of the maximum fifteen, but could they tack on additional charges at the end of the ten days to keep me behind bars, now that they had me in their claws? Were they working on them even now? The wretched flowerbed alone could support a charge of vandalism, carrying between one and three years' imprisonment, but what if they added a political charge—spoliation of that jingoistic slogan? Of course, I'd never heard of administrative detention turning into a real prison sentence without a trial, but who knew what they might do.

Eventually, the door opened, and the guard ordered me out. My legs were numb, leaden, my senses refused to cooperate. Slowly, still in a daze, I shuffled down a long hallway and up the stairs to an office, where an Estonian officer sat behind a desk. He began asking me questions. The interrogation did not take long; soon I was back in my cell.

And yet, everything had changed; a black cloud had descended upon me. They wouldn't have troubled interrogating someone who was about to be released from administrative detention. Clearly, my fears had come to pass. They were not going to let me go. I was going to do actual prison time—with thieves, with murderers, with swindlers, with people who had done evil things. I, who had done nothing wrong. In a Soviet prison, from which people so often came back injured, maimed, their health ruined . . . if they came back at all.

And indeed, the next day they brought me out again. They handed me a typewritten form and told me to read it. At first, I had trouble making out the words—the letters swam before my eyes, my vision was oddly darkened. Eventually I made out my name and the words "criminal charge" and "vandalism." They told me to sign, confirming that I had been made aware of the charges. I signed, adding my protest against an unwarranted arrest.

Back in my cell, my thoughts took a different course. The day was August 2, 1984. Four years of work—lost, destroyed. At least for me personally. Even if I survived prison and returned unscathed, I was now a marked man and, as such, useless to the Cities Project. Others would have to take the work forward, others would have to see if the structures I had built would endure. But the cause in which I had invested my entire soul was now closed to me—and what was left for me now?

* * *

With the filing of the criminal charges against me, my status had changed: I had passed from administrative detention to investigative custody, which involved moving me from the local lock-up in Võru to a pre-trial detention facility in the Estonian capital of Tallinn. Pre-trial detention was a major part of the Soviet penal system; a detainee could spend months in custody before his trial, with no access to legal counsel and no effort made to advise him of his rights.

I was relatively fortunate in that my trip from Võru to Tallinn took only one night by special prisoner transport train, its cars divided into sections with three-tier bunks behind bars, like cages. The train stopped several times to pick up new prisoners, until my compartment, which sat four on the bottom bunk, was crammed with at least twenty people.

We arrived at dawn. The prison was a gloomy old building, reportedly built by Catherine II, that had undoubtedly seen much use in the intervening two hundred years, judging by the worn-down stairs: what multitudes must have passed here, to have worn these depressions in the solid stone!

Tallinn prison building

The worn-out stairs inside Tallinn prison

Inside a large prison cel

In the enclosed prison courtyard at the foot of the stairs, I took a look at the crowd of prisoners surrounding me. Their appearance was a shock to me: the reek of unwashed bodies, the shaved heads, but most of all, their faces. Having spent most of my life among educated, intelligent people, I had rarely been exposed to the criminal elements of society, had rarely seen faces radiating such elemental violence. Truly, this was a different world.

Prodded along by foul-mouthed guards, we shuffled up the stairs and were sorted into transit cells. My transit cell was as big as a hospital ward, with two aisles of iron double bunks, enough to fit a hundred prisoners. The walls were filthy, the ceiling sooty from clouds of cigarette smoke rising upward, obscenities scratched or scribbled on every surface. There was already a line over in the corner by the toilet enclosure, men jostling one another, pushing newbies and weaker guys to the back of the line: the law of the jungle was clearly the law here.

After a while, I was taken to the showers—crowded, filthy, cold, and all too short—and then to the storerooms to be issued a mattress with a sheet and a pillow, a metal mug, and a spoon. I was now ready to be assigned to my regular cell.

The female guard opened the door of a cell with practiced movements: the lower latch with her leg, the top latch with her left hand while her right hand inserted the key into the lock and turned it. The door opened with a grinding sound; the door closed; I was inside. I had become one of the multitude of Soviet prison inmates, the *zeks*.

I took a look around. The cell was small, with a bunk bed and another bed. A small toilet was fenced off in the right corner; it stank but not too badly. In the middle, a metal table was bolted into the floor, and two men sat around it staring at me. One, a large, sturdy man of around forty, had an intelligent and somewhat predatory face. The other one was tall and clearly Estonian.

"Well, hello there," said the first man. "I'm Eugene Fastov, this here is Kalm, and who might you be? Come on in, put your mattress down, and tell us about yourself."

Fastov began to chat about everything at once. About life in prison, about the prison rules, how he had been arrested and convicted and got an eight-year sentence. Fastov was, apparently, a man of many talents: he had studied mathematics and other sciences and had even started a doctorate. He could have become an engineer but was drawn to business, a risky and illegal occupation in the USSR. The Soviet legal system punished economic crimes much more harshly than crimes against persons: theft or embezzlement of government property could easily bring a ten- or twelve-year sentence, or even the death penalty, while murder usually earned five or six years and never more than eight.

Fastov revealed a lot of sensitive details about his case. I was too tired to pay much attention to him, but out of sheer habit I did glance at the vents when he started talking about the things he had managed to conceal from the investigator. Wasn't it obvious that the prison cell was bugged? Not a place to spill one's secrets.

Interestingly, the next morning, the three of us were made to swap cells with the people across the hallway. The cells seemed identical, so what was that about? Perhaps the listening devices in the other cell were malfunctioning!

As soon as we were taken outside for our daily forty-five minutes of fresh air in the prison courtyard (partitioned into concrete boxes five meters by six meters, with a metal mesh overhead), I mentioned it to Fastov.

The prison courtyard

"It may not be a good idea to talk about these things out loud in the cell," I said, "what you told your investigator and what you didn't. They might use it against you."

Fastov snarled:

"They can all go to hell for all I care!"

Is that right, I thought to myself. No one could be that nonchalant about the possibility of getting caught lying in an interrogation. You weren't placed into my cell by chance, my friend, you're an informer. They think that you can soften me up, that your pretend confidences will make me want to respond in kind and spill my own secrets. Well, now I know. Thanks for the warning!

This also explained another anomaly: why Fastov and Kalm, both of them in post-conviction status, were being held in a pre-trial facility with people who were still under investigation, like myself, when by the rules they ought to be held separately. Fastov had mentioned that the authorities were crafting additional charges on top of his current sentence. Clearly, this made him vulnerable to blackmail: if he got me to talk and testified against me at the trial, he could hope for a shorter sentence.

The concrete box where prisoners took their walks

* * *

Prison life was chaotic and unpredictable. During the month I spent in pre-trial detention, Fastov and Kalm kept getting taken out to meet with their investigators and threatened with new charges. My own life was downright leisurely by comparison: I was only taken out twice and driven back to Võru to talk to the investigator assigned to my vandalism case.

During these interrogations I got a sense that the authorities were contemplating various new charges, trying them on for size, as it were. The first time, they took away an old jacket I had with me and returned it with every seam ripped apart, an obvious set-up for a potential drug charge. The second time, they brought in the mailman from Ähijärve and had him pick me out of a group of tall, burly, blond Estonians who were about as hard to tell apart from me as dump trucks from a bicycle: I was supposed to have offered him a bribe in connection with that broken mailbox at the holiday village. However, none of this seemed to be going anywhere. For the time being, the only charge against me was vandalism, which carried a maximum of one year in prison, unlike Fastov and Kalm's lengthy sentences.

But this didn't mean I could relax. The show trial the KGB had long promised required something far more substantial than vandalism. Clearly, they were cooking something up, and the fact that I couldn't see what they were doing was unnerving. I had a sense of impending doom that was almost physical in its intensity.

Chatterbox Fastov kept trying to draw me out, asking me about my case. Slowly, over time, I began to open up a little, always careful to share only those things already known to the KGB. Fastov seemed skeptical that the KGB would care about people teaching Hebrew; I even heard the words "delusions of grandeur." Evidently, I didn't look like someone who could stand up to the KGB, inspire demonstrations of support in the West, and so on. Still less did he and Kalm believe me when I told them that if the authorities persisted in fabricating charges against me, I would declare a hunger strike.

＊＊＊

We were fed three times a week: metallic-tasting tea in aluminum mugs and thin gruel in metal bowls with hunks of sour bread, all of this pushed through an opening in the door by one of the service

An inside view of a cell, seen through an opening in the door

zeks. These were convicts with relatively short sentences who had been allowed to serve out their time by working in prison. They were housed separately and fed slightly better. Because no one received this privilege without being recruited as an informer, service *zeks* were universally despised.

The overhead lights were never switched off. The only means to distinguish between day and night was the radio: it came alive at 6 a.m. and stayed on well into the afternoon, a never-ending flood of mendacious government news and propaganda, broken only by an occasional hour of classical music.

Sleep was a problem, not least because I tried to keep a different schedule from my cellmates. Fastov and Kalm sat up late at night talking and smoking, while I tried to tune them out and fall asleep so I could get up early and have some private time for prayer before Fastov woke up and latched on to me. An educated man, he liked to talk to me about everything from literature and music to tips on how to survive in labor camp.

Every tenth day was a library day: a service *zek* brought around a list of books available from the prison library, and we were allowed to order two books per person. As poor as the selection was, the first couple of days after the library day silence reigned while my normally chatty neighbors read their books.

We were also allowed to order things from the prison store. Each *zek* had a prison account into which his family could deposit money from the outside, that could be used to order small miscellaneous items, such as cigarettes, combs, paper and pens, or picture postcards.

* * *

My mother remembers

I remember every minute of that day, August 29, 1984. Grisha and I met up with Misha and Oksana downtown Moscow and went to a little park to discuss what to do next. In our bugged apartment, naturally, we couldn't discuss anything. The day was wet, cold, and cloudy. But no sooner had we brushed wet leaves off a bench and sat down than a young man sat down on the next bench and pretended to read a book while trying to eavesdrop on our conversation.

We moved to another bench, but the spy followed us. We started to walk around—and found ourselves in the middle of a small clot of people who all just happened to be there right next to us in an otherwise cold, empty park on a weekday morning. It was impossible to discuss anything, and we had to go home.

When we got off the bus near our house, I remembered that there was nothing to eat at home. Grisha went home, and I went to the store. When I came home, Grisha opened the door and, standing in the doorway, said: "Please don't be scared—there is a house search going on."

* * *

One day we heard quick steps outside; the door swung open. "I wonder who they're coming for this time: Fastov or Kalm?" I thought. At that point, the two of them were being called out on a daily basis while my case seemed forgotten.

"Kholmyansky, to the investigator!"

I stood up, shifting my weight from one foot to the other.

"What investigator? My investigator is in Võru. Are you sure it doesn't say 'transport'?"

"No, it says 'to the investigator.'" The guard twisted the paper in her hands. "It says so right here."

I shrugged and followed her, feeling a chill of anxiety. Had my investigator come here from Võru to meet with me? We went downstairs to the basement, where I saw a man pacing back and forth. Confident, middle-aged, an excellent suit, smelling of expensive cologne. A penetrating gaze, cold and sharp.

"Hello, Alexander, I am your new investigator, Colonel Chikarenko, special investigator for the major crimes unit. And this is my colleague, Major N . . . "

Caught off guard, I desperately tried to play for time in order to figure things out. Why did they feel the need to replace my lowly captain from Võru and give my case to these important gentlemen? When did my case escalate to "major crimes"? It must be major indeed if they were sending over the big guns from Moscow, two of them, even! Was this what I had feared?

"But I already have an investigator in Võru!"

"Your case has been transferred to us, Alexander; it is common practice that we take over cases from the provinces. Don't be surprised."

We went into the interrogation room.

Chikarenko turned to me.

"Alexander, we have something important to share with you. On August 29, a search was conducted in your apartment in Moscow. The search found a pistol, cartridges, and a quantity of anti-Soviet literature. Will you tell us now who gave you these items, and what was your purpose for keeping them at home?"

Simple words, but their meaning would not sink in at first, as if my body were covered with ice and they just slid off without being absorbed. And then suddenly, a burning sensation enveloped me. I was breathing heavily; my hands were trembling.

Here it was, the fabrication that I had been expecting! Here was that major case they were cooking up in order to bury me behind bars for real. And yet, I was strangely glad it wasn't drugs or something despicable or shameful. A gun charge had a certain dignity to it.

Don't show them your fear. Don't let them make their own transcript of the interrogation; I must control what is written down. As if reading my thoughts, Chikarenko handed me a blank transcript form (the *protokol*) to fill out.

"I must warn you, Alexander, that giving false testimony is a criminal offense."

I began writing down my testimony: "I affirm that I did not keep arms, ammunition or anti-Soviet literature at home." The pen danced in my shaking hands; my lines were coming out uneven, my letters were wildly slanted.

The interrogation continued:

"Please explain, Alexander, how is it that all those people who were vacationing with you came from different cities, and all of them are individuals of Jewish origin? Didn't one of them give you a weapon? What did you do during your vacation?"

I kept writing down my answers in the same uneven, shaky hand. Chikarenko kept asking the same question over and over in different words. But I held my line:

"These are extraneous questions that are not relevant to the case. I didn't keep a weapon at home, it was planted in my home during the search."

I stopped writing, and Chikarenko turned to me, saying in a mocking tone:

"I'm sure you know your criminal code, don't you, Alexander? Do you understand the penalty for illegal possession of a weapon? Up to five years' imprisonment. I'm not even talking about the anti-Soviet literature. I'm not even talking about the anti-Soviet literature. I suggest you begin to cooperate with the investigation. Nothing good will come of being stubborn. We'll chat again soon."

I followed the guard back up to the fourth floor in a daze on leaden legs and collapsed onto the nearest bunk, speechless. Hardened though they were, Fastov and Kalm were shocked at the sight of me.

"What happened?" Fastov asked impatiently. I waved him off.

"Come on, come on, what happened?"

I detected an unusually warm tone in Fastov's voice. Compared to Chikarenko, Fastov positively radiated warmth, almost as though he were family.

Alexander Kholmyansky

Moscow Hebrew teacher faces camp sentence

By JUDY SIEGEL
Jerusalem Post Reporter

A Jewish electronics engineer who teaches Hebrew in Moscow has been charged with "hooliganism," after falsely confessing to taking a letter out of a public mail box. Furthermore, a German-made pistol apparently planted in his apartment could lead to a very severe sentence, according to an Israeli who has just returned from a month in the Soviet Union.

Alexander (Ephraim) Kholmyansky, 34, who is unmarried and lives with his parents, applied for an emigrant visa to Israel in 1978 and was refused on the grounds that he allegedly had access to "secrets" at his work assembling TV and radio transistors.

During a vacation in Estonia with Jewish friends in July, one of the young women who had posted a letter home regretted what she had written, and asked her friends to help her retrieve the letter from the mail box. They were caught in the act.

Kholmyansky, who had not taken part in the extrication, took the blame upon himself and was arrested. He was charged with "hooliganism" and could face three years in labour camps.

"Moscow Hebrew Teacher Faces Camp Sentence," by Judy Siegel, *Jerusalem Post* (date unknown)

"A new charge... they've cooked up a new charge... weapons... a pistol and cartridges . . . and anti-Soviet literature . . . planted in my apartment . . . " I breathed.

"Wow," said Fastov, impressed. "They're really upping the ante. You could be right about your Hebrew: they wouldn't have done this if they didn't care. Do you know how long you'll get? Up to five years?"

"They hinted earlier at seven years imprisonment plus five years of judicial deportation," I muttered.

Fastov would not leave me alone:

"So are you going to start a hunger strike like you promised? Do you think you can do it?"

"Probably," I nodded hesitantly. "Bad timing though: I've just now got a care package from home . . . "

"A hunger strike, now, that's really something," Fastov chattered, sensing some entertainment coming. "In the morning, you hand a note to the guy who brings the grub that says that you've declared a hunger strike as a sign of protest and now refuse to accept food. And then the whole prison begins to buzz like a beehive that's been disturbed. Fun! and then they'll ship you out of here. They usually separate hunger strikers out."

Fastov and Kalm became engrossed in a discussion of the new stage in my case while I sat there, lovingly stroking the dried fruit Mom had just sent me in a care package and visualizing the start of my hunger strike the next day.

My mother remembers

When I came home, Grisha opened the door and, standing in the doorway, said: "Please don't be scared—there is a house search going on." No one approached me. I went into the kitchen, set my purchases down and quickly went to the toilet. I had Sasha's notes in my pocketbook, containing the names and addresses of people in various cities with whom he had been in contact. They were not to be destroyed except in an extreme emergency, which this clearly was. I tore them up and flushed them down the toilet, noting with amazement that no one tried to stop me, no one paid any attention to me at all. The reason for this became evident later. I went into the room.

There were seven of them in all: Bryksin, the investigator, the only one who showed his ID; two young men who appeared to be witnesses; and another four men, clearly KGB agents. One of these was a young man with a thin face and very dark, thick eyebrows, who was sitting at Sasha's desk, in his room, with some papers laid out in front of him. Another, a heavyset, energetic man, was stalking around the room with an air of authority despite his fussy, jerky movements. Evidently, he was the head of the operation. Two more pudgy, lantern-jawed young men were going in and out of the room. I fixed them in my memory: one had heavy thighs, the other, a big gut.

I sat down next to the desk, feeling tremendous pressure in my head. It was hard to think. I said to myself: "Maybe there's something you can do," and managed to get myself a little under control. The chief said in a soothing voice: "We're almost done."

At that moment, one of the pudgy men came into the room. He was holding a stick that we normally used to pull the curtains closed in Grisha's room. We always kept it behind the door. Now the stick was in the chief's hands. Several people crowded around the bookcase, as if trying to tilt it back. The chief bent down and began poking around with the stick in the small space underneath the bookcase. Then, suddenly, he pulled out some kind of dusty plastic bag, making it look as though he'd snatched it out from under the bookcase. "Well, well, what have we here?" he exclaimed with a show of astonishment.

He opened the bag and removed something that looked, at first glance, like a toy pistol. But when I leaned over the object, I made out the word Walther written on it in Latin letters. I had often heard that word, the name of an actual pistol, used during World War II; I felt sick, and all the voices seemed to be coming from a distance. With a tremendous effort, I returned to the terrible reality. I saw the chief counting something and saying: "Forty-three cartridges.

A pistol and cartridges; now that's a surprise! And here are the negatives of a book entitled Aliyah of the 1970s and a photocopy of a brochure by Markman, At the Edge of the World."

I shrieked: "These are not his! You've planted all these things here!" The chief, who had something of a professional actor about him, or a particularly sadistic magician adept at pulling things out of a hat, shouted in turn in a threatening manner: "Will you listen to what she's saying! You're going to have to answer for your wild accusations!"

No one paid any further attention to my protests. The chief ran to the telephone, and I heard him report his "findings" in an excited and satisfied voice. Then he began vigorously rubbing the pistol (probably trying to make it look as though his fingerprints had appeared on the pistol only at that moment).

After that, they began to bustle around, saying: "Now we're going to take a really good look around." And yet, their actions were just the opposite. They fingered a sleeping bag without opening it, pawed at the bookcase as though trying to pull it apart into little pieces . . . and then quickly left the room. Evidently, now that they had found the object they had planted, the rest of the search was just for show.

For instance, they didn't even try to look in other places where weapons or ammunition might have been hidden. There was a cabinet in the hall, where we stored tools and supplies for home repairs. It was big enough to hold an infinite number of cartridges. But they simply opened it, mumbled something, and closed the doors again. There was a crawlspace above the hallway, big enough to fit a whole machine gun, let alone a pistol: our suitcases were stored in there, all the way in the back, behind a stack of spare blankets. The chief climbed up on a stool and reached up until he could touch a blanket with his hand; then he closed the doors and got down again.

Finally, they were done, and the man at the desk began to write down an inventory of the items they had confiscated.

They were supposed to leave us a copy, but the copy they offered us was illegible. I said that I would make my own written copy straight from the original; otherwise I would not sign anything. Telling them what I thought of them helped restore some of my confidence and mental clarity. They began to fuss and fidget; they wanted our signatures in order to authenticate the record of the search. They seemed nervous and in a hurry.

Grisha and I refused to sign the inventory. Instead, we wrote on a separate piece of paper that we protested against the planted evidence. They took away the pistol and cartridges, the negatives and photocopies, without sealing them in an evidence bag.

* * *

After my meeting with Chikarenko I sat up all night, unable to sleep. Now the picture was clear; the uncertainty that had tormented me was gone. They had planted the weapon in order to paint us as a group of criminals, terrorists, who were only pretending to study Hebrew, Jewish culture, and Jewish civilization but were actually storing illegal weapons and ammunition—and why would we be storing them if not to use them for nefarious purposes? They were going to portray us as dangerous, violent people who must be incarcerated in order to protect society.

Yes, now it was clear. They wanted to break me and use me as an example to intimidate all the other members of the Jewish movement. They wanted the others to think that what was done to Kholmyansky would be done to each and every one of them, so that everyone would give in and stop resisting. And then everything would collapse; the Cities Project would turn to dust, as if it had never existed. Nor would the KGB content themselves with persecuting us quietly: no, they were going to put on a show trial, they were going to broadcast it on national TV so people would see me branded as a terrorist and criminal. And what would remain of the Jewish movement, what about those forty thousand *refuseniks* and people considering emigrating to Israel? They would see and hear all this and be terrified; what could we do to raise their spirits?

I owed it to them to stay strong. After all, the heroes of the Warsaw ghetto rose up against evil even knowing that their revolt had no chance of success. But we still had a chance!

What could I do to clearly show the world that I rejected these fabricated charges? I could declare a hunger strike! I was perhaps better prepared for a hunger strike than most, as I had fasted many times for medical reasons and for spiritual purification. I was thirty-four years old, at my peak both physically and mentally. Yes, a hunger strike was my antidote against KGB's poison, my true weapon. It was a double-edged sword: true, I would suffer; but so would they. I was ready.

Part Two

CHAPTER 6

I was startled out of my thoughts by a clatter of heavy boots from the hallway outside.

"Kholmyansky! To the deputy warden of the prison."

Major Kolk, a puny man affecting the penetrating gaze of a super-sleuth, launched into a verbal attack at once.

"So you want to declare a hunger strike, huh? Protesting, are you? We've seen this before. You think you're so smart, and yet you don't get it, you just don't get it: haven't you figured out who's running the country now?" (He meant the KGB, which had gained ascendance when its chief, Yuri Andropov, became head of the ruling Communist Party.) "Time is working against you people. On April 1 of this year, 1984, a decree was issued that says that refusing to accept food without good cause is considered a severe breach of the internal regime, and the offenders are to be sent to the punishment cell. *With no time limit*. Let me spell it out for you: if you attacked a prison guard, you'd get up to fifteen days in a punishment cell. But now you'll stay in there for as long as you keep on with your hunger strike. The only way to get out is either if you stop your hunger strike—or if you die. One or the other. I'll give you twenty-four hours to think about it, until tomorrow morning. Take him back to his cell!"

Back in the cell, Fastov and Kalm asked excitedly:

"So? What did he say?"

"I've got twenty-four hours to think it over. Either I stop the hunger strike, or they put me in the punishment cell tomorrow morning."

"And what are you going to do?"

"I guess it's the punishment cell for me."

The next morning, as expected, the guards yanked me out again and took me to see Kolk.

"Well? Have you thought it over, have you calmed down? Are you going to drop your hunger strike?"

"No, Major. A hunger strike is a sign of protest. It's the only weapon a prison inmate has."

"You're not an inmate yet, you're still a pre-trial detainee under investigation."

"I can't wait until I'm officially an inmate; by then, it will be too late."

"So that's your game! Don't like the charges, is that it? Not guilty, eh? Everyone else is wrong, but you alone are righteous? It's the punishment cell for you, then. We'll see if it won't cool some of your zeal. Maybe you'll come to your senses. Off to the punishment cell with you!"

Back we marched down the long prison hallways and down multiple flights of stairs, deeper into its bowels, into a little passageway with six iron doors on each side.

"Here's the punishment cell," the guard said amiably. "You're in number five. It's not fun, but people live."

I found myself in a stone pit. The guard lifted a cot—made of bare planks held in a metal frame, with no sign of bedding on it—and pressed it flat against the wall. A metal pin was pushed through from the outside, locking the cot tightly in place.

"Take off your clothes," the guard continued, handing me—to my amazement—a striped prison outfit made of the thinnest cotton, like something out of a Charlie Chaplin film. He also handed me a pair of flimsy slippers that did nothing to stop my feet from freezing.

"Make yourself at home," he said, and the door clanged shut.

I looked around me. So that's what it was like, this notorious punishment cell. This was the highest degree of punishment available to bring unruly *zeks* back in line. The only tools the penal authorities had that were worse than this were outright torture or the firing squad. The room was tiny, approximately 2.5 by 2 meters. Two metal supports were fixed into the floor: the cot rested upon them from eleven at night until five in the morning, when it was

Prison cot in the locked (upright) position

Metal pin holding the cot in a locked position (seen from the outside)

fastened to the wall. That was the window of time when I was permitted to use the cot.

Between the supports was a strange metal object, like a miniature stool, 12 by 12 centimeters, with sharp edges, too small for an adult to sit on. In the corner there was a tiny toilet partitioned off with a meter-high wall. The cement floor was fairly dirty. There was no window, no opening of any kinds for letting air into the cell; they must never air it out. So how was one to breathe? And it was cold, even though it was only the middle of September.

Well, here was the first miracle: there was a rag in the corner of the floor. I grabbed it and began to wash the floor, realizing that I would not survive in all this cement dust unless I made it as clean as possible. I scrubbed the entire cell before pausing to rest. The cell had probably never been this clean before, but then again, no one had ever moved in here permanently . . .

The cell was only big enough to take two steps in one direction. Two paces forward and two back: such was my little stroll, my exercise, if you will. My legs quickly began to feel tired, but there was nowhere to rest, no place to lie down or even to sit down. An overwhelming weakness came over me; that's what a hunger strike was like, and the first days were often the hardest.

At first, I tried to sit on the metal supports, managing a few minutes on one side and then the other. I tried curling up on that little stool, that brilliant torture device the likes of which I had never seen on the outside. Anything to pass the time until the evening. Anything to avoid lying down on the cement floor.

"Don't ever lie down on the cement floor," the *zeks* had told me. "Don't ever lie down, you'll catch TB right away. Whatever you do, don't lie down."

No lying down on the cement floor! That's the main thing. Perhaps I could somehow doze off standing up, first in one position then in another. Anything to hold out until the evening.

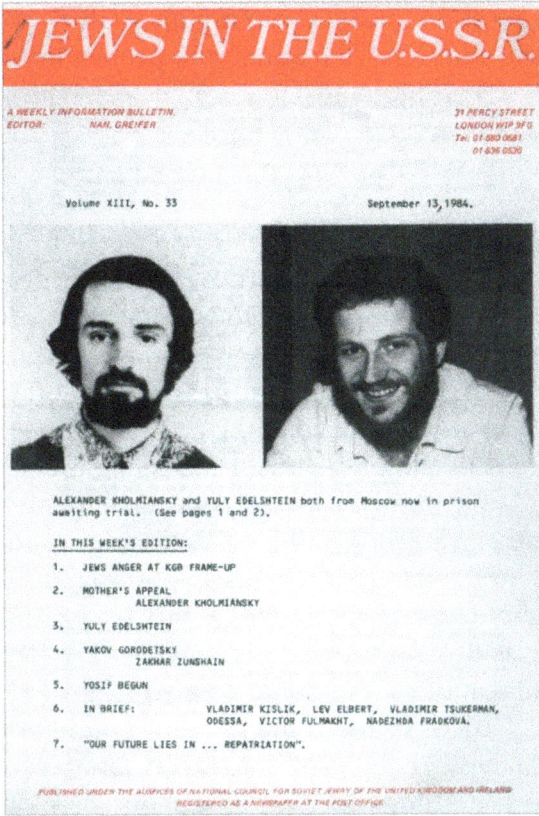

"Jews in the USSR," newsletter by the UK National Council for Soviet Jewry, September 13, 1984

Time dragged on with excruciating slowness, uninterrupted by clocks or trips to see the interrogator. I ought to pray but I didn't feel the strength to open my soul in this stone pit. Maybe a little later. At one point I did seem to doze off a little. I might try resting on my knees for a while; perhaps I wouldn't get sick from that. To pass the time, I started telling myself stories from books I had read, starting with Chekhov.

Before I knew it, evening had come. I heard heavy steps approaching: the duty guard was walking down the hallway, pulling out the pins holding the heavy cots up from the outside; the *zeks* inside lowered their cots. Now it was my turn: the guard opened my door and showed me how to lower mine—my bed, my couch of regal splendor, the object of so much longing—bare, chipped, rough-hewn boards held together by a metal frame, with no bedding of any kind. I took off my prison shirt and curled myself up on top of the cot in my undershirt, covering my shoulders with the shirt in a vain attempt to protect myself from the cold.

The moment I lay down (or so it seemed), the door opened again, and the duty guard shoved me off the bed: "Come on, move, it's five in the morning."

Shivering from the cold, too stiff to move my arms and legs, I slid off the cot. The guard pushed it upright, locked it in place, and shut the cell door with a clanging of the latches. I was left alone and bitterly disappointed to be jolted out of sleep, my only relief and protection against this harsh reality. My second day had begun.

My neighbors, the *zeks* in the other cells, were waking up; I began to hear voices. I was not alone in here: there were twelve cells in the punishment block, six on each side of the hallway. As soon as the guard was gone, the inmates began to call out to each other, shouting at the top of their lungs in order to be heard through two metal doors. I learned some important things from these shouted exchanges: for example, a typical stay in a punishment cell was three, five, or seven days, rarely ten, and fifteen was the legal maximum.

Most of the inmates were young, although a few were older. They were fed every other day, and even on feeding days the food was nothing to write home about: breakfast was a mug of hot water and a hunk of bread, hardly worth the trouble. The *zeks* found their few days in the punishment cell to be intolerable, whether because of the bad food or because of the isolation, and liked to toss around various schemes for getting into the infirmary. Few actually succeeded in doing so, unless they slit their wrists or managed to swallow something really nasty. Compared to the punishment cell, their regular cell felt like home and was remembered with affection and nostalgia.

Soon I, too, joined in the conversation. "Hey, guys," I yelled, "do they ever give anyone more than fifteen days?"

One of the veterans responded:

"That's when they really want to break someone, they'll give him fifteen days, then pop him back into the regular cell for a few hours and then bring him back here for fifteen more."

"Did you ever hear of anyone doing more than thirty days?"

"Nah, that's never happened."

Perhaps it hadn't, but now, evidently, it was going to. If the stay in a punishment cell was always time-limited, the administration must expect that the first few days would break me.

The next morning the door opened: "To Major Kolk!"

What did the grand vizier want from me now?

My fellow inmates peered through every peephole and crack in the doors as I was led away along the hallway. Since this was my first outing, none of them had laid eyes on me before. I heard soft gasps of astonishment; evidently, none of them had been forced to wear this outlandish striped outfit—I must be listed as the most dangerous inmate in here. Once again, we walked down the long prison corridors. I felt a grim pleasure seeing the guards escorting other *zeks* stop and stare at me in astonishment.

"We've talked it over," said Major Kolk, "and decided that your hunger strike can't really be considered open-ended. I know that's what you wrote in your declaration, but that was just your temper speaking. You've painted yourself into a corner, and we don't want that. Let's just agree that what's done is done, you've refused food for a couple of days, but now we'll reset and start over. We know you don't like being in a punishment cell, so here's a compromise: we'll feed you on the regular schedule, not punishment cell schedule.

You'll receive three meals a day; you're free to eat your ration or to leave it, but it will stay in your cell until they bring you your next meal."

Aha! My hunger strike was working. It bothered them; it was important to them that I should quit! I felt elated.

"I'm a man of my word, Major. I said 'open-ended,' and I meant it."

"But a hunger strike can't be open-ended! It must end sometime!"

"Let me remind you: I declared a hunger strike as an act of protest against the fabricated charges against me. If you want it to end, let me out and set me free!"

"Oh yeah? You'll die in here before they let you out!"

I returned to my punishment cell in a festive mood. As soon as I was inside, the door opened again: they were bringing me my so-called breakfast.

"Set it down on the floor. I refuse to eat."

They set it down on the floor. Now this was much harder to ignore. When a person is extremely hungry, the smell of food—even prison food—can be a powerful temptation. Now they would surely watch me closely to see if I took even the tiniest crumb, even half a teaspoon. No, I was not about to give them that pleasure!

In the meantime, my neighbors in the other cells set up a terrible racket. The punishment block was probably the only place in the entire prison complex where men and women were kept in close proximity, sometimes in adjacent cells. They couldn't see each other but they could hear—oh boy, could they ever! And so they let it all out, whatever came to mind, from crude flirting to all-out sex talk.

All this yelling was hard to take; a person on a hunger strike needs quiet. Each yell seemed to pierce through my thin protective shell. The noise, the obscenity was becoming unbearable . . . if only there was a way to switch them all off!

Only towards evening did my rowdy neighbors calm down. The noise died down, and then one of the gals began to sing in a surprisingly nice voice. These were the slow, mournful songs composed by men sentenced to penal labor in Siberia, old songs from the distant past, filled with anguish and despair. Several more people joined in. Evidently, these songs were widely known among this class of people; I was the only one in here who had never heard them before. And suddenly I felt a lump forming in my throat and an overwhelming wave of pity washing over me, not just self-pity but sorrow for those tens of millions of *zeks* whose lives had been ruined by the autocratic and totalitarian Russian state, in prisons and forced labor camps, over the past two or three centuries.

* * *

Kolk's orders were scrupulously obeyed. Three times a day the guards brought in my next ration and took the previous one away untouched. Often enough, they left the cot down, and I began to suspect that this, too, was done at Kolk's direct order so that the food would be closer to my face, the better to tempt me. I lay with my face to the wall, which radiated cold, saying to myself: "Nope, that's not actually food, it's inedible, it's like a piece of wood."

My mother remembers

Eventually, little by little, I began to recover from the shock of that house search and the planted weapons, until I was able to think and act again. Obviously, the first thing to do was to establish that the gun and the cartridges had been planted. I wrote out a detailed description of the search. In addition, when Misha read the inventory of the items that had been confiscated, he noticed that it did not specify the serial numbers of the pistol or the cartridges.

We had my description of the search translated into English and let some American diplomats read it; they said that it made for powerful reading. Misha and Oksana sent copies to many different government authorities in Moscow and Tallinn.

One of them was the Prosecutor General of the USSR whose job—at least in theory—was to verify that other government agencies did their work in accordance with the law. But our appeal produced no result. It soon became clear that the Prosecutor

General's office supported the fabrication, and we should expect no assistance from them. The KGB had free rein in this case.

They even told us this openly once. To gain time while the case against Sasha was being built, the office of the Prosecutor General of the USSR (a nationwide office) sent the file down to the Prosecutor General of the Russian Republic (a lower level in their federated hierarchy). Oksana and I went to the public reception office of the latter and asked the receiving official to let us see someone higher up, only to be told:

"They won't see you."

"Why not?"

"First of all, we no longer have your file. It was sent to us by mistake, and we've sent it back to the Prosecutor General of the USSR. And besides," he let slip inadvertently, "this case is being run by the highest levels of the KGB."

* * *

Meanwhile, my first week in the punishment cell was drawing to a close. Friday night was coming, my first Shabbat here. What could I do to celebrate it properly in here, to set that time apart, to make it special? I selected three of the prettiest postcards from the prison store and propped them up on the little partition that fenced off the toilet: my little bit of interior decoration to make Shabbat special. I washed the entire cell once again. Thankfully, it was quiet on the block; no yelling from the neighbors. And suddenly I felt strong enough in my spirit to attempt a proper Shabbat celebration in prison. You'd sung your songs, my dear neighbors, and now it was my turn to sing. I chanted portions of the liturgy, the *Kabbalat Shabbat*, those I could remember. My singing was far from perfect, but still I felt as if all the space above my head had opened up, reaching all the way up to the Source of Holiness, and energy flowed down to me—an encouraging, nurturing, uplifting sensation that gave me hope and support.

That magical Shabbat passed; Sunday came and went. Monday morning brought a summons—this time to see the warden himself, Maiboroda. I wondered how many of my neighbors had had that honor. My God, this was excellent: I kept getting these good omens that helped me bear this nightmare. If the warden himself was summoning me, it meant that my case was important to him, my hunger strike really bothered him. And therefore, every hour that I kept it up was another blow to the powers that be.

Maiboroda was the exact opposite of Kolk: a huge, imposing man who spoke in a confident, loud, angry voice and was clearly not used to being contradicted.

"Alexander, what are you trying to achieve? All you're doing is ruining your health. Do you think you're the first? We know how to deal with this; you don't think we'll let you die, do you? On day sixteen we'll begin to force-feed you. All this drama will die down, but you'll ruin your health for sure. You're an adult, after all; what's the point of these childish games? Think about your aging parents: why would you do this to them?"

"Do they know?"

"Oh, they'll soon find out. And I must warn you that you're not doing your case any favors. The behavior of a pretrial detainee during the investigation phase is very important, and the court always takes it into account during sentencing. Not only are you ruining your health, but you'll earn yourself a longer sentence."

Look at you squirm, I thought. Your words are like balm to my wounds. You're hating this situation I've created. Ha! The worse it is for my enemies, the better it is for me. And I turned to Maiboroda with a serene smile on my face.

Back in the punishment cell, I thought about the implications of his words. Apparently, my parents were not aware of my hunger strike. Were the authorities planning to keep it a secret? What could I do to let my parents and my friends on the outside know about it?

Suddenly, there was a soft knock on the door of my cell; it didn't sound like the guard. I went up to the door and heard:

"Hey, wanna get a note out to the outside?"

Astounded, I answered:

"Of course I do, but how? Do you have a way?"

"Yes!"

A *zek* stood on the other side of the door; I couldn't see him clearly through the tiny peephole in my door.

"What do I do?"

"You've got two minutes, write it quickly and get it to me."

"But how will I get it to you?"

"Through the crack in the door! Can't you see it, it's in the upper right corner."

"Where? I can't see any crack!"

"It's hard to see, but it's big enough to slip a note through."

"And then what?"

"I'll get it out."

"But how will you do that?"

"There's a women's transport leaving soon. I'll pass it to them through the kitchen. They don't usually search the women."

I grabbed the pen with a shaking hand and wrote a note addressed to my home address. Fortunately, I had been able to buy a pen from the prison store, and it was not confiscated during the search on my first day here. A minute later, my note was ready. My hands shook so badly from excitement that I had trouble slipping it through the crack.

"Come on, hurry up!"

Another second, and the note slipped through—my letter home, like a message in a bottle tossed out by a shipwrecked sailor.

*　*　*

The news of my hunger strike had spread all over the prison. No one believed it could succeed, especially not the older *zeks*, who twirled their fingers at their temples when they saw me out in the hallways to indicate that I was crazy. One of them whispered to me as I was being led past him:

"Are you nuts? Do you really think you can take on the entire government, the whole flippin' superpower? They'll just give you a little shot and say in the morning, 'Oh, his heart gave out.' And that'll be the end of you. You better quit before it's too late."

As I was gradually learning, these hardened criminals who were facing long years in prison or forced labor camps were not actually politically opposed to the regime at all, so that my notoriety as a supposed anti-Soviet agitator did not earn me any sympathy. My hunger strike, however, did. They contrived various ways of sneaking rags and newspapers into my punishment cell. These were really welcome: it had become so cold at night that if my hand or foot accidentally touched the metal frame of my prison cot, it really burned! I stuffed all the cracks in the boards with newspapers and wrapped the frame in rags. What a difference it made!

I was also lucky in my duty guards. Now and then they would leave the cot down for me, allowing me to snatch a few hours of rest when I could no longer stay upright on my feet. Who would have thought that jailers could be so considerate? Apparently, they weren't all beasts. Maybe these kinder guards were new, or maybe they had somehow managed to hold onto their humanity. They rarely took away my rags, and my handkerchiefs somehow remained in my possession after every search.

In other respects, Kolk's orders were still strictly observed. Plates of food were brought to me three times a day, and three times a day they were taken away untouched. Evidently, the effects of the hunger strike had begun to affect my physical appearance: every time I was led away for another chat with Kolk, I heard whispers in the cells and soft gasps: "So thin! How does he keep body and soul together?"

Incidentally, the feeling of hunger had disappeared. I wasn't feeling all that poorly. In fact, I had a new feeling of strength. I felt that I had seized the initiative: whereas before I had cowered like a trapped animal, waiting to see their next move, now they were reacting to me, trying to come up with something to get me to call off the hunger strike. Of course, a hunger strike was not an easy thing, but it was nothing compared with the feeling of impotence I had had when I was waiting passively to see exactly how the soulless beast was going to devour me and destroy my project, which I had created out of nothing and had cherished all these years.

My mother remembers

Here is a typical day: September 24, 1984.

At 9 a.m. I called Chikarenko. His first words were gruff: "Where have you been? I stopped by but no one was home."

Then he continued in a kinder and calmer tone:

"We need to talk."

"Talk about what?"

"About the gun."

"The gun was planted! Didn't you read the complaints I've sent to all the authorities?"

"We don't add complaints to case files . . . "

After this conversation, I went to the Central Committee of the Communist Party. From their public reception room, I dialed the number of a party official whose name I had been given. He told me to go see another party official, one Muranov, who was in charge of Estonia. Finally, after I raised a fuss, he said: "Leave your letter in the second window—we will consider it."

At 5:00 p.m. I called yet another official, one Maurer, the head of the Estonian Department of Investigations. I asked:

"Why is Chikarenko asking about the gun? Has there been a new charge filed, a new case opened?"

"No, there hasn't been, but naturally they're investigating, since it's against the law to keep weapons at home."

"So keeping them is against the law but planting them on an innocent man isn't?"

"You're out of line with your questions!"

* * *

Day sixteen of my hunger strike. I hear a heavy tread along the hallway, the bolts are unlocked, and my door swings open. "To the doctor's office," says the guard.

I haven't been in here yet. A nurse and an internal security officer are sitting in the room. The officer rises and addresses me in an official tone:

"Prison rules require us to begin force-feeding you on the sixteenth day of a hunger strike. Once again, I suggest that you start to accept food voluntarily. If not, take a look over here."

I look over—and gasp. The table is laid out with a whole range of tools and devices for force-feeding. The officer explains:

"This is a feeding tube, and these are special mouth gags for forcing the jaws open; this is for pulling out the tongue. This tip is inserted in the throat. And these are the handcuffs; the instructions require that you be handcuffed. Your mouth will be forced open, then the tube will be inserted all the way down to your stomach, to ensure that you can't vomit it up. A nutrient mixture will be poured into the tube. So, as you can see, we won't let you die. This will take the halo of martyrdom off of you in the eyes of the West since it won't look like a true hunger strike. But you'll still suffer. This is what you're doing to yourself."

"I won't take any food voluntarily, but neither will I resist. My hunger strike is still in effect; force-feeding won't change that. This is just another form of abuse. If you stop the force-feeding, I will continue to refuse food. But I'm not going to physically resist you."

> ### Hebrew teacher force-fed in Soviet jail
>
> MOSCOW (Reuter). – A Hebrew teacher jailed on charges of hooliganism in Estonia is being force-fed because he is on a hunger strike, members of his family said yesterday.
>
> Alexander Kholmyansky, 34, was detained for hooliganism on July 25 while on holiday at the Baltic coast. A full investigation was ordered after a search of his Moscow flat revealed a pistol and ammunition.
>
> Relatives said Kholmyansky had no knowledge of the weapon, and said it had been planted there.
>
> They said he began his hunger strike on September 13, and said a prison doctor had since told them he is being force-fed.
>
> The flats of five students and friends of Kholmyansky had also been searched. One friend, Yuli Edelshtein, 26, also a Hebrew teacher, has been charged with possession of narcotics and is also in detention, the family said.
>
> Kholmyansky's relatives said they believed the police action was intended to stop the two from giving lessons in Hebrew.

"Hebrew Teacher Force-Fed in Soviet Jail,"
Jerusalem Post, October 15, 1984

They insert the tube—roughly, painfully. My Lord, this thing is long! It feels like it will stay inside me forever. I feel something hot directly in my stomach. Then they yank it out, just as roughly, intentionally causing pain. They've damaged something; my throat hurts.

I'm back in my punishment cell. Now my throat is really burning. And yet . . . it could have been worse. They could have used actual torture, ripped my fingernails off with red-hot pincers. But this—it was just a feeding tube.

The officer did not show up for my second feeding. A different nurse came, an old woman, by herself. She looked at me:

"A hunger strike, eh? I've seen a lot of you people in my twenty years in here. Now you listen to me, sweetie. You sit like this . . . no, no, relax, don't tense up your mouth and neck."

In one swift, imperceptible motion she inserted the tube in such a way that I barely felt it. What a miracle—almost no pain! She pulled it out just as gently: a true master of her craft.

"Remember this, and you'll save your throat. But in general, it's better to drop this nonsense. I've seen so many of these hunger strikers, and it never helps. Just drop it, or you'll die."

And just like that, in one go, this good fairy with an ugly face taught me how do it. From that point on I was able to sit in such a way that the tube didn't hurt my throat—most of the time. I had learned to bear this painful procedure.

* * *

Thank God, now at least they stopped bringing me food and putting it in front of my nose three times a day. Glory to You, Lord! You had given me strength. I had withstood the temptation and had never touched anything. I continued to clean my punishment cell; there was no corner that I hadn't polished to a gleam. If there were a worldwide competition for the cleanest punishment cell, mine would be a shoo-in for first place.

* * *

Day twenty of my hunger strike. I raked my brain for a way to let the outside world know about it. Had my previous letter reached its destination? Or was it intercepted in Moscow? I must do something urgently: my time and my energy were not infinite. And whose address should I use? Best to make several attempts; let's see, whose addresses could I remember? My own home address, Misha's, Alla Sud's, Anya Yerukhimovich's: that's all. No, my memory brought up another address, a lady I knew called Inna Brokhina. I would start with her: she wasn't part of our project, so that's the last place the KGB would expect a letter from me. And if some of my letters were intercepted, that was OK so long as at least one of them got through. Now I could write openly; the time for secrecy was past. I didn't mind it if the KGB read what

I wrote. They knew I would try—that's why they had left me my pen and paper.

> My dears! I am still in complete isolation from the outside world. I have no idea what's going on. I have no access to newspapers or the radio. I am being held in a windowless punishment cell, 2.5 by 2 meters. October 13 marks a month since I declared a hunger strike. On day 16, they began to force-feed me through a tube. I'm feeling fine so far. My blood pressure is 90/60 on average, although it's unstable. My pulse is in the 80–100 range. I do feel weak and have trouble washing my underwear, but I can walk, albeit slowly. I can climb the stairs, eight or ten steps at a time. For a long time, despite my refusal to eat, they kept bringing in my meals three times a day and leave them where I could smell the food. They were hoping to break me that way. They've stopped now.
>
> My mood is good; I do not fear the future. They have failed to undermine my faith. And I know that I have a great many friends! My hunger strike is open-ended, and I am determined to hold out. I feel like a soldier going into battle, prepared to be wounded or to die. I am ready to die for the glory of His name (Kiddush ha-Shem). If they want a martyr, I'm happy to oblige.

After pouring my emotions out on paper, I felt better.

"Hey guys!" I called out to my neighbors. "How can I send a message out? I need to tell people about my hunger strike."

"OK, write your letter," a voice responded—probably a service *zek*. "I'm going to the infirmary, I'll take it and get it out if I can."

With shaking hands, I pushed my note into the crack in the door, where it seemed to get stuck at first until eventually it slipped through.

My mother's telephone briefing for Western supporters (October 7, 1984)

> In recent days, October 4–7, there were two house searches and interrogations. The first was in Moscow, at Michael Ratner's, where they found many books. Initially he told them that these were Sasha's books, then he said they were his own.

The second was in Kishinev, where they confiscated Hebrew teaching materials, books, and religious literature from Alexander Kogan. He received an official warning under Article 190 (allegedly, he'd been organizing meetings and distracting people from public activity; the commentaries on the Bible were declared anti-Soviet literature). During an interrogation they asked him: "How did you meet Alexander Kholmyansky? What books did you read and study with him, who organized your meetings and Hebrew summer camps?" He was told that Alexander Kholmyansky was in prison for organizing a "nationwide ulpan."

In the meantime, they began summoning the people who had attended Sasha's Estonian camp for questioning. Michael Ratner, who is one of Sasha's students from Moscow, came to see our son Misha, Sasha's brother, and told him that he had been interrogated by an investigator for major crimes in connection with Sasha's case. After the interrogation, the investigator told him to step into another room. There, a man who identified himself as a KGB officer Alekseyev told him that Sasha was held in a cell with a violent criminal who beat him; that Sasha was sleeping on the floor next to the slop bucket, which he had to carry out and empty every day; and that he prayed and sobbed incessantly.

Misha and Oksana felt that they must relay this to me and Papa. We both just shuddered at first but then refused to believe a word of it. This litany of horrors might frighten the young people but it didn't frighten us. Everything in the story was too crude, too contrived, the work of a primitive imagination. Besides, whenever they actually do such things, they usually try to hide them. And then, to imagine Sasha "sobbing" . . . that's just not him. Then we decided that if they'd fed us this story, we should figure out a way to use it against them.

* * *

My mother remembers

When we came to the Tallinn prison on October 11 to leave a food package for Sasha, the prison authorities accepted it without a peep. They even let us in, at our request, to see the prison warden. We passed through an iron door that slammed shut behind us and followed a gloomy corridor with many side passages branching off it, which took us to a large room with a T-shaped table. At the short end of the table sat the warden, and some other man sat along the long side. They seated us on the left, near the warden, a tall, imposing man, even somewhat handsome, with the Ukrainian-sounding last name of Maiboroda. The cat-and-mouse game began immediately.

"What brings you here? Didn't they take your food package?"

"No, they took it. We're here about our complaint."

"What complaint?"

"We wrote a statement protesting the appalling treatment of our son. We were told he is housed with violent criminals, that he is beaten and mistreated. We gave it to Major Kolk yesterday. He promised to give it to you. And if he didn't, I can recite it right now from memory."

I recited the text of our complaint.

"But this is utter nonsense. We're a European country, after all. Your son was here in my office just yesterday, he sat where you're sitting right now. He brought me a written complaint. Look, here's another one he wrote earlier."

And he handed me two pieces of paper written in Sasha's hand. Father and I studied them intently.

"You can see the kinds of things he feels deprived of, what he's complaining about. He wants access to major newspapers, he wants his exercise period back, he's even telling us what time is more convenient for him. Are these the kinds of things he would be complaining about if what you just told me were true? Someone's trying to frighten you.

"So did they take your food package?" he asked again.

"They did," I said mechanically, still digesting the new information.

"Pity he can't use it."

My heart sank. I stared at the warden and at the doctor he had called in during our talk, an old Jewish woman.

"What do you mean, why can't he use it?"

"He has refused to eat. So we were required by law to place him in isolation."

I started asking questions, trying to get answers from him first, then from the doctor, aware that they were hiding something. Then I couldn't go on any longer. We went out into the courtyard, sat down on a bench, and I began to sob. I had never cried before, not out loud, not for any sorrow—and there had been plenty of them in my life. But now I just couldn't stop. "He's not eating, he's not eating, he's starving, he's in a punishment cell!" I was gasping for breath. Grisha didn't know what to do, he walked around me begging me to stop, to calm down. But I couldn't stop until I was utterly spent.

We went to find a phone to call Misha.

"What's going on?" he asked impatiently.

"He's not eating!" I sobbed into the receiver.

"A hunger strike? Brilliant! Oh, he's awesome! Now the news will spread!"

"But, Misha, he's going hungry!" I repeated.

"Oh, stop it, Mom, don't you see how awesome this is!"

Michael Kholmyansky's telephone briefing for Western supporters (October 14, 1984)

There was a public meeting in Kalinin (Tver) where the authorities mentioned Alexander Kholmyansky and his group. They described Alexander as a dangerous, anti-Soviet criminal who had been found to keep a gun, ammunition, and anti-Soviet literature in his home. They said that his group had illegally kept a weapon and trained in its use under the guise of teaching Hebrew.

This is the first public statement about Alexander. It's very disturbing. It seems to be a trial balloon of some sort. The authorities want to see whether there will be any reaction abroad. We must react quickly and firmly to nip these practices in the bud.

We have learned that Alexander Kholmyansky is conducting a hunger strike that began on September 13, that is, a month ago. He is doing so to protest against the fabricated charges that have been filed against him and against the false evidence that was planted in his home. Alexander's mother was informed of this by the prison warden in Tallinn, who also stated that Alexander is being force-fed. When we asked about his health, we were told that it is consistent with that of any person who has been fasting for a month.

Immediately after the November state holidays commemorating the anniversary of the Bolshevik revolution, activists in Moscow are starting a chain of hunger strikes in solidarity with Sasha. In fact, they want to take it nationwide! Forty people have signed a letter of protest addressed to the Prosecutor General of the USSR, informing him of their hunger strike and demanding an immediate closure of the fabricated case against Alexander Kholmyansky. Similar letters have been sent to the Central Committee of the Communist Party of the USSR and the Presidium of the Supreme Soviet.

* * *

Meanwhile, I was taken to see Kolk again and found his demeanor markedly changed. Would you look at that! He was even being somewhat pleasant. Where were his usual threats?

"Alexander, we've decided to give you a chance to reform. The punishment cell conditions are very harsh; we don't want them to have a negative impact on your mental health. We will allow you to use the cot in the daytime and will even give you bed linens."

I couldn't believe my ears. This was my first small victory. They had realized that a frontal assault wasn't working, that threats weren't working. And what could they threaten me with now, anyway? What more could they do to someone who was already sitting in a punishment cell without food? What else could they take away from me?

Ah, so now they were giving me something that they *could* take away. And so they would, no doubt—but later. For now, I stood looking on while a service *zek* spread the sheet out on my cot. How strange it looked on these boards in a metal frame. Here was a second sheet, and a blanket; in a flash I dived under the blanket. Oh my God, this was heaven! If someone tells you that it's not possible to experience heaven in a punishment cell during a hunger strike, don't believe them. It *is* possible!

A new block commander came around, a man with striking, unusual facial features.

"Why is your cot open in the middle of the day?"

"I have Major Kolk's permission."

"That's impossible!"

"You see, sir, I'm in here because I'm conducting a hunger strike to protest against false evidence that was planted in my home, a handgun."

"A hunger strike? Planted handguns? That's impossible. I'm going back to look into this."

It didn't take him long and had an unexpected outcome: the duty guard came and took me to the commander's office.

"I bet you'd like to send a letter to your family?"

"What?"

"OK, listen well and then forget what I'm about to tell you. I'm an Armenian Jew. There are very few of us and few people know about us, but we help fellow Jews when we can. I'm coming to your cell in an hour as if to search it. Have the letter ready. Now go."

He did indeed come into my cell soon afterwards.

"Where's your letter? No, this won't do, don't seal it. Write down the address right here on this separate piece of paper and give me a blank envelope. I'll address it in my own handwriting."

My letter, the envelope, and the note with Anya Yerukhimovich's address disappeared into the inner pocket of his officer's tunic. Truly—a miracle of miracles!

Anya Yerukhimovich remembers

I went to visit my friend Clara Shvartzman in Kishinev for her birthday. When I returned to Moscow a week later, in the morning, I went straight to work without stopping by the house. At work I learned that a Jewish activist named Inna Brokhina supposedly had received a strange letter from Sasha; now she was trumpeting everywhere that she had a special relationship with him and was the only one who knew what was happening to him. "That was stupid," I thought, "he should have written to me."

With this thought in my mind, I came home and opened my mailbox. Inside were three letters from Sasha, addressed to me, to his parents, and to Misha. For a moment, I stood there in complete shock, absorbing what I was seeing. Then I came to my senses, looked at my watch and said to myself: "You idiot, if you're going to do something, do it now—it's already 11 p.m." And I ran out to the street to make a call from a phone booth (since our home phone was tapped). I called Sasha's parents first, but no one answered. I hesitated to call Misha: I had never met him; he didn't even know of my existence; the hour was late; Misha's own situation was precarious, with the KGB after him and his brother in prison.

Misha's telephone number was in the letter. I took a deep breath and dialed his number. I said I needed to see him; his reply was terse in the extreme: "If you need to see me, come on over."

It was already almost midnight when I arrived; not the best time for visiting strangers. Misha and Oksana greeted me coolly, with caution and suspicion. I came into the room. My old friend Michael Dinaburg, Misha Kholmyansky's student, was sitting on the couch. "Anya!" he greeted me joyously, and told Misha and Oksana who I was. The tension melted away immediately.

I handed Misha all three letters. He stared at them in astonishment. "Looks like his handwriting," he said, finally tearing himself away from the letters, "but how do we know that Sasha actually wrote them?"

"Look, right here is a hint, this is about the time he came to see me and I had nothing better to serve with tea than some bread rusks—the same kind they send to prisoners in care packages. We had a good laugh about the sad symbolism of the rusks."

"Was anyone else present?"

"Nehemiah, Sasha's student and friend. But he's above suspicion. Sasha is mentioning this on purpose because this is something that only he and I would know about."

"You might be right."

One day, at work, soon after receiving the letters, I was summoned to the office of the chief engineer. The chief engineer wasn't there, but two men awaited me inside—one who was clearly the boss, the other young and handsome. They started questioning me; I think I looked frightened, and answered all their questions with "I don't know, I don't remember." After a while, the boss man said:

"You're going to have to do better than this, Anna. We're going to make a transcript of this conversation, so we need actual facts, not your evasions and excuses."

At this, I came to my senses and realized that I must have been behaving unwisely. They were talking about making a formal transcript, the kind that they would want me to sign. I recalled Sasha's lessons about prudent conduct during interrogations and changed my tone drastically. I asked if they had a warrant to interrogate me. I said:

"What makes you think I'm going to sign anything? I haven't done anything wrong, and you yourself said you've come to chat, not to interrogate me. So we're chatting. But signing transcripts—that's a totally different matter."

"Would you look at that! I can see you've been trained. We've talked to a lot of you people, and only Kholmyansky's people talk like this."

I found this funny and gave a nervous giggle, even though I was terribly frightened.

"Look, Anna, we understand: you're in love, you're waiting for him. But you're going to have to face reality: he's looking at five years' imprisonment."

"That's up to the court. He hasn't been sentenced."

They gave me a meaningful look and laughed.

"You're an intelligent person. Deep down you know there's no point in waiting for him. To waste five years of your life—that's a long time for a young woman!"

* * *

These dramatic changes in my living conditions, courtesy of Kolk, and then the Armenian Jew taking my letters—these were two miracles, back to back. Oh, Lord, you were helping me! Was this a time of special grace? If so, it would be a sacrilege not to use it to the fullest, to the last drop. Later the same day, I got a third letter out:

October 11, 1984

My dears!

I feel good. My mind is completely clear. Of course, I feel weak (my blood pressure is 90/60), but I don't feel any hunger and feel no suffering or hardship. I've gotten used to this way of life. I believe I can continue like this for a very long time. I'm under constant medical supervision. Every few days the chief doctor of the internal prison hospital examines me and tries to persuade me to drop the hunger strike.

I'm doing my very best to keep in good shape. I do special toning exercises for the stomach and intestines, as well as deep relaxation and breathing exercises. My mood is generally excellent. I have no doubt that every day of my hunger strike brings tangible benefits in the global sense. I am sure that in the end everything will turn out just fine. And I know that everything possible is being done for me. Have patience, my dears, and don't be sad—the day of freedom will arrive. Happy Sukkot! Kisses.

* * *

Oksana Kholmyansky's telephone briefing for Western supporters (October 14, 1984)

The Prosecutor General's Office continues to insist that the gun they found belongs to Sasha. They claim that because it was discovered in the dust, this proves beyond any doubt that it was lying there before the search party came. The Prosecutor denies all allegations of fraud. They say they checked and found no violations of law. The Prosecutor's Office claims that it doesn't matter that three men who conducted the search were not identified in the protokol, even though article 141 of the Code of Criminal Procedure requires it. The Prosecutor's Office says that it is a routine practice not to record people's names in the protokol . . .

In general, we have a sense that they are preparing some drastic steps. They might not stop at a gun charge; they might have even worse things up their sleeve. Maybe they're preparing a big show trial, maybe even under Article 70 (anti-Soviet agitation and propaganda, their favorite charge against political dissidents, which carries up to seven years' imprisonment followed by up to five years of judicial deportation).

On the other hand, it looks like Sasha's hunger strike is making them want to be done with him as soon as possible, even though they say that his hunger strike doesn't bother them. The supervisor assigned to Sasha's case, Officer Salnikov of the Prosecutor General's office, told Sasha's mother that they had been instructed to "accelerate the termination" of the hunger strike. When asked how exactly they were planning to do so, he said: "By medical means. Our doctors know how to do it."

All of us, including Sasha's mother, are extremely worried by this statement. We cannot imagine how doctors can force Sasha to stop the hunger strike. We fear they might use psychotropic drugs.

* * *

My mother remembers

On our next trip to Tallinn, we had a stroke of luck. We managed to get the phone number of the prison doctor, the same elderly Jewish woman with whom we had spoken during our visit to the prison when we learned of Sasha's hunger strike. We could not imagine that a Jewish woman, herself probably a mother and a grandmother, could be indifferent to the plight of someone on a hunger strike. Clearly, she wasn't going to say anything that could jeopardize her official position, but we might still be able to learn something from her, if only we could find her number.

This time. Grisha took the lead. During his life-long career in industry, he had developed a special tone of voice for official calls: deep, confident, commanding. He called the prison's front office and asked for the doctor's telephone number.

"Who's asking?" said the soldier on duty.

"Andreyev!" I heard Grisha's curt, commanding reply. He sounded just like a big boss, angry that people didn't immediately recognize his voice and were making him identify himself. When I heard him bark out his reply and then saw him writing down the telephone number, I laughed so hard I had to sit down right there in the phone booth. The Soviet mind is programmed to obey the commanding shout of a superior without question. And even though we were in Estonia, it was being Russified so rapidly that the Estonian soldier couldn't be sure this wasn't, in fact, some big boss in his own chain of command who just happened to have a Russian-sounding name. So, thanks to Grisha's resourcefulness, we got the doctor's phone number. Later, officials kept asking us how we got this phone number, but, of course, we never told anyone.

We called the doctor. She was very surprised at first, but nevertheless answered our questions quite readily. From her words we got an idea of Sasha's condition. She told us how she had tried to persuade Sasha to stop the hunger strike, and what he had said. Those half-joking answers really did sound like him, as though it was his voice we were hearing. Later she started avoiding our calls, but sometimes we still managed to talk to her. We tried not to overdo it and called her only rarely . . .

* * *

Oksana Kholmyansky's telephone briefing for Western supporters (November 14, 1984)

We read in the November 6 and 7 editions of the national newspaper Izvestiya that US President Ronald Reagan has granted the demands of the American hunger-striker Mitchell Schneider by turning over a federal building to house the homeless, in order to put an end to his and his friends' hunger strikes. We hope that the leaders of the Communist Party of the USSR will show themselves no less humane.

We have a sense that the coming days will bring some fateful decisions, so the window of opportunity for exerting influence in Sasha's case is about to close. Afterwards, it may be too late.

* * *

Oksana Kholmyansky's telephone briefing for Western supporters (November 18, 1984)

When Sasha's parents were in Tallinn, the local KGB treated them quite rudely. They woke them up at 6:30 a.m. and hauled them in for an interrogation. Sasha's parents declined to testify. Upon their return to Moscow several days later, they were called in again for another interrogation. The KGB agents were extremely rough and tried to intimidate them, but once again, his parents refused to talk. The KGB told them, among other things, that if they didn't stop insisting that the evidence against Sasha had been planted during the house search and waging an international campaign, they could also lose their second son!

Similar threats were made to Misha Kholmyansky himself, who was brought in from work in the morning. He told them that he was willing to testify before an independent investigator from the Interior Ministry.

The attitude of the Prosecutor General's Office toward Sasha's parents has deteriorated dramatically. The officials don't want to talk to them. Moreover, Vsadnikov, the new supervisor who is assigned to monitor the case, said to Sasha's mother with unconcealed anger: "We have evidence that Alexander Kholmyansky knew that he had a gun in his home." The family is very concerned about this and suspects that the KGB have prepared a new fabrication or found false witnesses.

As many as 202 people from 13 cities took part in the massive hunger strike in support of the three illegally detained activists: Kholmyansky, Edelstein, and Berenstein.

* * *

Here it comes: another summons to see Kolk.

"We've discovered that you have smuggled out letters to your relatives in Moscow, illegally. This is a gross violation of the prison rules. Don't you realize that you are in prison? Don't you understand why you've been isolated—to let the investigation proceed without interference? We've made concessions, granted you privileges, allowed you to lie down in daytime, gave you bedding. And this is the thanks we get? I'm rescinding all special treatment and transferring you from punishment cell no. 5 to cell no. 4."

Well, I knew this was coming, didn't I? It was clear from the beginning that they only gave me all those privileges so they could have something to take away again. But I still felt lousy. My physical condition had taken a sharp turn for the worse; I felt a rapid pulse beating in my head; I had trouble focusing. Had I overestimated my strength? Maybe the end was closer than I thought. But if so, they would also pay a high price.

They moved me to cell no. 4: a metal box inside the stone cell. I hadn't felt such freezing cold in a long time! The metal walls were too cold to touch. So cold, so desperately cold. My physical exercises did nothing to keep me warm. I felt as though I were sitting inside a refrigerator, freezing from the inside. My teeth chattered. And there was no air to breathe. In a regular stone cell, there was always a bit of air that seeped through the pores in the stone, but here, inside a metal casing, it felt just like being inside a plastic bag. It was a cold death chamber. Well, if I was to die, let's hope it would be quick. But first, I must write a letter and get it out, quickly!

The door opened; the Armenian Jew stood in the doorframe. "Too cold, I'm about to die, there's no air . . . " I got these words out in a single breath, handing him a letter to Anya.

This time he seemed reluctant to take it but did it anyway. Barely an hour passed, and then, a new piece of luck: my door opened, and a guard handed me a brand-new warm jacket. "Your parents brought it," he explained.

Instantly I put it on. Whoever heard of a quilted jacket in a punishment cell, and a nice one, too! Where did they get this beautiful thing? I felt revived. Just when I thought that all hope was lost . . . Lord, thank You! This was Your Providence, Your salvation, a clear sign that my struggle was not in vain, was not senseless.

For three whole days I luxuriated in the warmth of the jacket, until block commander Litvinov appeared.

"We're moving you to no. 3. What's this? Who allowed this jacket in here? I'm confiscating it."

Litvinov opened the door to cell no. 3, and I stared in disbelief: in the middle of the floor sat a big, stinking pile of excrement, with dung flies buzzing around it!

"In you go."

"In there? Absolutely not!"

"Are you refusing to obey a direct order?" Litvinov hissed furiously.

"You can do whatever you want, kill me, hang me, but I'm not going in there. Go ahead, call Kolk!"

Like most petty tyrants, Litvinov was not used to *zeks* contradicting him, and my unexpected resistance took him aback. He made as if to hit me, but in the end his courage failed him, and he pounced on the duty guard instead with all his pent-up fury. In his surprise, the duty guard jumped as if stung and ran off to find the service *zeks*. In a few minutes, two service *zeks* appeared. Spurred on by Litvinov's shouts, they began frantically scrubbing the cell. I made them wash it over and over again, until all the visible filth was gone (though not the smell) before I would enter the cell.

What was that all about? A personal whim of Litvinov's, or part of a bigger game? Maybe they were checking to see if I still had the resolve to fight, to resist, to say no. If so, I had done well.

After just two days in the stinky cell, they moved me to cell no. 7, my fourth transfer. This one was oppressively hot and stuffy. In my weakened state, being constantly jerked around like that was destabilizing, and adjusting to a new cell was painful. I wondered if they were doing this on purpose, to keep up the pressure on me, or whether this was all a series of accidents—assuming anything that happened to me in here could ever be an accident.

I managed to get another letter out to Misha:

October 24, 1984

Dearest Misha,

Please take care of yourself. Be on your guard, they might target you, too. Communication, as you can understand, is very complicated. I may not get another opportunity to send a note, so don't worry if you don't hear from me.

Today, on the forty-second day of the hunger strike I feel much better than one might expect. The chest pains have stopped, my blood pressure has become more stable (it had dropped to 85/60 at one point). What bothers me is the condition of my throat and pharynx, my esophagus and stomach—the whole path through which the tube passes every day during the forced feeding. They're not always gentle about it.

My mind is clear. Psychologically, I feel quite good. They've moved me to another cell, this one hot and airless. They're clearly feeling the pressure from the outside. I am determined to continue the hunger strike even if my health deteriorates. I'm under very close medical observation, even annoyingly so. My weight is 51.5 kilograms. I am confident that we will survive all the challenges and come out of this stronger than ever! I am confident that I am contributing to our big, important cause, albeit passively. Don't worry about me. Kisses.

I thought of my situation with detachment, like a science experiment: no one I knew of had lasted this long on a hunger strike, especially in a punishment cell. It was interesting to see whether the human mind could withstand all this.

Despite the circumstances, my sleep was excellent. It was cold and uncomfortable in the new cell, and once again, like back in the first days, I had only the thin cotton shirt to put over my shoulders for a blanket, sleeping in nothing but my undershirt. This bed's metal frame had a metal strip running right down the middle so that, no matter how I lay, I couldn't avoid it; the strip was so cold that it burned my body on contact. I had to twist myself into an impossible pretzel in order to doze off—and yet, once asleep, I slept like a baby, undisturbed by nightmares or anything else. Sleep was my salvation. I was sure no ordinary *zek* in an ordinary cell could aspire to such good sleep.

My hearing was deteriorating: I could barely pick words out of the background noise. My sight was also weakening, though to a lesser degree. My coordination was also deteriorating, it was harder to walk; I kept tripping over my feet, and I felt weaker. My eyes had also become teary, oozing liquid for no apparent reason; Kolk and Maiboroda kept staring at me during our endless meetings, wondering if I was nearing the breaking point and one last push might tip me over, make me give up. So they pressed harder and harder, but I just smiled quietly in response.

I remember studying the elasticity of materials back in college. We learned that each solid material has a *yield point*, or elastic limit. Below that point, the material can withstand a small amount of stress without changing shape. As the amount of stress increases, the material behaves *elastically*, that is, it will change its shape but will return to its original shape when the stress is removed. But once the stress exceeds the yield point, the material begins to exhibit *plastic* behavior where even a small additional increase in stress produces a significant change in shape, a change that is permanent and irreversible and will persist even after the stress is removed.

I began to think that a similar model might describe human behavior. A person can withstand a small amount of mental stress without a change in behavior. As the stress increases, so long as it stays below a certain limit, the person's behavior may change temporarily but will revert to normal once the stress is removed. However, if the stress exceeds that limit, his behavior changes significantly, it becomes irrational, the person "breaks," loses self-control, and then, even when the pressure is removed, the behavior does not return to normal, to its initial state.

Our reaction to fear or threat is a good example. Whenever the KGB managed to sow fear in people's minds—that is, push them beyond his yield point—even a mild threat could tip them over afterwards into irrational panic behavior and total surrender. I was convinced that the KGB's entire system of intimidation was built upon this observation. They tried to find one's weak spot, implant fear there, like a virus, and then apply a threat when necessary. The virus of fear continued to live inside the person, erupting in full once the body had already been weakened.

A man who had resisted the virus of fear was much more difficult to overcome: he kept his freedom of choice. As Victor Frankl had said: "Everything can be taken from a man but one thing: the last of human freedoms—to choose one's attitude in any given set of circumstances, to choose one's way."

On the eve of the November 7 holiday (the anniversary of the Communist revolution of 1917), the punishment cells were emptied, and their inmates were returned to their regular cells. I savored the ensuing silence, finally free to lift my thoughts up to God without distraction, to cleanse myself mentally from all this filth. But I hadn't had long to enjoy it before a suffocating wave of blackness came over me, threatening to swallow me up. Screaming, I beat my fists against the walls, I pulled at the unyielding cot with all my remaining strength, I broke my comb into tiny pieces and set them on fire using my secret stash of matches. Very gradually, the fit passed, giving way to exhaustion and a strange sense of relief.

Suddenly, I heard the clanging of a door latch: a new inmate was put into one of the far cells on the other side of the block. He must have done something extraordinary to have earned a stint in a punishment cell on a holiday. The newcomer immediately began to call out: "Hello, is there anyone else in here?" *Zek* etiquette required a response but I was too exhausted for long introductions and too weakened to make my voice carry all the way to the far cell. I sat in silence for the rest of the day, ignoring him.

Of course, he realized there was someone else on the block when he heard the clanging of the bolts as they came to take me to my next feeding. Once I was back, he called out to me again. I answered him reluctantly and too softly for him to hear, prompting him to yell:

"Speak up, compadre!"

The Russian word he used meant "countryman," the accepted form of address among strangers in prison. It made me think of Kipling's *Jungle Book*, where Baloo the Bear taught Mowgli the proper greeting to use when meeting a strange beast in the jungle: "We be of one blood, ye and I." Kipling was a genius. Little did he know that prison was its own kind of jungle, with its own ritual greeting.

The next day, a nurse came alone, without a guard, to take me to my feeding. Apparently, during the holidays they operated with a skeleton staff. Once the door closed behind us, instead of stuffing the tube into my throat and pouring in the nutritive gruel, she suddenly plopped a bowl of it down in front of me and intoned, like a hypnotist:

"Eat . . . eat!"

I looked up at her in mute amazement, speechless, caught by surprise.

"If you're afraid of me, I'll leave. Don't worry, no one will ever know, eat up quickly!"

Without meaning to, I grabbed the bowl and gulped down the gruel in a sort of frenzy. A blissful warmth spread throughout my body, a long-forgotten feeling of satisfaction, of satiety. All I wanted now was to get back to the cell quickly and lie down on the cot. What a contrast with the dark mood of yesterday! Once back in my cell, I fell asleep with a feeling of heavenly bliss.

I woke up in the middle of the night, fear piercing me like a sharp needle. The shame, oh God, the shame! Why did you yield to temptation, you wimp, why didn't you resist? What if she wrote down in my medical record that I had started to eat? My entire hunger strike would have been wasted! Waves of bitterness and despair washed over me again.

Chapter 7

Several days later, Chikarenko was back to tell me the results of the forensic tests: no identifiable fingerprints had been found on the pistol!

No fingerprints?!

I was speechless with shock: I had fully expected them to forge my fingerprints, or at least to say they found them. Otherwise, why go through the trouble of planting the gun in the first place?

So what happened? What had changed out there in the world that no one in the KGB dared to sign off on a forgery? Was this because of my hunger strike and international pressure?

I sensed some great tectonic plates began to shift, I saw the great steamroller, poised to flatten me, falter and stall. Were we beginning to win? In a swirl of thoughts and feelings that had erupted in my mind, I had trouble processing Chikarenko's words.

Chikarenko interrupted my thoughts:

"Our ballistics experts have established that the pistol was in working order . . . "

Imagine that, I thought.

"Out of forty-one cartridges, thirty-nine were usable. The pistol had been fired, but they could not determine when it was last used."

Yes, I thought, I know what you're trying to say. The pistol could have been used to commit a dozen crimes, and you're telling me you might pin any or all of them on me. And yet, if you were afraid to forge my fingerprints, you won't dare to do that, either. In other words, I really have seized the initiative. This thing I'm doing . . . it's working!

But why did they bother with all of this to begin with—this fake investigation, this theater of the absurd? Why couldn't they just kill us outright, like their Nazi predecessors with their mass graves? Evidently, they couldn't. Evidently, there were rules that even the KGB must abide by. There were limits even to their lawlessness. And the more we persisted, the more we kept the eyes of the civilized world focused upon them, the less free they felt to oppress us.

* * *

It was getting harder to open my eyes and to keep them open. Now I kept my eyes closed during my endless meetings with Maiboroda and Kolk, because the bright light bothered me. It was getting harder to concentrate. I began to have vivid hallucinations—some of them visions of food, complete with the smell, taste, and sound of eating, others sexual in nature. I was King David, Alexander the Great, Napoleon Bonaparte. Each new fantasy was a blessing, helping me last another hour, win another small victory.

Too much was at stake. I could not allow them to intimidate the other Jewish activists, I could not let them paint us as bad guys who used teaching Hebrew as cover for violence and criminality. This false narrative must be nipped in the bud. I must hold out; I must not break or acquiesce in their fabricated charges; I must not let them have their show trial!

I continued to turn my thoughts to God. Lord, I prayed, break this evil empire, break it into pieces. I thought back to the prophecy of national ingathering in the book of Jeremiah, 31:9, which promised to "bring them from the north country and gather them from the farthest parts of the earth . . . since I became the father of Israel, and Ephraim is my firstborn." Lord, I prayed, let the USSR be the "north country" of the prophecy. Open the gates of this country and bring the Jewish people out the way You brought them out of Egypt in Biblical times and gather them in their own land.

I resolved to take the name Ephraim if I survived this ordeal. After all, in the Bible the name Ephraim is a symbol of the ten lost tribes of Israel, and we, Soviet Jews—Elie Wiesel's "Jews of Silence"—were also, in a way, like a lost tribe.

* * *

The pressure tactics continued.

The doctors informed me that my health was at a dangerous tipping point, that I was showing signs of progressive heart failure and was at risk of irreversible damage, including muscular dystrophy.

Chikarenko came back to ask me once again about the pistol and ammo and the anti-Soviet literature. He threatened me with a big show trial and the longest possible sentence if I didn't stop my hunger strike and begin to cooperate with the investigation. Once again, I responded that the items had been planted in my apartment, and I denied all the charges. "Surely," I added, "a man of your rank, your experience, can understand that the time for threats has passed."

At a meeting in Maiboroda's office, I found Maiboroda, Kolk, and four strangers, two of them with a demeanor indicative of a high rank. One of the strangers, who might be a psychologist, observed me closely throughout the interview. Another, who might be a doctor, came up to me and sniffed my breath, probably checking for the telltale smell of "hunger breath." Finding what he expected, he sat down, looking satisfied, and remained silent for the rest of the meeting while Maiboroda continued alternately to threaten and cajole me. I sat there with my eyes streaming involuntarily but said nothing, smiling quietly; I think my smile infuriated them the most.

* * *

Again and again, my thoughts returned to Anya Yerukhimovich. Her delicate figure with its long mane of hair often emerged from the depths of my subconscious, as if she dwelled there all the time. We had not spoken about our feelings before I left for Estonia, nor did I mention them in the two letters I smuggled out to her from my punishment cell. But when Fastov asked me, before my confinement in the punishment cell, whether I had a girlfriend, I said yes without a moment's hesitation. And yet, in my present situation, romantic feelings seemed like an impossible luxury. After all, I was a prisoner with a long tunnel of torment stretching before me, and then a long prison term still to serve. Wasn't it better to dismiss these thoughts — better for both of us?

***

One day, the guard came and took me down to the interrogation room in the basement, but Chikarenko was not there. Instead, a young, pleasant-looking man came towards me, looking at me with keen curiosity.

"My name is Mart Rask. I'm your lawyer, your defense counsel."

My *lawyer*?! How odd the word sounded. The very concept of defense, of fair trial, seemed utterly alien within these thick, lifeless walls, in this world of lawlessness and oppression. It belonged to that other world, the world of freedom and civilization that had come to seem unreal to me. And yet, someone had come here from there, someone who was on my side. Tears welled up in my eyes.

We sat down. Rask, evidently perfectly aware that the walls had ears, took out a note and passed it to me without a word. I recognized Misha's handwriting. The note said that Mart Rask was in fact our attorney and could be trusted. While I was reading it, Rask, making small talk, took out a longer letter from Misha and gave it to me.

I began to tell him briefly about the interrogations and about my health. He listened, staring at me intently, committing to memory every detail of my appearance and demeanor. He was the only one who had seen me in person; he would tell my family and the world that I was alive and unbroken, that I was keeping up the fight. That was the main point of his visit; our discussion about my case was perfunctory, since we both knew that every word spoken aloud would be known to the KGB.

"Unfortunately, there are quite a few issues we haven't covered. Your case is quite complicated. I'll be back tomorrow to continue our conversation," said Rask, making a sign with his hand that I should write a letter that he would take to my family, against all the rules.

Back in my cell, I read Misha's letter in a state of euphoria. I picked up the pen and began to compose a leisurely reply.

Dear Misha,

> I feel an immeasurable satisfaction that my isolation has finally been broken. This feeling cannot be expressed in words. Even though I felt strong before, this is different. I was expecting

Rally in New York in support of Soviet Jewry

A spoof of Lenin's mausoleum (tomb) that was staged in New York by the Coalition to Free Soviet Jews. The Russian word across the lintel, where Lenin's name should be, is "Freedom." The message: this is where freedom lies buried

to see a wave of repressions within the country and a successful international campaign in support of my case, but both have far exceeded my expectations. I was moved to tears by the news of all the people conducting their own hunger strikes in solidarity with me, the worldwide protests, and the news that I now have my own apartment on a kibbutz in Israel. I hope that our struggle will help achieve several goals:

To awaken the Jews in the West and in Israel, at least for a while. Maybe some will feel the need to live a Jewish life; some may be saved from assimilation; some may become motivated to study Judaism, some to help people, and some to make aliyah. For Israelis this may be a welcome distraction from the war in Lebanon, from inflation and strikes. Besides, if everyone's combined efforts help bring us together as Jews, that alone is no less important than the cause we have served all these years.

I would appreciate it if the campaign of support would not focus on specific Prisoners of Zion, but rather on Soviet persecution of Jews in general. We need to bring pressure to bear toward a general opening of the gates.

My personal freedom. I have no doubt that I will be released if I keep up my hunger strike long enough.

Isn't this a miracle? One would have to be blind not to realize that there is something impossible and improbable going on here. We have seized the initiative and we are dealing them a great blow—them, the giant superpower that sits atop a vast territory, with every conceivable natural resource and a servile population at its disposal. They thought they had nothing to fear: they had me in their hands, in the punishment cell, they thought they could do anything they wanted to me. But look at what's really happening. Isn't it wonderful? Each day that my hunger strike continues is of great value to all of us because if I were to quit, the public interest in our issues would dissipate immediately. So I intend to continue it for a long time.

* * *

Michael Kholmyansky's telephone briefing for Western supporters (December 2, 1984)

They have extended the investigative phase once again, this time to December 14. We think this means that someone very senior has

Michael Kholmyansky's open letter to the Israeli government (December 29, 1984)

Gentlemen,

We are seeing the first efforts by the government of Israel on behalf of the Prisoners of Zion. We are tremendously appreciative. We would like to remind you of the fate of Alexander Kholmyansky, who is in prison, continuing his protest hunger strike that he began on September 13. Alexander is protesting the regime's illegal treatment of him. It has gotten to the point where his life is in danger.

The time to act on his behalf is now, before his trial, when much more can be done for him than afterwards. We urge you not to waste precious time and to act resolutely to halt this wave of repressions. Save the Prisoners of Zion and show the Jews of the Soviet Union that the State of Israel accepts responsibility for their fate.

* * *

Oksana Kholmyansky's telephone briefing for Western supporters (December 29, 1984)

We are very concerned about the persistent rumors that Sasha's case will not be discussed at the upcoming meeting between Foreign Ministers Gromyko and Shultz. Just recently, Lawrence Eagleburger promised us that this issue would be raised at every level. A terrible disappointment!

* * *

January 3, 1985. I was barely awake when I heard a heavy tread out in the hallway, the grinding of locks. My heart started beating rapidly, expecting the worst. The door swung open.

"Come out with your things—you're moving to another punishment cell."

A prisoner in a punishment cell has little to pack. Two minutes later, I was ready. This time we walked all the way out of the punishment cell block and headed somewhere far away, to another wing of the building. The long trek was hard for me, I could barely drag my feet, but the guard was patient and let me shuffle along at my own pace.

The new cell was quite big, maybe seven meters by seven. Unlike before, this one was big enough to walk around in; that was good. My Lord, but it was freezing in here! The cold quickly seeped into my body, all the way into my insides.

A single stationary double-wide cot stood in the middle of the cell. A middle-aged man lay on it. He greeted me in a strong Estonian accent.

"Hello, my name is Yulo Modilian. I'm on a hunger strike, like you. I'm an Estonian separatist, I've been framed for murder. Have you been sentenced?"

Surprise and curiosity momentarily overcame the feeling of unbearable cold.

"No, not yet. Have you?"

"Yes."

"And you're keeping it up even after the verdict? Do you think you've got a chance?"

"I think I do," said Yulo in a hoarse and weary voice.

Well, what do you know, I thought. Once again they've put me in with someone who's post-conviction. That's against their rules: I'm a pre-trial detainee, I'm supposed to be with other pre-trial detainees. Chances are this Yulo is another plant, like Fastov and Kalm; I guess those two didn't get enough out of me, and now the prosecution wants another fake witness to build up their case.

The cold, though, was really something else.

"These cells are always cold," observed my new cellmate, "but this winter's been especially harsh—it makes it worse."

It was too cold to sit or stand still. I found I had to move around or I would start to shiver uncontrollably. In this way, with shaking knees, I began to recite the morning prayer.

This must be the final lap before the trial, so to speak. Now they were going to do everything they could to try and break me, force me to quit. How could I counteract their efforts, what could I do to escalate things? I could refuse to drink, though not right away: I would keep this in reserve, use it as a threat. A dry hunger strike is so damaging that I might not last long, and now that my case was a matter of public knowledge, they couldn't afford to let me die on their watch. I resolved to start on January 13, to mark four months of my hunger strike.

A new nurse came to take me to my feeding: apparently, this wing of the prison had different staff. She ripped into me right away:

"Hurry up, move your feet, you walking skeleton, I've got no time to wait on you. Come on!"

In the feeding room, she shoved the tube roughly down my throat, spilling part of the gruel.

Back in the cell, I wrote out my declaration of a dry hunger strike:

Whereas:
- the charges against me have been fabricated;
- I have been continuously kept in solitary confinement; and
- since January 3, 1985, I have been held in a freezing cell with a strong constant draft —

therefore, in protest, I hereby declare a dry hunger strike. Holding a person on a hunger strike in such conditions — extreme cold, leading to sleep deprivation and intensified hunger — is tantamount to torture and constitutes a violation of the Convention against Torture and Other Inhuman or Degrading Treatment or Punishment, adopted on December 11, 1984 by resolution of the UN General Assembly, to which the USSR is a signatory.

> **Prisoner of Zion steps up 4-month hunger strike**
> *Jerusalem Post Staff*
>
> Prisoner of Zion Alexander Kholmiansky, imprisoned by the Soviet authorities without trial since July 1983, intensified his four-month-old hunger strike this week and has stopped taking fluids.
>
> This was reported to activists for Soviet Jewry in Jerusalem by his sister-in-law, Oxana Kholmiansky in a phone conversation on Wednesday evening.
>
> Kholmiansky has been on a hunger strike against his detention without trial since September. On November 5, he was transferred to solitary confinement in a small cell. But earlier this month he was moved to a cell with a convicted murderer, after his blankets and clothes were confiscated, Oxana reported.
>
> Oxana and her friends have written to the central committee of the Soviet Communist Party that Kholmiansky's continued detention without trial violates Soviet law, and asked the committee to intervene.
>
> Kholmiansky was arrested after the police found a gun in his parent's home. Jewish activists in Moscow allege that the weapon was planted there.
>
> Meanwhile, the Hebrew University has decided to award an honorary degree to Prof. Alexander Lerner, a renowned cyberneticist from Moscow who is a veteran fighter for the right of Soviet Jews to emigrate.

"Prisoner of Zion Steps Up 4-Month Hunger Strike," by Judy Siegel, *Jerusalem Post*, the week of January 13, 1985 (exact date unknown)

Another feeding with the cruel nurse. Once again, she shoved the tube in roughly and too quickly, but then someone came in, and just like that, all her great hurry was gone. She started making disparaging comments about me to the other woman while I sat there with the tube down my throat, unable to utter a word, until she had had her chat and yanked the tube out.

On the third day, the gruel she fed me was completely cold, as if it had stood for hours after it was cooked. It gave me bad stomach pains for the rest of the day, and my heart began to race. Finding the gruel cold again the next day, I informed her that I refused to take it. She raged and ranted and threatened to call in the duty officer and have me handcuffed to the chair, but in the end I was returned to my cell unfed.

The cold was getting to me. My feet, especially, froze during the night and ached all day. Yulo and I shared the one bed, pressing our backs together. This gave us an illusion of warmth in our trunks but did nothing to help our feet. Yulo shared some plastic bags with me and showed me how to tie one over each foot; miraculously, this helped.

Yulo told me endless stories about Estonian nationalists, about KGB persecution, things that sounded plausible. He stayed in the cell all day without eating. They took him out once a day for a feeding; I wondered if he was eating real food or being fed through a tube like me. Of course, there could be no accidents or coincidences in here: Yulo was almost certainly a plant, but if so, he was a world-class actor. If all I had to go on were his stories and his behavior, I would never have suspected anything. I even tried testing him, asking him to get his friends to slip us some food in secret, but he declined.

On January 8, my fifth day in the cold cell, I was summoned to see Maiboroda:

"You have complained about the harsh conditions in the cold cell. We have decided to move you to another cell. I want to make it clear that you were actually placed in the cold cell for your own safety. A dysentery epidemic has broken out in the prison, and all the warm cells are temporarily being used as isolation wards," he said with truly Orwellian cynicism.

"If you're worried about my safety, you'll remove that sadistic nurse before she cripples me completely. I assume you received my protest?"

"We have no sadistic nurses here, Alexander. Our medical staff works in full compliance with the regulations."

"She deliberately tried to feed me liquid that was completely cold, I'm telling you. Yesterday I didn't let her put the tube in."

Maiboroda's face darkened.

"We're going to look into it," he said softly. "In the meantime, you and your neighbor will be transferred to a warmer cell. But not because of your threat of a dry hunger strike."

I smiled quietly. The new cell was, in fact, better: still very cold, but noticeably warmer than the previous one.

On January 10, the sadistic nurse was gone, replaced by the previous staff. Victory!

Meanwhile, my concerns about Yulo had gradually receded. Then one day he said to me:

"I need your help. I need to get a letter out to my friends in the Estonian independence movement abroad. Can you help me?"

I heard his request with mixed feelings. On the one hand, I must be on my guard; on the other, what if he had no other way of letting his people know about his hunger strike? After all, I myself had help getting word out. In addition, prolonged hunger and endless stress had eroded my resistance, made me vulnerable to the slightest hint of friendliness; I had trouble thinking straight. I told Yulo to write his letter, and the next day I gave it to my lawyer, Rask.

He read Yulo's Estonian writing with an extremely troubled face and wrote down his own note for me on a piece of paper: "*This is a trap. This Yulo is undoubtedly a KGB agent!*" He wouldn't even tell me what the note said. Damn. They almost got me, for all my vigilance, I thought bitterly. I almost took their bait.

On January 13, I stopped taking water, but the prison authorities didn't skip a beat: I found that the bowl of gruel was much larger, maybe doubled in size. They had simply added water to compensate for the lack of liquids.

Just before the trial, I wrote to Misha:

Dear Misha! They are using enhanced forced feeding methods to make me gain weight in order to discredit my hunger strike. Don't be surprised when you see me.

The trial is coming up. I look terrible, although I actually feel well enough. On January 16, I weighed 47.5 kilograms. My blood pressure is 90/60. My skin is a deathly pale, yellowish color, and I am as emaciated as an inmate of a concentration camp. Please prepare our mom so she won't be shocked at my appearance.

There is no doubt that my sentence is pre-determined, so it doesn't matter what we all say at the trial. I plan to speak bluntly and call a spade a spade. No more fear!

Please try to draw the attention of the Western media to the fact that in its treatment of me, the USSR is violating the new international convention against torture it has recently signed. This is the best way of stopping them from moving me to another cold punishment cell.

The zeks told me that one of them was told by his family on the outside that they had heard about my hunger strike on the Voice of America. So much for the punishment cell and isolation!

THE SOVIET JEWRY EDUCATION AND INFORMATION CENTER
REHOV ALKALI, 9, JERUSALEM (02) 636279
YOSEF MENDELEVITCH - CHAIRMAN, SHMUEL AZARKI - DIRECTOR

To: The Government of Israel

On 25th July, 1984, the Moscow teacher of Hebrew, Alexander Kholmiansky, was arrested. He was accused on a false charge of the possession of a weapon (which was in actual fact planted in his home). As a sign of protest against this provocation and this illegal arrest, Alexander began a hunger strike, which has continued for over half a year. From the 13th January he has also refused water.

The cold, the threatening conditions in the cell, and the attempts at force feeding him have changed a healthy and young man into a cripple. Alexander has been transferred to a hospital because of internal bleeding.

We, former Prisoners of Zion, turn to the Government of Israel with the request to do everything possible for the release of Alexander Kholmiansky.

Ruth Alexandrovich
Anatoly Altman
Hillel Butman
Mark Dimshitz
Efim Wolf
Solomon Dreizner
Sander Leibensohn
Lassal Kaminsky
Lazar Lyubarsky

Yosef Mishiner
Yosef Mendelevitch
Natan Malkin
Lev Poitburd
Reisa Palatnik
Boris Shilkrot
Silvya Zalmanson
Zeev Zalmanson
Yakov Suslenski
Ariyeh Knoch

Letter to the Israeli government from a group of former Prisoners of Zion

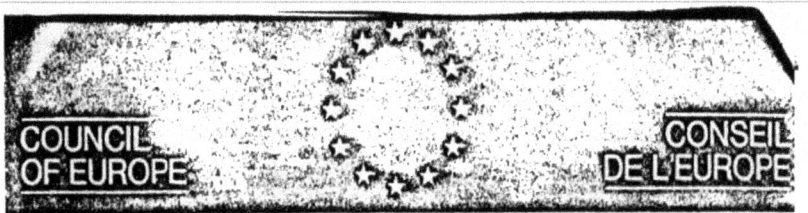

DIRECTORATE OF PRESS AND INFORMATION **DIRECTION DE LA PRESSE ET DE L'INFORMATION**

F (85) 4
30.01.85

F L A S H

APPEAL TO SOVIET GOVERNMENT

Deeply concerned by the continued harassement, arrests, trials and imprisonment of Jews seeking permission to be repatriated to Israel and the increasing persecutions imposed on Jewish culture and on its teaching of Hebrew in the Soviet Union, Mr Hugosson (Sweden), Chairman of the Commission on Relations with European non-member countries of the Parliamentary Assembly of the Council of Europe, launched today an appeal to the Soviet Government in favour of Yosef Begun and Alexandre Kholmianski.

Dr. Yosef Begun, Ph D in Applied Mathematics, aged 52, is serving a third term of imprisonment in the Soviet Union. The pretext for Mr Begun's prison sentences is his wish to emigrate to Israel together with his open struggle for Jewish culture in the USSR and the right to teach and study the language, history and traditions of his people. His wife, living in Moscow, was told that her husband has coronary insufficiency. According to her his life is seriously threatened.

Mr Alexandre Kholmianski, Hebrew teacher in Moscow, imprisonned on the same grounds as Mr Begun, has been held in complete isolation in prison since November 1984 for having started a hunger strike four months ago. His trial is due to open tomorrow 31 January 1985.

Mr Hugosson called upon the Soviet government:

- to release Mr Begun and Mr Kholmianski from prison;
- to give them all medical care they may need;
- to permit them to leave the Soviet Union.

Press release of the Council of Europe, January 30, 1985

Oksana Kholmyansky's telephone briefing for Western supporters (January 17, 1985)

In the Directorate of the camps, we have been told that the prison warden and the regional supervising prosecutor are going to meet with Sasha and once again explain to him the futility of his hunger strike. It's obvious that Sasha is resolute in his decision to continue the hunger strike. Moreover, he stopped taking water on January 13—to mark the four-month "anniversary" of the beginning of his hunger strike. His courage is amazing!

Although the investigative phase of his case is finished, there is a danger of new charges being filed under Articles 70 or 190.

* * *

Oksana Kholmyansky's telephone briefing for Western supporters (January 24, 1985)

The overall situation in the USSR is so dire that it's not even clear who is running the country: the heads of the Communist Party seem unable to rein in the KGB's abuses or to put an end to the antisemitism that is rampant in the country.

* * *

Anya Yerukhimovich remembers

Sasha's letters from the punishment cell had turned me into a member of the family, and when the date of the trial became public, it didn't even enter my mind not to go. But going wasn't a simple thing, it required me to leave work unnoticed—a very risky proposition. I told my aunt Inna Yoffe-Uspensky about my plans so she would know where I was if, God forbid, something should go wrong. Inna was taken by surprise: she knew that I was studying Hebrew, but a romance with one of the leaders of the Jewish movement—that was something else altogether. Seeing how agitated I was, she gave me a mild sedative pill to take with me, something to help me calm down.

I didn't know until the last moment if I would be able to sneak away. The day I had to leave, I sat there at work with my packed bag at my side. About an hour before the end of the workday, the door opened, and a KGB man came in—one of the pair who had interrogated me the first time. This one was the younger and less imposing of the two.

"Dear Anna, you left us with a bad impression last time. Let's see if we can fix that now," he said with an ingratiating smile and kept pushing this line over and over again. I answered at random, thinking about the trial and about not missing my train. Eventually, he gave up and left with nothing to show for his efforts.

Wasting no time, I grabbed my bag and dashed out the back door so the boss wouldn't see me. I flew into the second-class carriage and climbed up on the top bunk; since we bought my ticket at the last moment, this was the only seat that was available. Only then I did I realize that I was trembling and took the pill Inna had given me. It was not supposed to cause drowsiness, but the next thing I was aware of were voices that said: "What's this stop?" "It's Pskov Lakes." Oh, no, that was my stop! Still half asleep, I tumbled down from the top bunk and leapt out of the train car. The train pulled out right away.

I stood on the platform, alone, sleepy, and cold, in the dead of night. The darkness was complete; the only bright spot was the train, and it was moving away rapidly. A few minutes later, when my eyes had adjusted to the darkness, I noticed several more people who had come out of the other train cars. They all headed towards a single light, which I now saw on the platform. Near this lamp was a small building.

After a while, a bus to Võru pulled up to the building. I got on the bus and sat down in the second row. A guy in a sheepskin coat and fur hat sat down on the seat in front of me and immediately fell asleep. So did I. Soon I woke up briefly and found a fur hat and a kippah[17] in my lap, but I was so tired that I slept on. When

---

[17] A Jewish skullcap.

I woke up again, I saw that the guy was obviously looking around for something. Then I remembered that something had fallen into my lap and told him: "If you're looking for a fur hat, here it is." He picked up the hat, put it on, but kept looking around. "Was there something else that fell on you?" he asked me. I looked down and said: "Oh, yes, here's your kippah."

The word kippah sounded out of place in the Estonian wilderness. The man turned and looked at me closely. "Are you going there too?" he asked. That's how I met Lev Tukachinsky.

But when we arrived in court, none of us—Lev, me, or Oksana—were allowed into the courtroom. They said they only let in witnesses or family members, and apparently, not even a sister-in-law qualified as family. They said there were no seats left; as usual in such cases, the room was packed, filled with a hand-picked audience, with KGB men in the front rows.

* * *

January 31, 1985, 10 a.m. The trial begins. I sit on a hard wooden bench facing the judge. This is the same judge who had screamed abuse at me while sentencing me to my ten days' administrative detention. Today, he is still and impassive, radiating dignity and impartiality.

The courtroom is densely packed with hostile-looking Estonians. The prosecution opens with those old stories about the broken mailbox and the vandalized flowerbed, but it is clear that these are merely a lead-in to their real case, which is about the weapons. The first witnesses called to the stand to testify about the weapons are the two young men, Devyatko and Popov, who served as witnesses when my apartment in Moscow was searched. One after the other, they repeat their story. One of them remembers the serial number of the pistol as beginning with a 24, and the other remembers it as ending in 99K.

They both mention the large bookcase in my bedroom. Between its bottom panel and the floor—so the testimony goes—there is a small gap, two centimeters high. During the search, the bookcase was tilted forward, which had the effect of widening the gap.

A packet containing a pistol and ammunition was removed from under the bookcase; the gap was wide enough in that position that the packet was removed without effort.

Rask jumps to his feet:

"You two attend a leading technical university, I believe? If so, then you should know that if the bookcase were tilted *forward*, the gap would get *narrower*, not *wider!*"

Rask shows the audience a scale model of the bookcase, which clearly shows the gap narrowing in the forward-tilted position. Even the hostile Estonians in the audience seem to get it. Rask also hands the judge photographs of the bookcase, including one showing a matchbox placed against the gap to establish the size of the gap in the original, upright position. The pictures clearly show that there was plenty of room under the bookcase to slide a gun under it during the search without tilting anything.

Next, Fastov and Kalm are marched into the courtroom under guard. They present an appalling sight, sporting labor camp uniforms and close-cropped hair, with dull, lifeless eyes; evidently, they've been brought in straight from the camp. Fastov delivers his piece in a confident tone, without faltering:

"Kholmyansky is well-versed in weaponry. He kept talking about the strategic arms race between the United States and the USSR. Displaying an unusual expertise in the subject, he talked about the war in Lebanon, quoted lots of facts from memory, compared different kinds of military armaments and weaponry, the performance of different kinds of military aircraft. He asked me about liability for illegal possession of weapons *before* he knew the results of the search in Moscow on August 29. All this indicates that he kept weapons himself."

I speak up:

"I have a question for this witness. If you're saying that talking about a thing shows that one is keeping that thing in one's home, then—by your own logic—was I keeping a military airplane in my home, too?"

Giggles from the audience. The judge lets it go without comment.

Next, Misha takes the witness stand.

"On August 6, 1984, when my brother Alexander Kholmyansky was in jail in Tallinn, I interrupted my vacation and returned to Moscow in order to inspect the apartment my brother shares with our parents. We were expecting a search and were worried about a possible frame-up. From 8 to 10 p.m. that evening, together with Alexander Bayevsky, I made a thorough search of my brother's room, including the space under the bookcase where the weapons and literature were allegedly found on August 29. We both saw with our own eyes that this space was empty. The floor under the bookcase was covered with a thin, even layer of dust; our parents had moved out of the apartment on July 13, after having done a thorough house-cleaning, and my brother had left even earlier.

"When my family and I returned from vacation, on August 26, we learned that a series of house searches had taken place in Moscow in connection with my brother's case, and that in one instance, at the home of Yuli Edelstein, drugs had been planted. This caused us further concern. On August 27 my mother and I carefully went over the whole apartment again, paying special attention to my brother's room. At that time I saw, once again, that there was nothing under the bookcase.

"The testimony of Devyatko and Popov is false. For one thing, it is practically impossible to tilt that particular bookcase at all, because it's very large and heavy and reaches all the way to the ceiling. It consists of a cabinet and six shelves, holding about 1,000 books. The books would have fallen off the shelves if anyone had tried to tilt the bookcase forward, but in fact, no books fell off during the search. My parents have asked the investigative team to conduct an experiment recreating these events, but their request was denied."

Of course, the KGB did not need to physically plant a pistol with ammunition under the bookcase in order to claim that it was found there.

The judge announces a break. The guards help me shuffle down the hallway to the bathroom. We pass very close to my family and friends standing in the hallway; I can see them clearly, and they can see me. Mom gasps softly, but I wave cheerfully. I see Oksana and Anya Yerukhimovich.

After the break, Oksana, Anya, and Lev Tukachinsky appear in the audience. Only now do I realize how much it helps to have friendly faces in the audience. It's a strange feeling, as though the whole tenor of the room has changed, as though the forces on our side have increased! And then, toward evening, all the Estonians start leaving one by one. They are probably workers from nearby factories who have been drafted to attend the trial; now their workday is over, so they are going home.

It's 10 p.m. The first day of the trial is over. I am back in the local police lock-up in Võru, though no longer in solitary, reading a letter from my family that Rask has passed to me. When I'm done, I grab a pen right away to write a reply:

> It was an enormous pleasure and comfort to see you all! It felt almost like a visit home, like a family reunion—instead of what it is, which is a modern-day Dreyfus[18] trial.
>
> Something new is in the air, like a smell of spring: they are cracking under our pressure! I am very pleased that the international discussion is being framed broadly, including both the Prisoners of Zion and the issue of aliyah. So long as the plight of Soviet Jewry is considered as a whole, I'm confident that the problems of individual Jews will be resolved in due course.
>
> I'm not really worried about myself; somehow, I feel that all will be well. One thing is perfectly clear: my sentence has nothing to do with what's going on in court and everything to do with our continuing fight for our cause!
>
> I'm going to continue my hunger strike. It's like a medieval battering ram: we'll keep battering these walls until they crumble. This won't happen on the first try, but eventually the authorities will have no choice: they will have to do something about me and about the Jewish problem as a whole.
>
> Many thanks to all!

As I'm being taken into the courtroom for the second day of the trial, Misha manages to come close enough to whisper to me: "They've turned off all long-distance phone lines, the whole city's

---

[18] A reference to the Dreyfus Affair, the 1894 trial in France that resulted in wrongful conviction of Alfred Dreyfus, a French-Jewish artillery captain, on fabricated espionage charges, sparking a widespread political scandal.

been cut off from the rest of the world. That's how seriously they take us!"

The prosecutor begins his closing statement.

He speaks brazenly, harshly, rehashing all the false accusations, working himself up into a fury. Does this mean that my four-and-a-half-month-long hunger strike has achieved nothing; that the international campaign of protest and solidarity hasn't helped either? Does this mean that I am about to hear these accursed words: "Seven years of imprisonment plus five years of judicial deportation"?

But then a thought pierces me: this is not the show trial they had promised! They wanted a big production, with extensive media coverage and a harsh sentence at the end that would intimidate the Jewish movement. But if they have disconnected the city from telephone communication with the outside world, this means that things are not going their way and they want to hide that fact. No, this is not their long-awaited show trial!

The prosecutor reaches his conclusion:

"Therefore, we demand that the accused be punished to the full extent of the law and request a sentence of *two years and five months' imprisonment!*"

We all sit there, stunned. Is that all they're asking for? Not in my wildest dreams did I expect such a mild sentence! They never even mentioned anti-Soviet literature. Gasps of surprise and unrestrained delight erupt from the benches where my family is sitting. A wild, intoxicating joy sweeps over me. Did the prosecutor really say that? They can't give me more than the prosecution asked for. Unable to believe my ears, I rise from my seat. No, it's not a hallucination: anger and frustration are written all over the prosecutor's face. The judge, on the other hand, looks inscrutable, his face like a mask.

Now it's time for my own closing statement, the "last word" the law allows to the accused. It's the most dramatic moment of the whole judicial process. Oh Lord, give me strength to say everything I want to say, to say it like it is. I'll give them a show trial—a real one that will show the whole world exactly who they are and what they've done. Don't let me lose heart at the last minute, even if this turns out to be literally my last word!

The real question, if it please the court, is this: who is behind the planting of the gun and cartridges in my apartment? I'm confident it is the KGB. The record clearly shows that my initial arrest was wrongful, both because it was not based on any evidence and also because of the way the charges against me kept changing. I am convinced that the KGB picked the original charges of vandalism in order to gain time to get to their real goal. What they were actually trying to do was fabricate a major charge, like the weapons charge that is now before the court, one that would be serious enough and would put me away for a sufficiently long time to effectively isolate me and to scare off other Jews from studying and developing the Jewish culture.

That I am innocent of these charges is proved by two facts:

1. I left the apartment at the beginning of July, that is, almost two months before the house search, and have not returned there since then.

2. After my arrest, my room, and particularly the space under the bookcase where the weapon and ammunition were allegedly found during the search, was examined very thoroughly twice, on August 6 and 27, and on both occasions nothing was found.

A number of violations of procedural norms were committed during the house search. For instance, none of the serial numbers of the pistol or the cartridges were recorded in the written inventory of confiscated objects, and after the search, these items were taken out of the apartment unsealed.

As a result, it is not clear which specific pistol and cartridges were allegedly found during the search. There is no way to tell whether they were the same ones I am accused of keeping. It's not even known whether the pistol confiscated during the search was in working order. Clearly, any charges built upon such defective evidence are invalid.

To make the fabrication look more plausible, the witnesses Devyatko and Popov claim that each of them remembers two digits of the pistol's number. Since the serial number has 6 digits, there are as many as 100 different pistols whose numbers include the four digits remembered by these gentlemen. Which of these 100 pistols are we talking about here?

In fact, the gun I am accused of keeping, serial number 243199K, is very unusual. First of all, it is not registered in the National Registry of Firearms. The Head of the Investigative Division of the Estonian Ministry of the Interior found this fact so important that he lodged an inquiry with his national counterparts, the

Ministry of the Interior of the USSR, asking them to ascertain the prior owner and the date and purpose of purchase. In other words, the Estonian authorities did not feel that merely finding a gun during a house search—whether this particular gun or a different one—could support an indictment.

Secondly, the forensic experts failed to find fingerprints of sufficient quality on the gun with the serial number 243199K. If that was the same gun that was allegedly found in my home, where are the fingerprints of everyone who handled it during the house search?

I also note that the national authorities were unable to satisfy the request of the Estonian investigators. Virtually nothing is known about this particular gun. If it is the same gun that was planted in my home, it must have come from such highly classified storage facilities that even the senior officials of the national Ministry of the Interior were not cleared to access them.

Incidentally, the pistol is a Walther, a brand that was manufactured in the Nazi Germany in the 1930s for the Gestapo. Many Jews were probably killed with this very pistol; the planting of this particular pistol in my apartment is a desecration of their memory.

Another procedural violation has to do with the choice of witnesses attending the house search. The regulations governing house searches require witnesses to be chosen randomly from the general public; usually, they are neighbors or people who live nearby. There was no shortage of neutral witnesses in our apartment building, which houses as many as 1500 people. Yet the investigators hand-picked their own witnesses, the students Devyatko and Popov. The prosecutor even drove them to my apartment and back in his own car: was that because they were needed as accomplices in the frame-up?

In an effort to fabricate evidence and blacken my name, the prosecution resorted to using hardened, convicted criminals. This court heard the testimony of two of my former cellmates: Fastov, currently serving eight years for aggravated embezzlement, and Kalm, convicted of twenty counts of embezzlement. These men were placed in my cell unlawfully, because the regulations prohibit housing post-conviction inmates together with pre-trial detainees. They were placed there specifically as informers, intended to give false testimony at trial. Their testimony is not credible and should be disregarded.

Yet, it is Fastov's testimony the prosecution used in its closing statement, claiming that I asked him about the punishment for keeping weapons, allegedly before I even knew about the house search. They used it because they have nothing better to establish my guilt. Meanwhile, they refused to consider exculpatory evidence, such as a drawing or a photograph of the bookcase showing how easily the weapon and ammunition could have been planted, and rejected my parents' request to conduct an investigative experiment to verify the claim about the tilting of the bookcase.

Based on everything I have described and on the rest of the evidence, I have no doubt that the weapon and ammunition were planted in my home during the search, and that the prosecution is aiding and abetting this crime.

Therefore, I ask this court to dismiss all charges against me and to punish instead the real law-breakers—all those involved in this fabrication. I have no doubt that this entire case is a fabrication, that it is nothing more than yet another link in the chain of persecution of the long-suffering Jewish people, its culture, and traditions. I am determined to bear your verdict, whatever it may be, with my head held high and my sense of mission unimpaired.

My words have the effect of a bombshell that has gone off in the courtroom! The judge's face breaks out in red spots, and a strange, mirthless grin plays over his lips. The court withdraws. We all sit there on pins and needles, awaiting the verdict: what's taking them so long?

Finally, the court comes back.

"All rise!"

A solemn pause. Here it comes . . .

"One year and six months' imprisonment."

Jubilation seems to sweep the entire courtroom. Even the Estonian workers in the audience share our joy. Take that, you KGB goons! You didn't get your show trial! You didn't get your "seven plus five"!

As the guards walk me out, Misha once again slips in next to me, and I manage to whisper to him:

"Victory! An amazing victory! And yet it's not enough, since they didn't drop all the charges. I'm going to continue my hunger strike until our victory is complete!"

Anya Yerukhimovich remembers

Our wild delight knew no bounds! We all hugged and kissed each other. Then we moved slowly out into the lobby. It was late Friday night. Shabbat had started long ago. Lev Tukachinsky took out a bottle of wine and said: "Hey, everyone, I've got something here for the Kiddush!"[19]

We drank that one bottle—no more than a sip per person—in celebration of both Shabbat and our victory! The wine tasted amazing; but we were all intoxicated before the first drop passed our lips.

"Kholmyansky Sentenced, Sharansky Ill,"
Washington Jewish Week, February 14, 1985

---

[19] The blessing over a cup of wine that ushers in the Jewish Sabbath.

Chapter 8

Back in the police lock-up, I sat for a long time reliving the dramatic events of the trial and reveling in the afterglow of the love and support from my family and friends I had felt in the courtroom.

Victory! True, it wasn't the full acquittal we had demanded, but still: we, a handful of ordinary people, had defeated the almighty, malignant leviathan of the KGB! They didn't get all they wanted! This was virtually unheard-of in this country!

Of course, they would now try to get back at me, entrap me in some way so they could fabricate new charges in order to keep me behind bars for as long as they had originally planned. I couldn't imagine them not trying.

But in the meantime . . . as I was walking out of the courtroom, Misha had whispered to me that I could now request a visit from my fiancée.

My *fiancée?*

I had long pushed all such thoughts away: a man in my situation had no room for romantic intentions, indeed, no right to them. But now? Dare I speak my heart?

Yes!

If we were granted a meeting, I would formally propose to her. Oh, but could I even wait until then—and what if they denied us a meeting? No! I would write her a letter, and Rask would get it to her.

I sat down and began writing.

* * *

That night, the prison transport took me back to Tallinn. Cocooned in my euphoria, I carefully ignored all thoughts of tomorrow. But tomorrow couldn't be ignored for long: it still held a full year of imprisonment, more punishment cells, the continuation of my hunger strike.

Michael Kholmyansky's telephone briefing for Western supporters (February 8, 1985)

The authorities won't let us see Sasha. He is continuing his hunger strike and is still in solitary confinement. This is illegal! Under Article 360 of the Code of Criminal Procedure, even an inmate who is held in solitary confinement for a serious offense cannot be denied a post-trial visit from his family.

We ask everyone not to relax their pressure on the authorities. Although Sasha's sentence is lighter than expected, he is still unjustly imprisoned when he should have been acquitted and released. We must continue to raise this issue at every opportunity, in every public or private forum. Because the books planted in his home were not mentioned at trial, there is still a possibility that the prosecution may file separate criminal charges against him under articles 70 and 190 (anti-Soviet propaganda and slandering the regime).

The struggle for Alexander Kholmyansky's release is not over. Now everything depends on us, people of good will in the free world, governments and parliaments of Western countries.

Free Alexander Kholmyansky!

* * *

Mart Rask returned a couple of days later to discuss our next steps, that is, to decide whether or not to file an appeal. Logically, the verdict left us room for appeal because it was internally inconsistent: the court had cleared me of illegal possession of the gun but convicted me of illegal possession of ammunition, which was based on the same faulty evidence as the gun charge. Rask recommended appealing. I agreed, relying on his legal judgment and his knowledge of the local Estonian court system; I wanted to keep fighting. He left, promising to draft the appeal petition and bring it to me for signature.

Ten days later he was back, looking worried, even agitated; his Estonian accent, usually barely noticeable, was suddenly quite pronounced. He advised me against filing an appeal. When I questioned him, he explained that there was a catch. In the absence of an appeal, the verdict would take effect in a month and would then be final. He said that since I had already served six months of the eighteen-month sentence, I had one year left — but not more than that; even the KGB couldn't easily extend it. However, the mere filing of the appeal would have the legal effect of cancelling *all* the proceedings of the lower court, including the verdict. It would give the KGB another bite of the apple, a new opportunity to try and overturn the verdict and make it much harsher. To file now would be to open a Pandora's box.

I studied Rask's face. He looked uneasy. Clearly, he had been told something that had led him to change his mind, but he refused to tell me what it was. Well then: I would heed his warning. I could think of letting the sentence stand as a tactical retreat.

* * *

It soon became apparent that Rask was right, because once the authorities learned of my decision not to file an appeal, they literally went insane. Once again, I was taken to see Maiboroda, who launched into an incoherent, angry rant. In the middle of it, he received a telephone call, evidently from someone very high up, because his posture changed right before my eyes: he shrank, became smaller, no longer the big, powerful boss but a mere vassal, a serf, everything about him expressing servile obedience. I could hear the authoritative, commanding voice booming at him from the receiver, although I couldn't make out any words. This was clearly the KGB: they loved giving instructions over the phone, leaving no paper trail.

In the hallway on my way back I was accosted by an unknown man, likewise strangely agitated, who asked:

"Don't you realize that by not appealing the guilty verdict, by letting it stand, you're acknowledging your guilt? Is that what you're doing? Are you, in fact, declaring yourself guilty?"

> **THE NEW YORK TIMES, THURSDAY, FEBRUARY 14, 1985**
>
> **ABROAD AT HOME | Anthony Lewis**
>
> # Crime and Punishment
>
> ## The ordeal of a quiet Soviet Jew
>
> BOSTON
>
> He is a computer programmer, 32 years old, described by a friend as "a quiet, contemplative, unobtrusive man." An unlikely person, one might think, to be treated as a threat to the state. But Aleksandr Kholmyansky is a Soviet Jew who cared about his Jewish heritage. His story is instructive.
>
> On Feb. 1, in the Estonian town of Voru [sic], Mr. Kholmyansky was convicted of illegally possessing ammunition and sentenced to 18 months in labor camp. . . .
>
> On Aug. 29, three officials and a number of policemen searched Mr. Kholmyansky's Moscow apartment, which he shared with his parents. His mother said in a letter that the officials "found" under the cupboard "some items that were not there before the search, including a revolver and bullets. As soon as they made their "discovery," they "stopped the search and left in a hurry". . . .
>
> But the real charge, the real point of the crude tactics used against Aleksandr Kholmyansky, is not in doubt. It is part of a new and frightening campaign to suppress Jewish consciousness and culture among the two million or more Soviet Jews. . . .
>
> One last word on Aleksandr Kholmyansky: He reportedly began a hunger strike last Sept. 13. There is no word of his ending it; the authorities may be force-feeding him. What can the West do about all this? . . .

"Crime and Punishment," by Anthony Lewis,
New York Times, February 14, 1985 (excerpt)

"No, God forbid, of course not. I have the legal right to appeal or not to appeal. I'm simply exercising my legal right."

Next, they took me to see the prison psychiatrist, who spent hours trying to crack me, to find a weak spot, also trying to convince me to file an appeal. Yes, it looked as though Rask's source had been right. I didn't know who it was but it might have been someone close to the top echelons of the KGB, which would explain Rask's reluctance to disclose his identity. However, by all appearances, the KGB had indeed prepared a trap for me, and my refusal to appeal had foiled their plans. Now they would likely try something else. It was time for a pre-emptive strike on my part. What could I do? Should I try a dry hunger strike again?

Again they took me to see Maiboroda. He was furious, clearly about to lose his self-control. Watching him closely, I said:

"Don't worry about my appeal. I would like to inform you that as of tomorrow, I will be starting a *dry* hunger strike."

His face became purple, and he looked almost apoplectic:

"What? A dry hunger strike? We're doing you a favor by feeding you, keeping you alive, otherwise you would have died long ago. There's no limit to your impudence!"

I spat back:

"I never asked for any favors! You're not keeping me alive, you're just postponing my death, and ruining my health in the process. Your people threatened me with handcuffs and jaw clamps and tongue depressors—that's torture, that's not feeding! I never asked to be fed; you may stop it at any time!"

"Oh yeah? We will, then. If you don't like dying slowly, you'll die fast. Off to the punishment cell with you!"

* * *

The small punishment cell was still the same. Nothing had changed in here. This place was impervious to the power of time. Here were the same walls that smelled of damp and decay, the same cot locked into the wall, the same primitive toilet in the corner and the water tap . . .

The water tap. If I turned on the faucet, water would start running. I could open it again and again, and each time, the water would start running. I could keep it open, and the water would keep running. Water . . . such an ordinary thing for everyone—but not for me. I was on a dry hunger strike. I would not drink. I could wet my face and my hands, but I would not drink.

Water . . . flowing down the drain, into a great invisible ocean. I imagined myself floating in that ocean, a blazing sun overhead, tormented with thirst. Don't drink the water, it's bitter, it's bad . . .

They must have thought if they left me in the cell with running water, I wouldn't be able to stop myself. As usual, they'd underestimated me. Thankfully, I felt no hunger, but the skin on my arms and legs was peeling, and my tongue stuck to the roof of my mouth, too dry to lick my parched lips. And here was the water . . . clear, pristine water, a gurgling brook fed by underground streams. All I had to do was bend down and scoop it in my hands, and . . . I was back in the punishment cell, the faucet open, the water streaming down my hands and dripping on the floor.

I pressed my hands and my head forcefully into the rough wall so the pain might take my mind off my thirst. How many days had passed? Three? One could survive seven days without water. Perhaps the authorities didn't know that, and that's why they had left me alone all this time; probably not because they wanted to kill me now, right after the trial. They were still watching to see if I would break. They would come, but they might come too late.

The fourth day passed in a daze, my thoughts drifting toward oblivion. I was beginning to go . . . But if I died, I would die a winner. I had thwarted them. They had tried to intimidate us and failed; they had tried to paint us all as terrorists and failed; they had tried to put on a show trial and failed. I had won. If I died, it would be a good death.

On the fifth day, I tasted blood—maybe a nosebleed, maybe from my cracked lips. Surprisingly, I found myself able to pray. I sensed a confirmation: carry on, this is not in vain. I heard a great silence all around me. I was in a desert . . . To think that somewhere out there was a whole world of people who had no idea what it meant to be able to drink whenever and however much they wanted. And here I was in a desert . . . A wagon train was rolling through the desert with a great screeching of metal . . .

My cell door burst open with a great screeching of metal, and a whole delegation filed in, four people, maybe more; they couldn't all fit into the tiny cell. The short man in front was one Dimov from the office of inspector general of the Prosecutor's Office; massive

Maiboroda loomed behind him. Dimov took one look at me and gasped. He yelled at Maiboroda, but I could no longer make out his words. All I could see were two *zeks* racing towards me with a stretcher. They placed me on it and carried the stretcher out at a trot. I lay on it like a sack, unable to move.

They took me to the prison infirmary. As though through a mist, I saw several people gathered around my bed, all shaking their heads: I must have been a scary sight. A nurse fussed over me, trying to find a vein in my arm to start an IV, but my veins had collapsed. She poked here and there, until, at a particularly wild stab, I felt a sharp pain and lost consciousness.

* * *

Michael Kholmyansky's telephone briefing for Western supporters (March 10, 1985)

We have learned that three weeks ago, they stopped feeding Sasha. His weight has dropped to 42.5 kilograms (his height is 172 centimeters). He had begun hemorrhaging blood and was hospitalized. As of three days ago, at least, he was still in the prison infirmary. When his health improves, they will send him to a labor camp. Please send a letter to the US Secretary of State George Schulz and to the heads of delegations at the US-Soviet arms race talks in Geneva.

* * *

I woke up and looked around. I was in a large infirmary ward with ten beds, all of them occupied. The window was barred, like in my cell—but the door, surprisingly, was not. I wondered if ambulatory patients were allowed to walk down the hallways on their own.

Time became an endless sequence of infusions, injections, medical examinations; they were clearly making a serious effort to fix me back up. Two weeks later, they told me:

"Your weight is back up to forty-six kilograms. We've pulled you out of critical condition. You'll receive intravenous nutrition and a vitamin complex. This will help, but if you're stubborn enough to continue your hunger strike, you will inevitably return to critical condition."

Gradually, I began to feel much better and was able to get out of bed and walk several steps down the ward. By the middle of the third week, I gathered my courage and stepped out into the hallway. I was able to take a few steps but found myself unable to straighten up and walked bent over.

Letter to my family, March 11, 1985

My dears! My verdict is now in force, and this means that all the limitations on correspondence are dropped. I'm in the prison infirmary, feeling better. There is nothing to worry about. My mood is excellent, as always.

* * *

"Hey, you there, you look like you just got out of Auschwitz," a cleaning lady, gruff but friendly, hailed me in the hallway.

"What, don't you like my looks?"

"Ugh, dead people on their way to the grave look prettier than this!"

"Eh, I'm not ready for the grave."

"Ready or not, you look like you've got one foot there already."

"Nah, I'll live, I'm tough."

"How old are you, tough guy?"

"Almost thirty-five."

"Got a wife or kids?"

"No, I'm not married yet."

"Most people are married by thirty-five. You got a girlfriend, at least?"

"Yes, I do, she's waiting for me. We'll get married when I get out."

"Married? If you keep on with your hunger strike you'll ruin all your plumbing till you're no good to her at all!"

* * *

Breaking news: Chernenko, the Communist Party chief, has died. The whole country waits with bated breath to see who will preside over the burial commission: by a macabre, Orwellian tradition, this task always falls to the designated successor before he is announced as the new Secretary General of the Communist Party of the USSR. Against all expectation, it goes to Mikhail Gorbachev, a virtual unknown.

* * *

Michael Kholmyansky's telephone briefing for Western supporters (March 12, 1985)

We have a request: Tomorrow, after Chernenko's funeral, a reception will be held in Moscow, at the Kremlin. Foreign dignitaries will attend. Could any of them raise the problem of Soviet Jews and the plight of Prisoners of Zion at this reception? Would the UK representatives consider doing so?

An open letter from Alexander Kholmyansky's parents

Dear friends:

Tomorrow, March 13, marks half a year since our son Alexander Kholmyansky has been on a hunger strike protesting against his illegal arrest on fabricated evidence and his unjust sentence.

He has declared that he will stop his hunger strike on the first day of his release. Alexander is fighting not only for himself, but for all the Jews of the Soviet Union who want to emigrate to Israel.

Throughout his struggle you have been disseminating information about him and his plight in the media in Israel and the Diaspora. This information has touched so many hearts and has caused an unprecedented wave of solidarity and support in Israel, Europe and America. We greatly appreciate your efforts.

At this point, our son's condition has deteriorated so severely as a result of his prolonged hunger strike that we have reason to fear for his life. We ask that you redouble your efforts to attract media attention to his heroism and his desperate situation. Please speak out!

Please urge the Government of Israel, the Israeli public, and Jewish communities around the world to take immediate actions for his release.

* * *

In the evening of March 18, after almost four weeks in the prison infirmary, I was shipped from Tallinn to Leningrad by special prisoner transport train. I rode in a tiny compartment behind bars, like a death row inmate or one severely ill, with special round-the-clock guard posted out in the aisle.

The infamous Leningrad prison Kresty looked for all the world like an enormous railroad terminal, with *zeks* and their guards rushing chaotically to and fro. They put me in a large cell holding around eighty men, where I witnessed the establishment of the prison pecking order—the brutal hazing of newcomers by a pack leader and his sidekicks. Watching their cold, detached, ruthless cruelty, I wondered how far removed these people had become from ordinary human notions of right and wrong.

Thankfully, I was able to sit unnoticed in the corner until the evening, when they led a group of us out to a prison van and drove us to the train station. There, another prisoner transport train was waiting at a siding, away from public view.

I found myself in another tiny solitary compartment, while the rest of the train car was crammed full of men sitting on triple bunks. We rode through the night. In the morning, the *zeks* set up a great racket, screaming and banging on the door, demanding water: they had been fed salted fish for dinner but had had nothing to drink. After a full hour of this, the guards brought in water. Sometime later, they came to take people out to the toilet, starting with me; the *zeks* pressed forward, craning their necks to get a look at me as I passed, whispering: "That's him, that's the dude on a hunger strike." Some of them called out words of encouragement, others made fun of my appearance.

But where were we going? The train seemed to be heading east. The *zeks* thought we were going to Sverdlovsk, to the largest transit prison in all of the Soviet Union, the major stopover point on the route to Siberia.

Michael Kholmyansky's telephone briefing for Western supporters (March 24, 1985)

We have learned that on April 7, a delegation of the US House of Representatives, led by House Speaker Thomas (Tip) O'Neill, arrives in Moscow. Two days later, a delegation of the US Senate, including Senator William Cohen (R-Maine) and Senator Carl Levin (D-Michigan), is arriving here.

We ask that our friends in the United States approach them via American Jewish organizations and ask them to meet with Jewish activists in Moscow.

Before Sasha was sent on to labor camp, he submitted a declaration to the Presidium of the Supreme Council renouncing his Soviet citizenship, but never heard back. At this time, Sasha's case calls for quiet diplomacy. Please contact all the delegations and influential people heading to Moscow and ask them to do something on his behalf.

We were not able to get Sasha warm clothes before he left, so he was sent on wearing what he had on when he was arrested last summer.

* * *

In Sverdlovsk's storied transit prison, I spent the first few days in medical quarantine—or what passed for it: a regular cell with five other *zeks*. One, a first-timer convicted of aggravated embezzlement, couldn't keep quiet in his excitement:

"They never found the money! I won't even be old yet when I get out—and I'll still have the dough!"

From there, I was transferred to the infirmary, a large, busy facility, and hooked up to an IV. My arms looked like two massive bruises from all the unsuccessful attempts to find a vein. Teams of doctors monitored me, but everyone was businesslike and detached: unlike in Tallinn, no one here seemed to care at all about my hunger strike. The amount of liquid nutrition they were pouring down the tube seemed to have been increased significantly.

Time passed, with absolutely nothing happening to distinguish one day from another, and yet it also seemed to stand still. A week passed, then a second one. By the end of March, I felt strong enough to amble around my ward and walk out into the hallway. At the next medical check-up, they told me that my weight was up to 48 kilograms, and my blood pressure was 90/60.

There was a new paramedic assigned to do my daily feedings. Unlike my previous nurses, this one was friendly—perhaps a bit too friendly for a prison paramedic. At each feeding, he would ask me a question or two, tell me a little story about himself, all quiet and low-key.

On April 8, when a guard brought me in for my feeding, the paramedic dismissed him and told me:

"You sit here a minute, it's not ready yet."

I sat there, half-listening to his chatter, while he continued to cook something in front of me, a sort of thin porridge with milk. All of a sudden, instead of sticking the tube down my throat as usual, he plopped a bowl of porridge in front of me, adding a good-size chunk of butter!

"Go ahead and eat," he said, "there's no one here to see, and I won't tell anyone."

Taken off-guard, I stared at him in a daze. The long-forgotten smell of fresh, wholesome food tickled my nostrils. A cube of butter was slowly melting in the middle of the bowl. A hot wave of irresistible desire washed over me, my mouth filled with saliva, and in a fit of frenzy I grabbed the spoon and devoured the whole portion in no time.

"Well done," said the paramedic with a fatherly smile. "Wipe your lips now."

I wiped my lips, and he called the guard to take me back. In a state of ecstasy beyond words, I lay down on my bed, filled to the brim with a sense of physical well-being, and slept like a baby.

The next day, the paramedic again dismissed the guard and placed the bowl in front of me.

"No, no, take it away, I didn't mean to break my hunger strike!"

"Oh, come on, no one will know, I won't tell. You ate yesterday, and it was all right, wasn't it?"

"Yesterday was an accident. Of course they'll know, they can tell the difference."

"But I've already cooked it and poured it, look! Come on now, just one more time, just today. Tomorrow is another day."

I fell for it.

Unable to control myself, I gobbled down the bowl of porridge and once again felt a sense of physical bliss fill my whole body — who can describe this feeling?

On the third day the Chief Physician of the prison infirmary stopped by on his rounds.

"I'm glad, Kholmyansky, that you've finally come to your senses and have begun to eat. Believe me, you'll never regret it!"

I felt my face turn crimson. Oh God, I fell for it, I caved! They used a trick to do what they couldn't do by force. I lay on my bed all night writhing, unable to close my eyes for a moment, tormented by shame and remorse.

Only in the morning did I begin to feel some relief. A new thought came: Why should I be so down on myself? What had I done that was so wrong? Had I cheated anyone, had I broken a promise? My goodness, I'd spent a total of five consecutive months in punishment cells, I'd been on a hunger strike since September 13. How long was that? I took a piece of paper and began calculating. It added up to 207 days! A new world record — maybe something for the Guinness Book of World Records, if they kept track of such things.

OK, they'd tricked me into interrupting my hunger strike. Fine. I would respond by changing my strategy. After all, the possibility of new charges hung daily over my head like the sword of Damocles; the KGB didn't get the long sentence they wanted and might try to drum up other weapons charges or something based on "anti-Soviet literature." Now I would let myself start eating again so as to recover a bit, get stronger. This way, I would be in a position to threaten them with the resumption of my hunger strike if they tried something, and since I had proven my ability to abstain from food for really long periods, the threat alone might deter them.

Besides, I wasn't going to stay here in the Sverdlovsk transit prison forever: I had several months of labor camp ahead of me.

That would be a big transition; I should give myself space to plan and prepare, and that was another reason to begin eating now.

* * *

Meanwhile, my thoughts kept returning to my dear friends on the outside who were continuing the Cities Project, with all of its risks and dangers. How were they holding up?

Dov Kontorer remembers

Ze'ev Geyzel and I found ourselves having to take over the Cities Project at the worst possible time. There were the two high-profile arrests in Moscow—you and Yuli Edelstein; in Kiev, Joseph Berenstein was tried and convicted; there were house searches in other cities across the USSR, where the police confiscated educational materials and gave official warnings. For a short while, our operations were paused. First, we were all so emotionally caught up in your trial and your hunger strike. Second, we had to assess the damage that your arrest had caused to the project. But the pause was short-lived. Already by autumn of 1984, the Cities Project came to life again. The two of us split the leadership duties between us informally, but we often stepped in to replace one another and worked in overall harmony, without any friction or competition.

Our first task was to assess the damage and find out which of our participants were psychologically intact, that is, unafraid and willing to carry on despite the risk. People in the cities had reacted in different ways. Most knew you personally, and your arrest, of course, had affected them greatly.

So my first trip after your arrest was an inspection tour. I visited the cities along the Volga River, then took a short break, then went on to Central Asia and eventually the Baltics.

One thing I should mention is that the Cities Project was funded in part with proceeds from the sale of items, mostly photo cameras, that our foreign visitors brought with them and gave us so we could essentially fence them for cash. We tried to keep the sales process separate from the project's core operations: for example, the messengers delivering the cameras to the dealers were supposed to be different people from those who traveled to the cities to deliver Hebrew materials to our project activists. But we were short-handed, especially after your arrest, and it did occasionally happen that the same person did both. Even then, the same person was not supposed to carry books and cameras on the same trip.

But there was one time when the project ran out of money. I was going on a book run to Saratov and saw no other option but to take two expensive Japanese cameras with me to sell there. This was against all our rules and extremely risky, especially since I had no proof of purchase for the cameras and wouldn't be able to prove that they weren't stolen goods if I were stopped. And that's when an incident happened that I consider a small miracle, an indication that our project was blessed and guided by Divine Providence.

My first stop was in the city of Penza, where I intended to stay for a couple of days and to leave some of my books with our people there. I left my heavy, twenty-five-kilogram backpack in the locker at the train station and went into town. I returned in the evening with Gennady Raikh, our man in Penza, to collect the backpack—but the combination I punched into the lock didn't work: the door of the locker wouldn't open. I tried again and again—in vain!

I realized that I was in serious trouble. Our rules required me at that point to abandon the luggage and leave the city immediately. I couldn't very well ask for help from the train station personnel without describing the bag and its contents, and what would I tell them—that it contained twenty-five kilograms of material the KGB would love to get their hands on? No, I had little chance of getting the bag back and every chance of getting arrested while trying.

That's what I would have told any of our messengers to do in this situation: forget the bag, go home, put together an alibi and hope the KGB doesn't trace the fingerprints to you. However great the financial loss to the project, nothing was worth the risk of getting caught!

And yet . . . the project itself was at risk: we were out of money. We had worked so hard to organize this trip. I could not give up.

I sent Gennady to wait at the exit from the train station, with instructions to call Moscow if I didn't show up within an hour and say a particular code phrase that meant I had been arrested with the luggage.

I went back to the left luggage room, contemplating the futility of what I was about to do. I began to fill out a luggage retrieval form: name, address, date of arrival, purpose of visit, contents of the baggage—basically a one-way ticket to jail. Armed with this document, I sent up a fervent prayer for a miracle and went to find the attendant.

Just as I was handing him my form, I noticed the number of the locker in front of which he was standing: B-435. But . . . that was the number of my own locker! It dawned on me that I had been trying to open the wrong locker: A-435 instead of B-435!

Quick as lightning, I snatched the form from his hand, muttering some nonsense, like "I forgot to add two shirts and a jar of jam." I went straight to the men's room, tore the form into small pieces, and flushed it down the toilet. Then I waited until the attendant walked away before going to the right locker, which opened easily. A minute later I was walking out with my backpack to find Gennady and calm him down.

During the winter of 1984–1985, we resumed operations wherever it was possible. Gradually, we worked back up to the same level as during your time, twenty active cities, and eventually even surpassed it, operating at our peak in about thirty cities.

In the summer of 1986, I organized a large, successful summer camp near the city of Samara, where we gathered new teachers from the Volga and Baltic regions. We also held smaller summer camps.

Valentine (Benny) Lidsky and Michael Volkov became more actively involved in the Cities Project.

* * *

On April 23, late at night, they took me out from the prison infirmary and put me on a prisoner transport train headed to the labor camp. I sat in my tiny compartment, lost in anxious thought. Nine and a half months of labor camp. A whole new world, totally different from prison, with its own rules and customs that I must learn. No more solitary confinement: I was going to be housed together with a hundred or two hundred criminals in a barrack. I had heard enough from Fastov and others to know that labor camp, like any closed group, like the holding cell in the Kresty prison, was sure to have its own brutal hierarchy, its own pecking order, in which I must establish myself right from the start to avoid being trampled down. I had to act quickly upon arrival: I had only one chance to make the right first impression. I had to seize the initiative; but how to do that?

It was also essential to position myself correctly vis-à-vis the camp authorities. I would resume my hunger strike for about six weeks, until my birthday. This would bring it to about eight months total; not bad at all. Then I should stop and spend the remainder of my sentence eating normally and recovering, getting as much of my strength back as it was possible to do in labor camp. There was a good chance that the KGB, cheated out of the long sentence they wanted, would try to stage some sort of incident that would result in new charges. They would likely try to do that toward the end of my sentence. By that time, I should be as strong as possible and prepared to renew my hunger strike in protest against the new charges.

Towards morning we arrived in Kamensk-Uralsky. The train stopped at a siding far out of sight of regular travelers, and we trudged across a web of tracks to waiting black vans, flanked by rows of guards holding ferociously barking dogs on leashes. A bumpy ride, a screech of metal gates; the van doors opened; I was in the labor camp.

Where, it turned out, it was already spring. The sun peeked out between clouds; the birds chirped merrily. Unlike the camp's human denizens, the birds were free. And the air! In all my time in prison I had forgotten how delicious fresh air could be. I wanted to savor it slowly in little sips, to breathe it in big gulps, to drive the cement dust of all those punishment cells out of my lungs.

A guard walked me to my assigned barrack. Though I could barely drag myself along in my weakened state, I gazed around me with urgent attention, taking in my new surroundings.

We walked along the line of sturdy brick barracks. Each opened into a small yard enclosed by a high wire mesh fence. The inmates of a barrack were forbidden to leave their yard on pain of incarceration in the camp's prison or even in a punishment cell. The only accepted way of leaving the yard was as part of an organized group under guard, and then only to go out to work, to the dining room or to the bathhouse. We passed an administrative building on the left, called "the headquarters," then another building, squat and low—the dining room.

"Here's your unit," said the guard.

We walked into a large barrack filled with double bunks, enough to fit as many as 200 men, although no more than 140 or 150 were actually inside: the rest had probably gone out to work.

"Here's a new arrival," said the guard, and 140 pairs of eyes turned as one and stared at me.

"I'm a religious Jew," said I in as loud and confident a voice as I could muster. "This is my time to pray. Which direction is Jerusalem?"

140 jaws dropped, their owners frozen in shock. Who would do such a thing—announce himself as a Jew right off the bat? Weren't Jews miserable, cowardly creatures who did all they could to hide their Jewishness? Such was the antisemitic image the average Russian was raised with. It offered endless scope for sadistic fun—uncovering these hidden Jews, revealing their shameful secret, exploiting their fear and mortification. But here was this weirdo trumpeting it for all to hear. Jerusalem . . . prayer . . . *what*?

"Well, guys? which way is Jerusalem?"

Some of the *zeks* shook themselves out of their stupor, crowded around me and began pointing in different directions.

"The south, I need the south. Which way is it?"

Having located the southerly direction by means of a majority vote, they left me alone while I said a short prayer. Once I was done, they surrounded me and started asking questions, with genuine interest and respect.

"Who are you, compadre? What are you in here for?"

"Article 218, part 2. Illegal possession of firearms."

With this declaration, I gained another measure of respect.

"What was your weapon?"

"It wasn't mine; they planted it in my home during a house search. They framed me."

"Who did?"

"The KGB."

"Why would they do that?"

"We, ah, don't get along too well, the KGB and I."

I heard some *zeks* mutter under their breath: "I'll be damned." Some of them prudently melted away while others persisted:

"But why are you so thin and green-looking? Are you sick or something?"

"Not sick. I'm on a hunger strike, to protest the frame-up."

"Have you been at it for a long time?"

"A really long time. I took a little break recently but now I'm doing it again."

Soon, a service *zek* from the camp's infirmary came in bearing a bowl of fresh porridge for me.

"No, take it away, I'm on a hunger strike."

"I know nothing about that, no one told me."

"Here's my written notice of my hunger strike, take it back to them."

The service *zek* put the bowl on the bedside table in front of me, took my note and left. I lay down on my bunk with my back to the bowl of porridge. My neighbors, shaken to the core, kept coming up to me and poking me:

"What's wrong with you, compadre? It's fresh porridge, they brought it in specially for you! Do you think they're going to do this every day?"

"No, guys, I'm not eating. This is my protest against the frame-up."

Soon, I was summoned to the commander of the labor camp, Zeranov.

"What are you up to, Alexander? I know you kept up a prolonged hunger strike in jail, probably hoping to influence your sentence. We're not going to debate whether it had any effect. But now your sentence is final, nothing you do will change it; you're going to serve it to the end. So to resume your hunger strike now will be viewed as nothing more than a refusal to work. Because, obviously, we're not going to make you work in your current condition. But a refusal to work is a very serious offense, punishable with isolation in a punishment cell.

"And that would be a shame, especially since you've already served half your term and are entitled to many privileges: visits from relatives, care packages, access to the camp store. A hunger strike automatically takes all these privileges away.

"You have until tomorrow to change your mind. I'm asking you to be reasonable and quit your hunger strike. If you don't, I will have no choice but to send you to the punishment cell for ten days."

Back in the barrack, I sat for a long time, unable to make a decision. I was left alone while others were led out to work and continued to reject the special deliveries of porridge. Zeranov was right, of course; everything he said was true. I had done what I could to establish myself in the barrack; there was no point in continuing. It was time to work on rebuilding my health so as to be ready if and when the KGB made their move. Even if they didn't stage a new incident, there was still that "anti-Soviet literature" they hadn't used against me. But to quit now . . . I had been at it for so long that I simply lacked the resolve to utter the magic words: "I'm ending the hunger strike."

Thus debating with myself, I missed Zeranov's deadline and found myself in the camp's punishment cell. This one was nothing like the one in prison: large enough to walk around in, and the cot stayed down. It must be freezing cold in winter but now, in spring, it was bearable.

* * *

A couple of days later, I was summoned to Zeranov again:

"Alexander, your parents are here. They came all the way from

Moscow to see you. Remember, you can't see them until you end your hunger strike. Here's your mother's letter, urging you to do just that. Here, read it."

My mother's letter was the last straw. Only a heart of stone could reject an appeal so powerful and raw in its intensity. It brought me the rest of the way toward the decision I had more or less already made.

"What do you say?"

"I guess I can stop now; I've done what I could and now I need to recover. In case I have to restart it again. Which I will do at the first sign of another attempt to implicate me in anything or any other illegal move against me. But for now, I'm ending it. Effective today."

"You are?" Zeranov asked, a note of mounting excitement in his voice.

"I am. With conditions. I want two weeks in the infirmary, a month on special rations for faster recovery, I want to see my parents, and I want out of the punishment cell."

"Deal!" said Zeranov, his voice back under control. "I can't let you out of the punishment cell, that's out of my hands, but once your time is up you'll have your two weeks in the infirmary, and I'll get you bedding and toiletries and your special rations and a visit with your parents. And one more thing."

"Yes?"

"You will sign a formal statement that you're ending your hunger strike, and we'll have a doctor and an officer attend you as witnesses when you actually end it."

"Done!"

* * *

I sat in the punishment cell, trying to comprehend what had just happened. I had ended my hunger strike. It felt like the end of an era, a major and very significant period. Now I should reset my thinking, develop a new strategy, focus on rebuilding my health as much as possible.

A paramedic came in, accompanied by an officer and bringing food. So they had meant it about the witnesses. They had actually taken me and my hunger strike seriously! I ate a few spoonfuls of porridge, feeling a soft, spreading languor, a blissful warmth in my stomach, reveling in the delectable taste.

And this wasn't stolen pleasure like that time back in prison when they had tricked me into eating. I had earned this.

The paramedic handed me a form to sign: a declaration that I had taken food voluntarily.

Elated by all the formality and drowsy from the food, I fell into a kind of surreal slumber.

The officer attended my feedings for the next two days but after that they just sent a nurse. The food was not the meager punishment cell rations but more nutritious food served in the infirmary.

Soon enough, even with a better diet, my solitary confinement began to weigh on me. It had been tolerable during my hunger strike, when it was for a good cause, when each passing hour felt like a small victory. But now that there was nothing else to strive for, time seemed to stagnate like water in a swamp.

On the tenth day, they took me to the headquarters building without explanation. At the end of the hallway sat an officer, eyeing me curiously. He got up and unlocked a door right behind me, in what looked like a blank part of the wall. I stumbled into a room equipped with two glass cubicles placed a meter apart, a supervisor sitting between them: I was in the room for family visits!

Oh my God! Here were Mom and Dad and Anya—right there in front of me! We stared at each other, unable to utter a word. "Finally!" my mother breathed out. We devoured each other with our eyes. My God, how much had happened since I said goodbye to my parents before leaving for summer camp, almost a year ago!

"Sasha," Mom said urgently, "you know there's no kosher food in here. Please don't make an issue out of that. We've checked with the rabbis; it's OK to eat non-kosher food to preserve your life, there's a rule about that.[20] They even gave us a special ruling

---

[20] *Pikuach nefesh* (saving a life). The principle in Jewish law that preservation of a human life overrides most other religious commandments.

just for you: you are specifically allowed to eat anything in here, anything at all, even pork! They told me specifically to tell you this."

"I know, I understand."

I turned to Anya.

"How are you?"

She gave me a shy smile.

"I have something to say to you ... something very important that I've wanted to tell you for a long time ... but couldn't ... I think you know why I couldn't ... "

She blushed. God, how our souls yearned for each other! But our time was up; the guard declared the meeting over; we parted. I returned to the barracks, floating on air.

Anya remembers

Your face was terribly puffy and swollen—a classic edema of kidney dysfunction. "Look, he's gained some weight, praise God," your mom said. I didn't say anything but I knew what this was from my own past health issues: fluid retention from impaired kidney function. You looked just like a labor-camp convict, exhausted and unhealthy.

Michael Kholmyansky's briefing for Western supporters (May 30, 1985)

On May 26 Alexander was allowed to see his parents and his fiancée. Mom says he looks better than he did in court. It has been a little over a week since he resumed eating normally. Of course, it will take him many months to recover fully. He spent another ten days in solitary confinement in a punishment cell, bringing his total time in a punishment cell up to an unbelievable five and a half months.

We ask you to keep talking about Sasha's case in the media, at least until his birthday on June 5. After that, assuming no new troubles, it's better to stop, so that media attention won't complicate his situation in camp. However, we must be vigilant and prepared to launch a massive new media campaign in the event of new attempts to further frame or implicate him or extend his sentence.

Please convey our sincere thanks to the Jewish community of New Orleans, and personally to Rabbi David Goldstein and his wife, Shannie.

* * *

Zeranov kept his promise: on May 30 they moved me to the infirmary, where I became completely absorbed in observing my digestion. For two weeks, the world outside my own stomach simply ceased to exist. Time stopped . . .

A letter to Anya (May 30, 1985)

Anya, my darling,
I'm in the infirmary and doing all right. I am eating quite a lot. I finished the little box of baby food you guys sent me and tried the bouillon cubes, which went down so easily that I finished them in one go. I've slowly been trying some of the solid food they serve for lunch, though with less success. But breakfast here is mostly edible, and supper usually is, too.

So things are on track, and hopefully, a full recovery is just a matter of time. Strangely enough, I don't feel much different, but at least I'm not feeling worse! Progress is taking longer than I would wish. But the doctors all say that it's a matter of months not weeks. At least I'm walking much better and can even walk up the stairs by myself.

I'm so glad you're getting along with my parents. You seem to have clicked into place, as though there was a slot in our family that was designed for you — predestined. God willing, it will always be like this!

Birthday cake baked by residents of Kibbutz Rosh Tzurim (Israel) in honor of my birthday on June 5, 1985. The cake is shaped like a Hebrew-Russian dictionary and reads in Hebrew and Russian: "Next Year in Jerusalem." The picture on the wall is captioned: "Prisoner of Zion in the USSR"

A letter to my parents, June 9, 1985

My dear ones,

I received an absolute flood of birthday wishes—telegrams, letters, and postcards. They took up half the bed when I laid them out! I'm so touched and even a little embarrassed, I never expected all this.

It's hard to believe I'm already thirty-five. I feel ready and able to start something new. My health is gradually improving, though it's still unstable. But there are new breakthroughs all the time. I've been able to eat a wider variety of solid food and greater amounts (though not to excess), and am gaining weight quickly. Since May 17, when I started to eat normally, I've gained about six kilograms, or about two kilograms per week. At this rate, I'll be like Pooh Bear and won't fit through the front door of our apartment!

I'm very glad that you are getting along with Anya. It sounds like things have fallen into place very naturally.

Chapter 9

On June 15, they sent me back to the barracks to begin the labor part of my labor camp sentence. No more special treatment for me. Our unit was divided into three work gangs: one worked in a mechanical workshop, the second gang were weavers who made oversize mesh bags, and the third were the "guard-free"—the elite group who were taken out to work outside the camp without a guard being posted.

I was assigned to the weavers, who made huge mesh bags for vegetables, almost one meter long. What kind of nonsense was this—making them by hand, in this industrial day and age? But what did it matter? At least this wasn't logging, the work was indoors, it didn't require a lot of physical force...

What it did require, as I soon discovered, was a fair amount of skill and dexterity. Not only did I lack the skill but it turned out that my hunger strike had greatly impaired my coordination, my fine motor skills. My fingers refused to obey me, they moved slowly and awkwardly. The quota of five bags a day seemed completely out of reach: I barely made half a bag a day in my first few days. My fellow weavers sniggered, giving me contemptuous looks. The foreman groused: I was bringing their numbers down. Well, at least individual food rations were no longer tied to the work gang's overall output like they had been under Stalin.

Of course, for slackers there were always punishment cells, though I doubted they would do this to me. I had my own reasons for striving to make my quota. They could do other things to me: suspend family visits, care packages from home, my camp store privileges. The care packages and the camp store were my two additional sources of nutrition to supplement the camp's meager rations. Without additional nutrition, it was nearly impossible for me to recover, so compliance was good policy at this point. I had already showed my fangs and left them in no doubt of what I could do if they tried anything.

So now my goal was to survive, adjust, fit in.

I noticed that everyone except me was using a sewing shuttle: apparently, this was a necessity in weaving.

"Hey, guys, where can I get a shuttle?"

No one answered at first. Then a gaunt, weedy-looking youth, one of the "juveniles," said:

"I can get you one, but it costs money."

"Money? There's no money in camp, it's forbidden, isn't it?"

"There's money in camp if you know where to look."

Hang on a moment! I had something I could use instead: beautiful postcards with 3D pictures that were in the last care package I had received. I had heard that they could be used in camp as a form of alternative currency. I showed one to the boy, tilting it this way and that to reveal the holographic image.

"How about one of these?"

"It'll do. I'll get you a shuttle."

Indeed, two days later he brought me a shuttle. But how was I to use it? Seeing my awkward attempts and the blank, helpless expression on my face, the boy laughed.

"Here, lemme show you, 's not hard."

He himself seemed to have mastered this craft perfectly. Like other young zeks, he easily made his five mesh bags even before the lunch break. After a few days of his training, I was able to make one and a half bags a day.

I began to feel real sympathy for the young man who had given me such invaluable help, and he, starved for attention, rewarded me with sincere affection.

"Why are you so thin, compadre?" I asked him.

"Heart disease. I've had it since I was little."

I took a closer look at him. He wasn't merely thin and weak: his lips had a sort of bluish tint. Poor thing!

"Did you come here straight from 'juvie'?"

"Yep."

"What about school? How many grades did you complete?"
"Seven."
"Would you like to study some more?"
"Sure, I even got my books here with me, 'cept I done forgot everythin'."
"Bring your books. I'll try to help you."

His gaunt face lit up with a mix of joy and suspicion. The next evening he brought his books, and I spent some forty minutes explaining the material to him—discovering, to my own delight, that my mind had remained more or less intact despite all the ordeals and stresses I had been through. I was thinking more slowly, my hearing and my vision were impaired, I couldn't walk far without getting out of breath—but my mental health was fine. I hadn't lost my mind or my soul.

* * *

I worked hard. I was always the first to start work and the last to finish, but despite all my efforts, I couldn't do more than two bags in a shift. In the meantime, my friendship with the scrawny boy continued to strengthen.

"Hey, don't kill yourself with these stupid bags. I'll make you one every day if you want. No one'll notice. I'm disabled, I got a reduced quota anyway, but I'm done with my five bags by noon. Can't leave your station so I'm just sittin' around anyway bein' bored."

What a gift! Wordlessly, I squeezed his hand in thanks.

Sometimes while my hands were weaving automatically, I would begin to drift off in thought. Occasionally I was able to tune out the sounds around me and pray.

* * *

Although I established my standing early in the closed little society of the barrack, navigating these relationships was a delicate matter. The *zeks* were not predisposed to like either Jews or Muscovites, considering the latter to be conceited snobs.

"What about me?"
"You're kind of OK, but still . . ."

Some of the weavers were moved to work outdoors, including me. What a blessing: after many long months in punishment cells I still hadn't had my fill of fresh air. I made myself comfortable in the shade and prepared to relax with my shuttle, but it was not to be: there was a virulent anti-Semite in our group!

"You Jews, it's all your fault. Russia's starving while you're getting rich. You're keeping the common people addicted to drink! You sat the war out hiding behind others' backs! Hitler didn't kill enough of you! He died too early!"

I kept my cool, with difficulty, but he would not shut up. When he started up again on the second day, I felt my blood begin to boil. No one else said a word; they were all enjoying the show—this was more fun than weaving. I looked at the man closely. Was this the KGB move I was expecting, was he trying to provoke a fight that could be used against me? No, this didn't feel staged, the man was sincere—a sincere flaming bigot, his face distorted with a grimace of anti-Semitic fervor. My restraint seemed to feed his rage.

"You kikes, you're all the same! There'll be no peace in the world so long as you're around!"

Blood rushed to my head. Gripping the shuttle like a knife, I advanced toward the anti-Semite with a determined step. Kill the bastard! A step, then another, then another. I raised my hand to stab downward—but instead of parrying my blow, he suddenly went limp and fell back.

"Come on, man, what's your problem?"

The other zeks began to jabber:

"Forget it, man, he was just talking sh* t, come on, it's not worth it."

"Don't talk sh* t if you want to keep your face," I said to the bigot.

I returned to my place, breathing heavily. What a mercy that it wasn't staged—I had totally lost control of myself. I could have actually killed him. They saw it in my eyes.

This little episode did much to raise my standing still further. The criminal bosses from the elite guard-free gang began to invite me over to drink second-brew chifir, a sign of great respect. *Chifir* was super-concentrated black tea made by brewing a hundred grams of tea in half a liter of water; it produced a high very similar to a drug. The bosses drank the first brew themselves, then added more water to produce the second brew; this was offered to a select few guests. I declined once but soon got another invitation. Must tread carefully now; I couldn't afford to antagonize them.

"Thank you, guys, appreciate the invite, but my heart can't take it after the hunger strike. Gives me chest pains. Sorry about that."

That worked: it allowed everyone to save face. They let me be without hard feelings.

* * *

Oksana Kholmyansky's briefing for Western supporters (July 6, 1985)

There's been a hit piece in a Soviet English-language newspaper on people engaged in subversive activities. They named ten people, including the Kholmyansky brothers. And all this time they're continuing to deny our applications to emigrate. This is unbearable!

They arrested a Jewish activist who broke down and named everyone in his testimony in open court: Sasha, Misha, Tanya and Yuli Edelstein, Fulmakht... Dear Lord, what else are they plotting?

* * *

Lunchtime. In theory, each unit was supposed to eat together at an assigned time. In practice, there was always a line to get into the dining room, especially since we had to wait until all our three gangs came back from their different work locations. It wasn't cold now, in the summer, but in winter it must be brutal waiting outside in the cold. Even so, the long wait was excruciating because I was famished—as I always was these days.

Some *zeks* from another unit tried to cut in line; *zeks* from our unit ran over to shove them back out. Only the arrival of the guards put a stop to the scuffling, screaming, and cursing.

Finally we were inside. The servers tossed ten aluminum bowls on each table: dented, cracked bowls, so beat-up they were virtually impossible to get clean, and so greasy they slid around on the filthy table. Each table was assigned a senior *zek* to ladle out the food.

I peered into my bowl: a nasty mess, scraps of pork meat floating in a broth with globs of fat and pieces of skin with sparse remains of bristles on them. I felt my gorge rising in disgust.

Eat, I told myself. Eat so you can recover. Mom told you the rabbi said to eat everything, and specifically including pork!

I closed my eyes, spooned up the meat and put it in my mouth. The broth went down all right but the muscle effort of chewing, in my weakened state, was a problem. It always took me a long time. Every day I was the last one to finish, still chewing while my unit left the dining room and the next one came in. Once I was done, I dragged myself back to work, exhausted by the effort of eating and wishing I could lie down and rest. I went alone, hoping not to run into one of the guards who were always lurking around the dining room and not to get busted for walking alone, without my unit, against all the rules.

After lunch, nobody talked; everyone sat around weaving mechanically, absorbed in his own thoughts. I wasn't quite there yet, I still had to watch what I was doing, but even my own fingers had begun to move with more skill and speed. If I got to where my hands could truly work on autopilot then they would be the only part of me that was in bondage. The KGB could enslave the body but not the spirit!

Early in July, I began receiving my month-long special rations. Zeranov had kept his word. Not from any noble motives, surely; it must mean they were happy with my good behavior. And no matter the reason, the extra nutrition was vitally important. I was ravenous all the time, and although I felt marginally stronger, still I could barely lift my feet.

Oksana Kholmyansky's briefing for Western supporters (August 4, 1985)

Alexander's parents were finally granted a long visit with him. They spent three days together, alone in the same room. We don't have the details yet, but they seem very encouraged. They had to wait two weeks in Kamensk-Uralsky for their visit, supposedly because there was an outbreak of some infection in the camp but in fact because the KGB wanted them out of Moscow during the World Festival of Youth and Students that has just ended, and away from all the visiting foreigners. Alexander received many letters from supporters in France and got reprimanded by the camp commander for that.

* * *

A quiet evening in the barracks. For once, no one was cursing or squabbling. The guard-free crowd sat in their own aisle drinking their *chifir*; over in the far corner another group softly sang old prisoners' songs, mournful and poignant, to the accompaniment of a plinking guitar. Two aisles over, more *zeks* huddled together over a crossword puzzle. I had just borrowed a book by Dostoevsky from the camp library and was hoping to do a little reading, but just then, the crossword puzzle solvers got stuck on some scientific word.

"Hey, professor, come over here, what's a word that fits in here?"

"Come on, guys, I'm not a professor. And I'm not good at crossword puzzles either . . . OK, fine, let me see."

By chance, I found the right word. Raising their hands in grateful amazement, they bent over their puzzle once again. I went back to my reading, but five minutes later they called out to me again.

"Hey, professor, come back here, here's another tricky word."

Once again I got the word right. I returned to my book but not for long:

"Come back, professor, you're good at this!"

"Let me see . . . nope, I can't guess this one. Let me be, guys, I want to read."

They left me alone after that, but apparently, news got around that I had guessed two words out of three correctly. Soon, one of the guard-free *zeks* approached me with an unusual request.

"Look, professor, can you help me write a letter to a girl?"

"To a girl?"

"Yeah . . . See, I'm getting out soon, but I don't have anyone to go back to."

"So who are you writing to?"

As he explained, once a *zek* was "inside," his girlfriend usually dumped him and went on with her life. There were other single girls, however, who were willing to meet with ex-cons upon their release; lists of their names and addresses circulated among *zeks*. One could write to one of these girls and might perhaps find a new girlfriend; stranger things had happened.

But, evidently, there was a problem. Many *zeks* were barely literate and certainly not good at writing romantic letters; the skill set they acquired "inside" was very different. Surprisingly, these rough men felt self-conscious, nervous, they didn't know how to begin.

I finally understood what he was asking me to do:

"You mean I should write a letter for you, as if it's you writing?"

"Yeah, that's it!"

I sat down and looked closely at the would-be suitor. No Romeo he; where could I find the inspiration, how could I get into the role? What a funny situation. But wait, there was no need for me to make things up; I could just say something about feeling lonesome. I got my thoughts together and produced a plausible one-pager. I read it over—not bad, really! I handed it to my customer. He was delighted!

"Here, want this?"

He handed me a big, fresh onion. What a brilliant reward for my efforts—vitamins, so badly needed, so scarce in my meager camp diet! Speechless with gratitude, I grabbed the onion and sniffed it again and again, feeling my mouth fill with saliva.

I never knew what came of that particular letter but it brought me a lot of business from other aspiring suitors, and each gave me food in return. The surge of love letters lasted about three weeks and then abated. But I wasn't idle for long: a *zek* came to ask me to write him a good, persuasive complaint to the authorities. This was followed by another request, then a third, and soon I was in the business of writing legal letters. Here, I had ample experience from my years of Jewish activism. And lo and behold—one of my letters actually helped! My status in the barrack rose still further.

***

Though bag weaving didn't seem like hard work, by the end of the day I was always exhausted to the point of seeing spots dance before my eyes. I was often the first one to start work and the last to leave. I tried to weave an extra bag every day beyond my quota so I that by the end of the week I would have my Shabbat quota done, too, and wouldn't have to actually work on Shabbat—just show up and pretend to work. Very occasionally, I was able to barter an extra bag from someone else in exchange for one of those 3D postcards my family sent me. This, however, created problems of its own, since these extra Shabbat bags had to be securely hidden all week.

In fact, leisure time was almost nonexistent in the camp; I found myself always busy with something. Besides constantly moving the extra bags to a new hiding place, I had my scrawny young friend to help with his studies, my letters home to write; I had my shuttle that needed fixing, my letter-writing business, all the petty bartering that was always going on . . . This constant mental effort was the last thing I had expected to find at the labor camp.

***

Suppertime. Evening meals were a problem. Breakfasts were usually edible: some kind of hot mush, easy enough to chew and swallow, even if it did occasionally smell of something like motor oil. But for supper they often served semi-rancid fish that made my gorge rise; I couldn't make myself touch it, even though most *zeks* scarfed it down with no problem at all.

Each barrack opened into a small courtyard surrounded by a mesh fence about five meters high. Our yard, about thirty meters long and ten meters wide, adjoined a similar yard attached to the next barrack. One Sunday—our only day of rest—we were all ordered outside, and I noticed a man in the next yard, right across the fence from me. He had a vaguely Mediterranean appearance (could he be Jewish?) and an interesting, intellectual air about him. I called him over, and we introduced ourselves.

No, he wasn't Jewish, he was half Armenian and half Russian, he'd gotten in trouble over reading something politically incorrect and was imprisoned on a fabricated criminal charge, just like me.

He seemed about twenty years older than me and looked quite ill. Apparently, he was having an even tougher time in camp than I was: unlike me, he had no international support, no relatives and friends on the outside trying to help, and no noble cause to struggle for. It was just him and his wife.

A human mind is a peculiar thing. Now that I had met someone even more vulnerable than myself, someone I could help, I felt ten times stronger and more determined than I had been just ten minutes ago! I began to look for ways to get some clothes and food to him. We began snatching brief moments chatting across the fence on Sundays and quickly became friends. These stolen moments with someone from a more or less similar background, a good man I could relate to, combined with my determination to help him, gave me a new sense of purpose: I felt as though my batteries had been charged with new energy.

This lasted for about six weeks. Then, to our surprise and bitter disappointment, his entire unit was transferred to another barrack at the far end of the camp.

I sat for a long time, stunned, struggling to come to terms with my loss. Of course, this was no accident, it was definitely a swipe at me. Someone had told the authorities that I had a new friend. No doubt, the KGB had me closely watched, even when nothing seemed to be happening. There was no reason whatsoever to swap units, other than to cause me pain.

What should I do? My friend was a sick man, he needed food. I had less than five months left in my sentence while he had more than a year. I would take all the food I had saved up and get it to him. I couldn't do it regularly but I would go over once and visit him and give him all I had. This was against all the rules but at least it would disabuse the authorities of any illusion that I had no fight left in me. And if they slammed me in a punishment cell, then so be it.

A week later, I found a free moment between supper and the evening roll call and walked across the entire camp to my friend's barrack, carrying my bag of food. I gave the headquarters and dining room a wide berth, hoping not to run into any guards, who would undoubtedly confiscate all my food on the spot. Luckily,

I made it safely to the distant barrack. Every *zek* turned to stare at me when I walked in.

"Where's X?"

I gave them my friend's name. Shrugging, they pointed me to his bunk. Judging by their expressions, he wasn't high on the totem pole, certainly not someone in the habit of having big bags of food hand-delivered to him. And there was my friend, looking even worse than when I last saw him, poor thing.

"Hang on, my friend, you've got to hang on!"

I did my best to cheer him up. We embraced; were we ever going to see each other again? Feeling happy about my good deed but also sad not to be able to do more, I walked openly back across the camp. I made it safely to our yard, where the *zeks* were just beginning to assemble for the evening roll call.

The next morning I was summoned to Zeranov.

"What happened, Alexander? You've been on your best behavior, you've done all your work—and now this. A gross violation of internal discipline. You know what this entails? The loss of all privileges: no camp store, no family visits, no care packages! We could send you to a punishment cell for a stunt like this. You, of all people, know what that's like—so why would you risk it again? Can you at least tell me why you did it?"

"I wanted to help a sick man. I've always felt that the most important thing is to act like a human being, regardless of circumstances. That's my guiding principle."

"Go!"—Zeranov cut me off angrily.

Perhaps this is for the best, I thought walking back to my barrack. Let them not imagine that I've become a rule follower. They should remember that I'm like a compressed spring—I can uncoil at any moment and punch them!

In the event, nothing came of Zeranov's threats. I received no punishment for visiting my friend in the distant barrack.

* * *

In early October, I got a new neighbor. The man who moved into the next bunk was one of the guard-free, a middle-aged guy, a welder.

"Hey, compadre, do you know where I can get smokes?" he asked by way of introduction.

"Why do you need more when you work outside the camp—you can get what you want there."

"That's not enough for me, I'm a heavy smoker."

"Well, OK, I guess I can help you out. I can buy cigarettes for you at the camp store—is that what you mean? And maybe you can do something for me in return. Don't you welders get rations of milk because your work is classified as hazardous?"

"You want my milk? You can have it all, I don't drink milk at all!"

What a stroke of luck! I never dreamed I would be able to get milk in here! With the first cup of milk, I felt something wholesome and vital enter my system. Thus began the next stage of my long, difficult recovery from the effects of a protracted hunger strike.

* * *

Every Sunday, after lunch, we got three hours free time—until five o'clock, when they herded our entire unit into to a special room for a couple of hours of political brainwashing. An officer came in to give us a talk on the evils and hardships of Western capitalism. Then the officer showed us an ideologically correct TV film and stayed in the room while we watched it. The TV set was kept inside a metal casing to prevent the inmates from watching it on their own; only the officer was allowed to unlock and open it.

I was always interested to see the reactions of the *zeks*, who usually sat there nodding their heads approvingly. These men actually identified with the regime that had trapped them behind barbed wire and kept them in these inhuman conditions. They still saw themselves as good Soviet people, ever vigilant against any whiff of anything alien or "anti-Soviet."

One Sunday, the lock on the TV set got stuck. It had always worked before but now it just wouldn't open. The *zeks* waited, fidgeting and muttering, while the officer fiddled with the lock, but in the end everyone dispersed, feeling cheated out of their weekly entertainment.

As it turned out, all the other TV sets worked fine that day, and all the other units got to watch the television show, which was about a recently exposed group of Jews engaged in anti-Soviet activities. A dozen people were identified by name, including the brothers Kholmyansky.

Not everyone in camp knew my name but the *zeks* in the next barrack certainly did: our names were written on our shirts and quilted jackets. Three of them got especially worked up. Impelled by a terrible suspicion that I might be that Kholmyansky who was mentioned on TV, they headed straight over to our barrack to expose me.

"Is there a Kholm . . . Kholmovsky in here?"

"Do you mean Kholmyansky? He's right over there."

In a blink of an eye I found myself surrounded by three tough guys, their faces red, their eyes bulging, ready to pound me to a pulp.

"Are you the f* cker from that anti-Soviet group on TV?"

Hearing loud and aggressive voices, the *zeks* from my unit began to converge around my bunk. These were strangers who barged in on our turf, and they were bothering one of "ours"—especially since I was fairly well regarded in our unit. My neighbor, the welder, also came over and tried to deescalate the tension:

"Come on, boys, chill, have a seat, let's talk about it."

By that time, around twenty men had gathered around us, surrounding my bunk on all sides. Even one of the bosses from the guard-free group came over, authority and menace in his voice:

"What's the problem here?"

The intruders explained, softening their tone a bit—but not their zeal:

"Didn't you see the TV show at five? They talked about this anti-Soviet group that just got busted in Moscow—they named names—and this a* * hole was one of them!"

"Could it be a different Kholmyansky?" asked one of our *zeks*.

"I don't think so!" the intruders persisted. "That's an unusual name. It's gotta be him!"

I spoke up:

"Don't you all know what I'm in here for? Article 218, part 2. Illegal firearms possession. What does that have to do with anti-Soviet activity? If I was such a big deal that they talked about me on national TV, would I be in here with you all? I'd be with political prisoners."

"That makes sense," the boss of the guard-free group backed me up. "If these people's names were given on national TV, that means they were all caught long ago and their anti-Soviet group is out of business. Besides, they don't put famous politicals in here."

The intruders left, defeated, but I sat there for a long time, shaken. Oh God, what did this mean? Was there a new criminal case looming over my head—and Misha's? Or was this the KGB trying to sic the criminals on me and get me killed? It must have been one heck of a TV show—it must have really played on people's paranoia—to make these men go after a *zek* on another unit's turf: this was not only not done in camp, it was actually dangerous for the intruders themselves!

And what if the lock on the TV case had opened and the *zeks* in my unit had seen the show? The same men who came to my rescue would have turned on me and torn me to pieces!

And wasn't it remarkable that the day the show aired was the day the lock wouldn't open, when it had always worked before? What was the probability of that? Clearly this was the hand of God, protecting me. Let's see if the lock opens next Sunday, I thought...

The next Sunday, and every Sunday after that for the rest of my time in camp, the lock opened without any problem whatsoever.

* * *

The worst part of the day was the evening roll call. The day was always filled with work and all the other business, but after 8 p.m. there was a short period of free time after supper for reading or writing letters home. So it was all the more jarring when the guard came in around 9 p.m. to begin herding us out into the yard. The roll call almost never started when it was supposed to, at 9:30 p.m., so we waited there, out in the cold, for almost an hour with nothing to do. We were still in summer uniform, even though it was already really cold in the evenings. It's hard to say which was worse: the cold or this enforced idleness that drove me pacing back and forth across the yard like a caged animal, ready to howl at the moon from the deep, aching misery in my heart.

Eventually the roll call would start. Our unit, all 200 of us, would line up in front of the officer, who called out our last names from the list. Each of us had to reply, stating his first name, the article of the criminal code he had been sentenced under, and the date of his release. This last part was torture for me: each of the others knew with certainty the day he would be free—except me. I was the only one who didn't know if they would actually let me go on that day or figure out a way to keep me in longer. So my date of release always stuck in my throat.

Today, though, was November 2. Barring the worst-case scenario, I had exactly three more months left on my sentence.

A couple of weeks ago, a young *zek* had plopped down on my bunk after supper—one of the guard-free group. I tensed up and turned to him, anticipating an attack. But instead, he whined in a bored teenager's voice:

"Tell me a story . . . "

Ah, I thought. You're another one of the "juveniles." Your education, your human development abruptly ceased when they locked you up, but your soul can't help longing for more. What shall I tell you? I can't say no, that would be seen as a hostile move, but I don't want you to latch on to me and take away my few precious moments of alone time.

I spun him some yarn of moderate interest but evidently not boring enough, because he stuck to me like a wet leaf for the next two weeks—until one day, when he saw that there was no one around, he sidled up to me and whispered in my ear:

"Hey, listen, I'm working in the camp infirmary right now. I have access to medical records. Want me to steal your chart? You can smuggle it out to your people, to prove that you really kept a hunger strike. I'm guard-free, they don't search us."

I shuddered. Here it was, the set-up I was expecting. Right on time, too: I had less than three months left before the end of my term! That's how they planned to pin a new criminal case on me. Surely this bright idea didn't originate in this young punk's

```
The Rt. Hon. Roy Mason M.P.

                    HOUSE OF COMMONS
                      LONDON SW1A 0AA

                                              25th January 1986

Dear Mr Gorbachev,

We, two United States Congressmen and two British Members of Parliament,
are writing to you on behalf of a Soviet family who have been refused
permission to go to Israel, in the hope that you may reconsider their
application. Each of us has met with Mikhail and Oksana Kholmiansky,
residing at Kirovogradskaya 24-1-191, Moscow, and would be grateful if
you felt able to reconsider their application, together with that of
their son Maxim, their parents Gregory and Rozalia, and their brother
Alexander.

In February of this year Alexander is due to complete a short sentence
in labour camp in Siberia. Each of us would sincerely hope that upon
his release, there would be no obstacle in the way of this family
receiving its exit visa. Any help that you could give in expediting
this would be much appreciated, not only by us four, but by several
other western Parliamentarians who have seen the Kholmiansky family in
the past.

In the hope that you may give your favourable consideration to this
case, we are, yours sincerely

               (signed)....Roy Mason.
                          Rt. Hon. Roy Mason M.P.

                          ....Ivan Lawrence....
                          Ivan Lawrence Q.C.,M.P.

                          ....Steve Solarz....
                          Congressman Steve Solarz

                          ....Edward G. Markey....
                          Congressman Edward Markey
```

Letter to Mikhail Gorbachev from a group of US Congressmen and UK Members of Parliament, January 25, 1986

primitive mind—especially the bit about proving my hunger strike. That was good bait. Of course it would be nice to see my medical chart. But what was the point? Proving that I had kept a hunger strike—to whom did I need to prove it, who would doubt it? Then again, who cared what the prison nurses wrote down in my chart. Obviously, they wrote whatever the KGB told them to write. This chart might say that I had gobbled their food down every day since last September and asked for seconds, for all anyone knew. It had no evidentiary value whatsoever. Let them keep it as a souvenir to remember me by!

The young dude wouldn't take "no" for an answer and continued to badger me. It took him another two weeks before he finally realized that he wasn't getting anywhere and left me alone.

A letter to Anya (January 5, 1986)

Anya, my darling,
Every evening I watch the moon and I'm happy to see the crescent moon getting thinner and thinner. It's a sign that the new moon, the first day of the Jewish month of Shvat, is approaching. I'm waiting for it with eager anticipation since it will be the last month by the Jewish calendar I will spend in here.

* * *

Finally, there were only three weeks left on my sentence . . . two weeks . . . ten days . . . My last week began. The fewer days remained, the more it seemed to me that time was like a spring stretched to its breaking point! Were they really going to release me in seven days? Was the KGB really going to stop trying for those additional long years of imprisonment and deportation they didn't get the first time? Did they have nothing more up their sleeve besides the offer to steal my medical chart and the TV program?

Three days before the end of my sentence, I—along with three other *zeks*—had my picture taken for my Certificate of Release, a head and shoulders photo. They gave each of us the upper half of a shirt, with a tie sewn onto it, to put over our camp clothes. Evidently, it was thought inappropriate for a free man to look like a *zek* on his identity papers.

An apt metaphor for the entire regime, I thought to myself. The Soviet Union displayed a civilized façade to the world, pretending to be a moderate and reasonable country, but underneath it was one big prison, cruel and barbaric. I chuckled at the thought and felt better for a moment.

* * *

Saturday, February 2, 1986. My last morning in the camp . . . hopefully. It takes tremendous effort for me to focus on my Shabbat morning prayer, to keep myself from rushing through it or being distracted. And yet, today true, intentional prayer is more important than ever: my fate hangs in the balance.

The hands on the old-fashioned wall clock show 9 a.m. Any time now, the duty guard's phone will ring ordering me to headquarters. I've heard from many *zeks* that the call always comes on time.

Time moves ever so slowly, as if filled with lead.

9:15 a.m. Some sort of technical problem? No need to worry just yet . . . How slowly the time passes.

9:30 a.m. Oh no. Are they not going to release me after all? I immerse myself in fervent prayer. The world recedes, my soul is lifted up in communion with Heaven . . . while my thoughts race ahead, reviewing my options. Another hunger strike? But God, I can't take anymore, I have no more strength left, either physical or spiritual!

9:45 a.m. It's no longer fear but a fit of despair that presses me to the ground. I sit hunched over in the corner of my bunk, clenching with numb fingers the small bundle containing all my worldly possessions. I'm having trouble breathing; my heart is pounding, every heartbeat like a blow, an impenetrable darkness before my eyes.

10:00 a.m. I hear the guard's voice:

"You still here? I thought you were released an hour ago."

"They haven't called," I say, trying to sound calm. "Are they sometimes late with the release call?"

"Not that I can remember . . . Well, sit tight."

10:15 a.m. The guard is back with a clumsy joke covering creeping doubt in his voice:

"They still haven't let you go. Maybe they've decided to keep you?"

I jump to my feet and begin to pace back and forth like a caged beast. Merciful Father, Oh, hear my voice! Don't let them gloat over my misery!

10:30 a.m. OK. It's all too clear now what's going on. Calm down, I tell myself; worrying won't make any difference. Get yourself together and get ready for what's coming. It's like what they did last time at the end of my ten days of administrative arrest: they held me back, and only later did they trouble to tell me what they were doing. Is this a repeat? A wave of heat washes over me, I feel like I'm dancing in a frying pan. Almighty God, please intervene!

10:50 a.m. I can't control myself any longer. I jump to my feet, grab my bundle and head out.

"Where are you off to?" asks the guard, surprised.

"Out! I'm going to get released today one way or another."

The camp is empty: at this hour everyone is at work. With difficulty, waddling heavily on legs that feel like they're made of cast iron, I make my way over to headquarters. The deputy chief of the camp steps in front of me.

"Where are you going?"

"I'm going to get released. I've done my time, today is my last day."

I scrutinize his face for signs of trouble. A momentary light flickers behind his faded eyes.

"Is it, now? All right then, go get released, and don't get caught again."

A hot wave of hope floods me. Surely he would know if there was a new plot afoot, but his face is totally blank and vacant, even bored. So all hope is not lost! I fly to headquarters as though I've sprouted wings.

"Who's the officer on duty?" I demand, emboldened. "Are you aware of what time it is? I'm due to be released, my time is done. So what are you doing? Why are you not beginning my discharge procedures? Are you trying to hold a free man behind bars? That's a criminal offense!"

The duty officer responds with genuine surprise:

"Have they not called you yet? Let me see what's going on. Is anyone else due for release today? Three more? Call them all in."

He disappears for a moment and quickly returns with a bunch of keys in his hand. He opens the safe, takes out three files, leafs through them quickly.

"Your file . . . " his voice falters. "It's not . . . it's not in the safe. Someone took it and didn't sign it out. Now we can't release you, or those three other guys either. They've been waiting since early morning, too."

Ah, so it has begun. Damn them and their damned state. Lord, break apart their evil empire! Obviously, the KGB had the file removed. The duty officer clearly doesn't know a thing; it's the KGB. They've cooked up something new.

I take a sheet of paper and write a note to Zeranov: *"If I am not released now, as required by law, I will once again begin an open-ended hunger strike and declare you personally responsible for the consequences!"*

The secretary takes my note and disappears. Silence spreads, broken only by the pounding pulse in my head. Another half an hour passes. The three other *zeks* due to be released today are brought in and sit down on the couch beside me. It strikes me as funny that we are sitting on the couch like free men, not squatting on the floor like *zeks*. "That's how I'll sit from now on," I say to myself. "Like a free man!"

People keep coming in and out; I sense that some unseen drama is taking place behind the scenes.

"What time is it?" someone asks.

"It's already 12:20 p.m.," says the duty officer reproachfully.

At this moment the door opens, and a higher-ranking officer bursts into the room. His hair is disheveled, his face red, his forehead beaded with sweat. He's holding a file in his hands.

As if answering my unasked question, he says:

"It wasn't me, the file was requested by High Command, I don't know why. Follow me, let's get you out of here. And you three also."

We walk down a narrow hallway and turn the corner. The checkpoint is only a few meters away. I see my mother and father

Back from imprisonment—
the family reunion
at the Moscow railway station
February 2, 1986. My mother is
on my right, Anya is on my left,
Oksana is next to her

behind the barrier. The officer hands the guard my file and my Certificate of Release. The guard, barely literate, takes forever to spell out my name on my Certificate. Finally, my mother elbows aside a soldier standing outside the checkpoint and comes inside.

"Stop this nonsense!" she says to the guard in a commanding voice—and he obeys!

The guard opens the door. I step out.

Mom grabs my arm. Silently, wordlessly, we leave the camp; the only sound is the snow crunching under our boots. We cling to each other, afraid to let go for a moment. The air is bitterly cold and still. The pale winter sun shines indifferently upon our solemn procession.

The camp recedes far into the distance, but I'm still reliving the turbulent events of this day. I'm out! Despite everything, I'm out! A wild, boundless joy explodes from the depths of my heart. The KGB didn't win! They didn't get their show trial, they didn't

My brother Misha (left)
and myself, my face
still swollen

get to intimidate the participants of the Cities Project or the Jewish movement at large—and they didn't get to keep me inside!

This is an enormous victory, the glorious outcome of our great fight. We, a mere handful of Soviet Jews together with our friends abroad, have forced the superpower to do what it didn't want to do! My fight has prevented new arrests of our project activists; no longer can the KGB pretend that the Jews were terrorists plotting evil "under the guise" of teaching Hebrew!

I am elated. Few people get to enjoy such a great triumph in their lifetime! Lord, oh how I thank You! I know that You made this miracle, that You gave me the stamina to endure, to overcome, to withstand things that were utterly beyond my humble human abilities. This is Your triumph first! And I must make this miracle known to all!

We arrive in Sverdlovsk and board a train to Moscow. The trip takes all day and all night—a badly needed period of transition. How I love transitions, those moments when neither the past nor the future have a claim on me and I am free to savor the present. I need time to disconnect from the past: from the prison, from the camp, from the hunger strike and punishment cells. I need to change my internal settings, to take myself off the permanent state of high alert, the constant readiness to react to plots, threats, and provocations. I leave them all behind; they belong to the past. The train hurtles me forward towards the future, so very different from the past. It will take me time to adapt to it. Once again, I sense that I have been given many different lives to live; this one is now receding behind me, and a new one lies ahead. Tears of liberation and cleansing come to my eyes.

We are almost there. The train slows down as it reaches the platform, where only my immediate family—Misha, Oksana, Maxim, and Anya—are waiting to welcome me home. The family has prudently declined offers of a grand reception ceremony made by the leaders of Moscow's Jewish movement, who wanted to fill the entire platform with people, to invite foreign correspondents, photographers . . . We had no doubt that there were multitudes willing to come in order to welcome and bless me, but these were dangerous times. Other returning Jewish activists had had lavish receptions that ended up getting them in trouble with the authorities.

Anya remembers

You still looked very much like a prisoner. The swelling in your face might have gone down a little bit. But your eyes never stopped moving, shifting restlessly back and forth. You were obviously still under terrible stress. It affected me too.

Dov Kontorer remembers

The first time you met with the project team after your release, you made a memorable statement: "Nothing I've seen in prison is so bad that it should scare any of us who are still on the outside into giving up our principles." These were strong words from a man who had clearly left a big chunk of his health behind in prison.

For obvious reasons, you couldn't return to the Cities Project, so it remained under my and Ze'ev Geyzel's leadership.

Chapter 10

The phone did not stop ringing. Hundreds of people wanted to see me. The leaders of the Jewish movement wanted me to hold a general reception, a big public event. But I felt totally incapable of socializing. Being with people caused me almost physical pain. I felt depleted, turned inside out. My initial euphoria had given way to a sense of infinite weariness. A fog seemed to have come down and covered everything. I felt as if my skin had been peeled off; the slightest touch caused me acute pain.

But people's impatience was so great that they began showing up uninvited, in small groups. Each such meeting left me so utterly spent that finally I decided it would be easier to go ahead with the big reception.

On that day, our apartment was densely packed with people. I talked for hours, trying to convey it all to them: my lived reality of imprisonment and the hunger strike; the extreme psychological pressures I had endured, summoning up every last bit of my strength; all the miracles large and small that carried me to survival and ultimately to a resounding victory. Once I started talking, I could not stop. Breathlessly, feverishly, I poured out all my emotions, all my bitterness and tension. They bombarded me with questions. Midnight had come and gone but no one wanted to leave . . .

* * *

Days passed, but the tension remained inside me, like a coiled spring that I couldn't seem to release. How odd it seemed: only recently, while still a prisoner, I had felt enough inner strength to move mountains—but now, free and reunited with my loved ones, I was like a latex balloon that had lost its air and had drifted down to the floor in a limp and useless heap. It was as though I had spent all of the mental and emotional energy allotted to me. I couldn't walk far without feeling short of breath; I had trouble focusing and often found myself sitting and staring at nothing in particular, my thoughts drifting aimlessly.

I embarked upon an intensive and prolonged therapy, everything from conventional medicine to massage, acupuncture, and Chinese herbs. Little by little, the telltale facial swelling began to go down. After the first few weeks, I began to sense the beginnings of a change. I felt a bit stronger physically, and as though a thin new layer of skin had grown around my soul, enabling me to deal with people without major pain . . .

Four months after my release, the doctors said my health had improved significantly. So Anya and I began planning our wedding.

We wanted a traditional Jewish marriage ceremony with a *chuppah* (bridal canopy). What better place to hold it than the Moscow synagogue? But the synagogue management, ever anxious to avoid trouble with the authorities, turned us down flat. Apparently, even free, I was still seen as such a dangerous figure that they were afraid to allow me this, the most natural of Jewish religious ceremonies. Clearly, in the eyes of the KGB I was not a private figure, and hence my *chuppah* was not a private matter either.

Come to think of it, they weren't wrong. My wedding would indeed be a symbolic event—a public acknowledgment that the KGB had failed. Hadn't Maiboroda told me more than once: "We'll bury you! Nothing will be left of you but the number on the grave marker in the prison cemetery!"

Oh well. Never mind them; we would have our *chuppah* at home. Our friends enthusiastically offered their help. Overnight, our small Moscow flat was transformed—all the furniture packed into one room, all interior doors taken off their hinges and turned into tables.

Finally, the solemn moment arrived. A *tallit* (prayer shawl) was spread above us to form the *chuppah*. Reb Lippa, the one elder from the Moscow synagogue brave enough to officiate, read the benedictions. I saw my mother's eyes fill with tears. Finally . . . our hopes had come true!

Our front door stayed wide open throughout the ceremony, people coming and going in a constant stream.

Finally . . . our hopes had come to pass!
Ephraim and Anna Kholmyansky's wedding ceremony

Anya remembers

The mood of the audience was so special—festive, joyful, jubilant! Everyone felt that this was not merely a private celebration but our joint triumph over forces of evil. It felt as though something that had nearly died had now come back and was triumphantly, vibrantly alive!

* * *

After the wedding, my health improved dramatically. I felt more energy, more interest in the world around me, a desire to start doing something new.

I analyzed the situation in the country carefully. Change was in the air; many signs pointed to an impending political liberalization. Though it would likely be temporary, it created a window of opportunity that must not be missed. I considered many ideas before settling upon three main courses of action.

- *Establish a group of former Prisoners of Zion.* Some of them had already been released; others were expected to be released soon. These were people who were not afraid of the KGB and had achieved name recognition in the West. If we were to speak with one voice, it would be heard.

    Our mission was clear: to fight for the release of the remaining prisoners, against all forms of persecution of Jews, and for free emigration. This group could also take on the work of protecting and speaking up for any of our people who were harassed by the authorities. They could become the single point of contact for anyone in trouble. All these years I had dreamed of having something like this alongside the Cities Project, and now, for the first time, it could become reality.
- *Establish a women's group.* I knew of many highly influential international women's organizations. Maybe we could get them to take an interest in the cause of the Soviet Jewry from the standpoint of women's rights. Persecution of women naturally tended to evoke a strong emotional response internationally, and the KGB might hesitate to use crude force against women.
- *Promote Holocaust awareness.* The Soviet regime had always banned any public events commemorating the Holocaust, but now the time had come to confront the authorities. Unlike women's groups, or Hebrew teachers' groups, or Prisoners of Zion—all of them small, niche organizations—the theme of the Holocaust naturally lent itself to mass gatherings of people. This was especially important in a country where civic freedoms like those of speech and assembly were unknown. I felt that, even though we were still in the early stages of liberalization, the KGB would find it difficult to suppress such gatherings.

* * *

"We're going to have a baby," Anya told me.

This tremendous news transformed our family. I felt that the last thread connecting me to all the horrors of the past was finally severed. Where my life had slowly ebbed toward extinction, there was now renewal; a new life had come into being; a new heart had begun to beat! On hearing this wonderful news, my mother shed ten years.

* * *

My proposal to form a group of Prisoners of Zion met with enthusiastic support. Several of my fellow ex-prisoners—Vladimir Kislik, Boris Chernobylsky, Vladimir Slepak, Victor Brailovsky, Lev Elbert, Alexander Yakir, Roald Zelichenok, and Vladimir Livshits—joined me. Soon afterwards, our group received an additional boost when we were joined by Joseph Begun, a prominent Jewish activist. Released from his third term of imprisonment, he became an instant celebrity, his apartment so crowded with correspondents from leading news agencies and TV crews from around the world that he barely had time to accommodate all requests for an interview. Joseph's support lent our group added weight.

A lobbying group of former Prisoners of Zion and Jewish activists. From left to right: Boris Chernobylsky, Alexander Yakir, Vladimir Slepak, Vladimir Kislik, Michael Kholmyansky, Lev Ovsisher, and Victor Brailovsky.

A lobbying group of former Prisoners of Zion. From left to right: Boris Chernobylsky, Ephraim Kholmyansky (holding the red folder), Lev Elbert, Joseph Begun, and Vladimir Slepak (partially seen)

Our group began operations immediately after the Jewish High Holidays in the fall 1986. Our first task was to organize a strong lobbying effort in support of the remaining prisoners: Joseph Berenstein, Yuli Edelstein, Alexey Magarik, and Ari Volvovsky. We set up meetings between their wives and influential foreign visitors to Moscow such as correspondents and diplomats, and also prepared a number of international petitions and protests. Once this campaign was launched, we began another one—in support of Ida Nudel, a Jewish activist deported to Siberia who had been released but was forbidden to move back to Moscow.

Joseph Begun and I organized a series of street protests in Moscow that began to attract foreign media attention. I took on the work of media relations, working especially closely with Dominique Dhombres of the leading French newspaper *Le Monde* and Peter Arnett, CNN's Moscow correspondent. The KGB reacted quickly: each time I headed to a demonstration, their goons would stop me openly outside the metro station and take me into custody for several hours. But the times had changed: now they showed ID, they made no other effort to keep me away from the media, and they did not disconnect my home phone.

* * *

Around the same time, I also started talking to people about establishing a women's group. We decided that the group should be small, no more than fifteen members, mostly wives and mothers of prominent refuseniks. The group began operations under the name *Jewish Women against Refusal*. It had no formal leader; Yelena Dubyansky became the group coordinator, and my sister-in-law, Oksana, also became very active in its work.

The group "Jewish Women against Refusal."
From left to right: top row: Ada Lvovsky, Mara Abramovich, Yelena Dubyansky, Rimma Yakir, Zhenya Lukatsky. Bottom row: Naomi Leibler (a visitor from Australia), Victoria Lifshits, Inna Yoffe-Uspensky, Rosa Yoffe, Yelena Krichevsky, Yulia Lurye, Victoria Khasin

They first reached out to *The 35s,* a UK-based women's group, a highly professional, active, and influential organization led by Rita Eker. They also worked hard to find contacts with highly placed women in parliaments, governments and women's organizations around the world. Their work soon began to bear fruit, winning support among influential international women's organizations seeking new arenas where they could flex their muscle. Our cause— the struggle for the freedom of emigration from the Soviet Union— appealed to many of them because it had justice on its side but also lent itself to measurable results and seemed to offer reasonable chances of success.

From the outset, the group showed a remarkable ability to work together in a collegial manner, making decisions by consensus, all pulling together—an unsinkable force. Although the KGB soon began spreading rumors, trying to discredit the group and sow discord within it, our women proved immune to their efforts.

Dov Kontorer remembers

By the end of 1986, Ze'ev Geyzel and I felt that we were on the KGB's short list. Our names kept coming up during interrogations in various cities, and the KGB's direct threats to us were becoming more and more specific. And yet, at the same time, in winter of 1986-1987, it became clear that the country was undergoing dramatic changes and that our fates were no longer dependent on the KGB's graces but on the progress and extent of perestroika— Mikhail Gorbachev's new policy of openness and liberalization.

* * *

Finally, at the beginning of 1987, I began to focus on our Holocaust awareness efforts. Despite the prominence, indeed the ubiquity of World War II in Soviet discourse, journalism, and art, the regime had worked hard to erase awareness of specifically Jewish martyrdom from the minds of the Soviet people at large and the minds of the country's Jews in particular. Though monuments had been erected at the sites of the worst massacres of Jews, such as Babi Yar, they were styled as generalized memorials to slain Soviet citizens; none of them explicitly stated that the victims were Jewish. And though Jewish soldiers had fought Nazism in significant numbers and with exemplary courage (500,000 fighters; over 140,000 slain in battle), public awareness of Jewish heroism had been expunged even more thoroughly than that of Jewish victimhood.

I decided to challenge the long-standing prohibition against memorial events at the sites of Jewish massacres and stage our first mass rally on Holocaust Remembrance Day on April 27, 1987. This would also be the first mass rally of Gorbachev's newly announced *perestroika*, making it all the more awkward for the authorities to suppress it. And if they did so, we were more than prepared to make headlines in the world media.

But where should we have our rally? *Perestroika* or not, we would never get a permit to hold it within the city limits of Moscow. And even if we did, the authorities would inevitably turn the event into a farce: they would push their own people forward and disrupt our independent speakers. We must find a place outside the city where it will be hard for them to prevent our gathering, even without a permit. Where could we find such a place?

I racked my brains, trying to come up with ideas, when suddenly it occurred to me: we could hold it at a Jewish cemetery just outside Moscow! How could the authorities stop people coming to a cemetery? Nothing more appropriate than honoring the Holocaust Remembrance Day at the cemetery. Better still: let's hold it right outside the cemetery, where it would be even harder for them to disperse it.

Along with several fellow activists, I went to scout out the area—and indeed, we found a large open space near the entrance to the cemetery. We rented megaphones and prepared speeches. We kept our preparations strictly secret until two weeks before the Holocaust Remembrance Day, when we convened a press conference for foreign journalists and announced the rally. The authorities seemed to be taken aback.

When the day came, people flocked to the appointed place in their hundreds. Several dozen policemen and a large group of KGB men in civilian clothes stood nearby, but their presence failed to intimidate us. One by one, people began to speak, blunt and unsparing in their criticism of the authorities. They spoke about the regime's ongoing efforts to rob us of our memory, to silence our pain, to rewrite history, to blot out the heroism of the Jewish soldier.

I also spoke out:

> The lessons of the Holocaust are not about weeping or being crushed by the weight of the terrible loss. They call us to action. We must act in order to prevent another catastrophe—both physical and spiritual; we need to prevent our own cultural and

Holocaust remembrance rally. I'm holding a sheet of paper, next to me is Colonel Ovsisher; below me, wearing a kippah, is Joseph Begun. Other Jewish activists are holding a video camera and a tape recorder, making a record of the meeting (at significant personal risk)

physical assimilation. And in order to accomplish this, we must bring about a mass *aliyah*!

The police and KGB men stood by in impotent rage, listening, unsure of the limits of their power during *perestroika*. And . . . they decided not to intervene.

The rally was a resounding success. At least five or six hundred people had attended. This was the first mass Jewish protest rally in living memory.

After the rally, everyone in the Jewish movement felt a change. The long-internalized sense of powerlessness in the face of the Soviet leviathan gave way to a new sense of strength.

* * *

Happy smiles never left our faces throughout Anya's pregnancy. And finally, it happened: Anya gave birth to a daughter! Her arrival felt to me like a quantum leap to a new reality, a new dimension. It was as though the whole house was filled with new light!

Grigory Kholmyansky with baby Dora

There was an existential immensity to this birth that went beyond the physical event. Our daughter was a new link in the chain of generations of the Jewish people, a new offshoot of the "Jews of Silence" whom everyone believed to be doomed to extinction. Just when all hope seemed lost for us as a group, the process of redemption had begun. And my daughter's arrival was a sign of this redemption!

She would undoubtedly know worries and challenges in her life, but I hoped she would never have to fight for her physical or political freedom. Her generation would be a generation of freedom. To symbolize this hope, we named her Dora.[21]

* * *

Though the terrible events of my arrest, trial, and imprisonment were behind us, we were still *refuseniks*. Several influential Jewish organizations and a prominent British historian, Sir Martin Gilbert,

---

[21] *Dora* sounds similar to the Hebrew words *dor* ("generation") and *dror* ("freedom").

were working tirelessly to secure an emigration permit for our family. Dorrit Hoffer, one of our brave Israeli friends, worked wonders as they contacted powerful international political leaders and influential personalities and urged them to get involved in our case. Our story received broad international recognition. Our family was added to a select list of names prepared by the prominent US Senator Edward Kennedy and mentioned by US Secretary of State George Shultz in a meeting with Soviet Foreign Minister Eduard Shevardnadze. At that meeting, Shevardnadze told Schultz that our "problem" had been "resolved." Senator Kennedy's secretary later told me this, as did the leadership of the National Conference on Soviet Jewry—the largest Jewish lobbying organization in the United States. Nevertheless, we received yet another notice that our application to emigrate had been rejected.

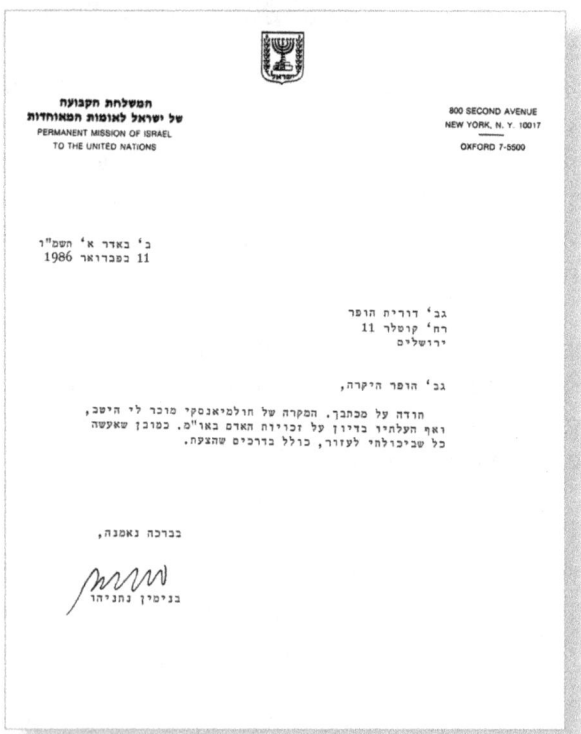

Benjamin Netanyahu's letter to Dorrit Hoffer. Translation: "Dear Ms. Hoffer, thank you for your letter. I am very familiar with Alexander Kholmyansky's case, and I have even brought it up in a discussion on human rights at the UN. Of course I will do everything I can to help, including the steps you suggested. Yours truly, Binyamin Netanyahu, Israeli Ambassador to the UN"

At the end of August, my brother Michael, his wife Oksana, and their son Maxim were finally allowed to leave for Israel, where they immediately added their own efforts in support of our cause.

In light of these events, our family felt that it was time to take action for our own *aliyah*. We applied for a permit to hold a family protest demonstration in front of the Foreign Ministry. Predictably, our request was denied, but we decided to go ahead with our demonstration on September 14, even without a permit, and notified members of the foreign media. A parallel demonstration was scheduled for the same day in Tel Aviv. Among its organizers was my brother, as well as some friends and fellow Soviet Jewish activists who had made *aliyah*, such as Yuli Edelstein and his wife Tanya.

A parallel solidarity demonstration in Tel Aviv. From left to right: S. Schneerman, C. Chesler, M. Kholmyansky, J. Mendelevich, Y. Edelstein, T. Edelstein, A. Landa, an unknown protester

We made our posters out of pillowcases, as other activists had done, cutting openings in them for our heads and arms so they would be easy to put on but hard for the KGB to take away. Anya spent the evening before the demonstration writing out the words "Minister Shevardnadze, keep your word!" on the pillowcases in big bold letters.

Finally, there we were, in front of the Soviet Ministry of Foreign Affairs, a massive building that exuded unshakable imperial power. The plaza in front of the building, usually empty, was now crowded with dozens of people who were milling around, clearly waiting for us. We lined up in front of the building: myself, my parents, and Anya with the stroller slightly off to the side. I pulled my own pillowcase on over my head and began helping Mom and Papa with theirs.

Immediately, a police officer and ten KGB men in civilian clothes pounced on us. The KGB men surrounded us on all sides, tearing at the pillowcases, yelling insults, and waving their hands in our faces. They began to push Papa and me, lightly at first but then more and more roughly. I had steeled myself not to respond, holding myself ready for any provocation.

Soviet Ministry of Foreign Affairs

The police officer stepped forward:

"You are breaking the law! This is an illegal demonstration!"

"Why, are you afraid of a couple of posters? Afraid to hear a word of truth?"

"You're going to answer for this. You're blocking the flow of pedestrian traffic!"

"What pedestrian traffic? We're off the sidewalk, there's no traffic here!"

At this moment, one of the KGB agents pushed my mother. My father, still remarkably strong at seventy-eight, shoved him aside. The police officer turned on him:

"This is hooliganism! You're under arrest! Follow me!"

My father followed the police officer, and the wave of KGB men receded, replaced with two dozen rough-looking women dressed as construction workers. In a carefully choreographed display of spontaneous public outrage the women rushed at us, brandishing brick trowels, as though intending to hit us, but stopped right in front of us, almost close enough to touch, and began yelling insults—shrill, hysterical, and gradually increasing in volume. One particularly large matron led the charge, spitting saliva:

"Traitors! Stay where you were born! Cowards! Our country has fed you and schooled you, and now you want to run off abroad? Ingrates!"

After about an hour of this, we began to turn around to go home. The women piped down immediately, as if an invisible hand had thrown a switch. Quietly they moved about fifty meters off and surrounded one of the KGB men, who checked their names off his list. The spontaneous outrage of the working masses was over.

That evening, international radio stations reported that, in the course of a peaceful demonstration by the Kholmyansky family held to protest the breach of Eduard Shevardnadze's promise to George Shultz, Alexander Kholmyansky's seventy-eight-year-old father had been detained for several hours. We wondered how the KGB let this happen: did they not know how ridiculous this made them look?

The authorities, however, did not give up. Four days after the demonstration, *Izvestiya*, the second-largest Soviet newspaper with a circulation in the tens of millions, printed a hit piece entitled "Who's Unhappy with Our Perestroika?" It mentioned Anya and myself, among others. Back in Stalin's times, such a mention would have been enough for a person to disappear into the cellars of the KGB, but times had changed. These days, it seemed to be merely part of the psychological pressure. Nevertheless, we couldn't help feeling some anxiety.

***

We began planning a memorial ceremony at Babi Yar in Ukraine, the site of a 1941 Nazi massacre of tens of thousands of Jews. Our Prisoners of Zion group published an open letter, where we announced our plans and said that the event was open to the general public. This was a move against the unwritten rule forbidding such events: no public memorial events had ever been permitted at the sites of the massacres, and even individuals who showed up to pay tribute to the victims' memories have been detained for several days. One of the previous attempts to break this rule was undertaken in 1966 on the twenty-fifth anniversary of the tragedy, when an unsanctioned meeting was organized. Dissident writer Victor Nekrasov was one of the people behind the gathering. Russian and Ukrainian dissident writers Vladimir Voinovich and Ivan Dziuba came to Babi Yar and gave speeches at the meeting. Needless to say, this initiative of the local liberal intelligentsia was severely punished. But now that times had changed, we decided to put an end to this appalling state of affairs.

On September 28, 1987, the day before the anniversary of the massacre, sixteen of us took the train from Moscow to Kiev. The train was packed with KGB men, who did everything they could to harass us. They ran past us back and forth with a menacing air, snapped endless pictures of us while talking in sinister whispers with the train attendants, came up close to stare intently into our eyes . . . We all felt the intimidation but none of us gave in.

In Kiev, we were joined by about thirty local Jews, mostly elderly people. As we walked toward the Babi Yar monument, we could already see a group of KGB men awaiting us and a busload of police. As we got closer, the KGB men surrounded us, keeping us away from any casual visitors to the memorial. In this way, inside the ring of KGB men, we climbed to the top of the hill and reached the monument.

And finally, we were there: for the first time in many years, Jewish activists were back at the Babi Yar Memorial. Our women laid wreaths at the monument, including one that said: "To the Generation of Suffering from the Generation of Hope." We wore white mourning armbands. The candles were lit, and we observed

At Babi Yar. I'm at the center with a sheet of paper; Mom is next to me, Alexey Lorentson is holding a candle. A KGB man biting his lip can be seen in the background

a moment of silence. The *Kaddish* (the Jewish mourning prayer) was recited. Now it was time to say a few words.

I said:

> On Passover, every Jew has a spiritual duty to think of the Exodus as though he had lived through it personally. I think we have a similar duty toward the tragedy of Babi Yar. We all were murdered here! And yet, to this day, the inscription on the monument doesn't say that most of the victims were Jews. The Government's efforts to erase the specifically Jewish nature of this tragedy are not an accident: this is a deliberate and deeply inhuman policy. Everyone who helps hide a crime, and especially mass murder, becomes an accomplice of the murderers! In 1941 we were murdered here, and now we are being denied the right to remember, to commemorate; they are trying to steal even our pain from us!

Alexey Lorenzon said:

> I came to Kiev six years ago to commemorate the fortieth anniversary of the Babi Yar massacre. I managed to take no more than a few steps down the platform before I was arrested

At Babiy Yar. With the local residents

for "hooliganism." I got fifteen days of administrative arrest. While in custody, I met two other young men who, like me, had travelled to Kiev from Leningrad to get to Babi Yar. After my release, an official put me on the train heading back and told me: "Tell your friends not to come to Kiev with wreaths again!" I asked him: "Why not?"—but I got no answer."

An old woman wearing glasses, who held a child by the hand, spoke out:

I've been coming here every year for many years. At first there was no monument here, just a stone that people gathered around. Then it became illegal to gather here at all. I remember boys who came here from Kharkov, from Novosibirsk, from other places... and the police harassed them, pushed them, grabbed the candles out of their hands, and then arrested them. I saw some of those boys again in the synagogue on Yom Kippur. They told us how they'd been kept at the police station and abused until three o'clock in the morning! ... What a blessing that you're here, that I've found you here ... Are you going to start coming here from now on?"

A young man introduced himself as A.E. Schvets, saying:

I'm also Jewish but I don't understand why you keep stressing that the victims were Jews. That's not the point, is it? Weren't they killed because they were Soviet citizens, not because they were Jews? It's inappropriate to hold demonstrations here: a minute of silence would be more respectful!

Another old woman replied: "How can you say that? It's not true! The Nazis gave their order specifically to Jews to leave their homes and gather here, and then they killed them!"

Dov Kontorer said:

We're told that it doesn't matter that the victims of this massacre were Jews. But it does. It mattered to the murderers, and it matters to those who have been trying to hide the victims' identity for the past forty years. If millions of defenseless and innocent human beings can be brutally killed just for being Jewish, that shows us that being Jewish is not something incidental or insignificant. If that is something that is so hateful to our enemies, it should be all the more precious to us!

A tall, balding, middle-aged man interjected: "I am also a Jew. And I'll tell you this: what you're doing here is a mockery of their memory! This is place for weeping, not for public meetings!"

Two women, with tears in their eyes, said: "Oh, what a pity we missed the beginning! Where are you from? Moscow? Thank you ever so much for coming. We're so glad we found you. What time should we come next year?"

*　*　*

On October 18, Anya started her own hunger strike, which lasted for twenty-four days. The authorities responded on December 6 with another hit piece in the *Trud* newspaper targeting us, entitled "Let's Be Honest." It looked as though nothing had changed.

But a few days later, something started happening behind the wall between our apartment and that of our neighbor-snitch Valery. We heard sounds of scraping and noticed a smell of fresh paint. We assumed the neighbors were renovating their home and prepared ourselves for weeks of breathing in paint fumes. However, the work on Valery's side ended in a matter of hours—and then work began in

> EDWARD M. KENNEDY
> MASSACHUSETTS
>
> *[handwritten: Copy to: Yuri Shtern — Here is a copy of a letter we sent to Michael Kholmiansky in response to the letter on the info you sent us. Best wishes, ...]*
>
> **United States Senate**
> WASHINGTON, DC 20510
>
> October 26, 1987
>
> Mr. Michael Kholmiansky
> 1 Ben-Dor, Ent. 3
> Jerusalem, ISRAEL
>
> Dear Mr. Kholmiansky:
>
> Thank you for your letter concerning your brother Alexander.
>
> First, let me take this opportunity to express to you my warmest personal congratulations on your recent emigration to Israel. While your struggle has been long and difficult, let us hope it has brought freedom closer to the countless others who remain behind, especially Alexander.
>
> As you may know, I had been working on your case and that of your brother. You may be assured that I will continue to work diligently on you brother's behalf until he too is allowed to leave the Soviet Union. I believe that it is my responsibility to press the human rights issue forcefully, and I will continue my efforts until all those who wish to emigrate are allowed to do so.
>
> My thanks again for your letter and please continue to keep me informed of any new developments in your brother's case.
>
> Sincerely,
>
> Edward M. Kennedy

A letter from US Senator Edward Kennedy to Mikhail Kholmyansky,
October 26, 1987

adjacent apartments all around us. There was noise everywhere, the sounds of drilling and scraping. There was even someone working above our ceiling...

And suddenly it dawned on me: My God, they're dismantling the eavesdropping equipment!

My mother had told me that after I was arrested, a Danish expert in surveillance equipment paid them a visit. A brilliant engineer, he had managed to smuggle his special detection device into the Soviet Union in pieces, put it back together in his hotel room and was amused to find a plethora of bugs in his room. He began to visit the homes of *refuseniks* with his device, discovering numerous bugs in homes of the more prominent activists. After a thorough investigation of our apartment, he told my mother: "The KGB took you very seriously. If you were to get all the money they've spent on the eavesdropping equipment installed here, you would have enough to live on for the rest of your days!"

But now they were taking it all down. There was probably an officer who was personally financially responsible for each and every "bug," so they must be thorough.

"We're about to get our emigration permit!" I told my household confidently.

Indeed, three days later we got a phone call from the visa office. "Why aren't you coming in to pick up your emigration permit?" said a truculent voice.

Our decade-long struggle was over.

Dov Kontorer remembers

Geyzel and I made aliyah almost at the same time, in the spring of 1988. After I got my permit, I delayed my departure for three weeks so I could hand over the Cities Project to Benny Lidsky and Michael Volkov.

It seemed to me that despite the euphoria and feeling of freedom that had gripped the country, the project should remain secret. That way, if and when perestroika was over and persecution resumed, we would have an effective framework that had proven itself. But things continued to open up, and in the summer of 1988 the summer camps were held openly for the first time. The project had emerged from the underground!

* * *

January 25, 1988. We arrived at Moscow's Sheremetyevo airport. How many years had I dreamed of this moment! How often had I come here seeing others off on their way to freedom, how many goodbyes had I said! Was it my turn now—could it be...?

Would they let us aboard?
Would they let the plane take off?
Yes!

Arrival at Ben-Gurion Airport, January 28, 1988 (2 a.m.)

On January 28, 1988, after a short layover in Bucharest, we landed at Israel's Ben Gurion Airport at 2 a.m. A representative of the Israeli Liaison Bureau ran up on board as soon as the doors opened, calling out our names. We were the first to leave the aircraft. Dan Meridor, Member of the Knesset who had monitored our case, stepped out of a car waiting right by the gangplank and embraced us. His car brought us to the terminal entrance, where we saw "Welcome to Israel" written in many languages over the door. Despite the late hour, the arrivals hall was packed with well-wishers who had come to welcome us. We saw Rabbi Haim Druckman, Liaison Office Director Yakov Kedmi, Yuri Shtern, Dorrit Hoffer, Rivka and Yoav Barzilai, Ari Landa, Sarah Hammel, Aryeh and Ora Rutenberg, Misha and Oksana, my friends from the Cities Project, and many, many others.

With Dora in my arms, surrounded by jubilant friends, I started dancing. Tears filled my eyes. After all the stress and despair, pain and suffering—what a reward, what heavenly joy!

Chapter 10

The next day I appeared on the Israeli prime-time evening news to be interviewed by an attractive TV anchor, mildly impressed that a man who had made *aliyah* only yesterday was speaking to her in fluent Hebrew.

"Finally, thank God, you've arrived in the country you dreamed of for so many years, for which you struggled so valiantly and suffered so much. Are you a little afraid of disappointment? Do you feel any apprehension that your dream might not survive an encounter with real life?"

"You've raised a very important issue. I realize that real life can't be like a dream. On the other hand, who can live without dreams? Once a dream has come true, what then? I think that our dreams are like an image of perfection, like our guiding star: we must hold it deep in a secret place within our hearts, to preserve it from erosion by day-to-day worries."

We went to visit Kibbutz Rosh Tzurim, to show our gratitude to this tiny community that had adopted me on the initiative of Rivka Barzilai, Ari Landa, and Shmulik Drory. This small kibbutz had dared to undertake a tremendous campaign of support: hunger strikes, solidarity vigils, media campaigns, lobbying in the Knesset. These few kibbutzniks managed to rally half the country to our cause . . .

A triumphal ride

A victory banquet. The sign displays a quote from the book of Isaiah: "And the redeemed of the Lord shall return, and they shall come singing to Zion"

* * *

And now, of course, on to the *Kotel*—the Western Wall in Jerusalem, the Jewish people's holiest place on earth. With awe and trepidation I approach the Wall. This is it: the culmination, the moment I've dreamed of for so many years, that I imagined so many times! I draw closer and closer . . . A powerful pillar of energy, unique in its beauty, descends upon me from above.

I extend my arms forward, almost touching the wall. Another step, and my cheek presses into its rough surface. Only a little while ago, this cheek had pressed into the rough wall of a punishment cell . . . I stand there for a long time, rubbing my cheek against the wall as if it is the face of a long-lost beloved and I can't tear myself away . . .

Master of the Universe! How much these heavy stones have seen! They have witnessed a sea of suffering, false hopes, and unfulfilled dreams. How many of our people's greatest sons through the centuries had yearned in vain to stand here. But our generation has been granted this blessing! And I myself have been granted a true miracle—nay, not one but a whole chain of them: the miracle of salvation, the miracle of fulfillment, the miracle of victory! Will I be able to tell others about it? It all seems so intimate, delicate, and vulnerable...

I press gently against the wall. A hot wave of gratitude washes over me. A torrent of energy penetrates into every chamber of my soul. I hear unearthly music. And then, as if from the innermost depths of my soul, I feel a song well up in response. At first it is soft, almost inaudible, a barely perceptible tune that grows louder and louder until I can hear it quite clearly... What can it be? This must be the voice of my soul; it has finally broken free and now merges into the eternal song of the Western Wall. This place has awaited me and missed me from the beginning of time, because the music was not complete without my part!

This marks the end of yet another of the many lives that have fallen to my lot. And at this moment, a new life takes root—an entirely different one, with its own rules, sorrows and joys. A new melody has come into being. I know this tune won't be simple; there will be times when I gasp and falter; but I'll try to sing it to the end without a single false note.

At the Kotel

List of figures

Introduction
Map of the Pale of Settlement. Source: Wikimedia   13
   Commons (author: Claude Zygiel)

Chapter 1
With parents and older brother   20

Chapter 2
Map of the USSR in the 1980s. Source: Wikimedia   46
   Commons (public domain image)
Yuli Kosharovsky with wife and son   47
Yuli Edelstein   49
Misha Kholmyansky with wife Oksana and son Maxim   49
Edda (Yehudit) Nepomnyashchy   55
Ari Volvovsky   57
Jewish song festival in Ovrazhki   58

Chapter 3
Rivka Barzilai   63
Reuven Ben-Shalom   65
Golda Akhiyezer   65
Joseph Berenstein   69
Clara Schwartzman   69
Felix Kushnir   74
Dorrit Hoffer   79

Chapter 4
Map of the Crimea. Source: Wikimedia Commons   91
   (public domain image)
Ze'ev Geyzel   102
Dov Kontorer   107

Certificate of Hebrew proficiency issued to Alexander Kholmyansky by the Oxford Centre for Post-Graduate Hebrew Studies, May 17, 1984	109
A rare moment of happiness (from left to right): my Mom, I, Shannie Goldstein (New Orleans), Papa	117
Valentin (Benny) Lidsky	119

Chapter 5

Map of Estonia. Source: Wikimedia Commons (public domain image)	121
Tallinn prison building	129
The worn-out stairs inside Tallinn prison	129
Inside a large prison cell	129
The prison courtyard	131
The concrete box where prisoners took their walks	132
An inside view of a cell, seen through an opening in the door	133
"Moscow Hebrew Teacher Faces Camp Sentence," by Judy Siegel, *Jerusalem Post* (date unknown)	137

Chapter 6

Prison cot in the locked (upright) position	146
Metal pin holding the cot in a locked position (seen from the outside)	146
"Jews in the USSR," newsletter by the UK National Council for Soviet Jewry, September 13, 1984	147
"Hebrew Teacher Force-Fed in Soviet Jail," *Jerusalem Post*, October 15, 1984	157

Chapter 7

Rally in New York in support of Soviet Jewry	181
A spoof of Lenin's mausoleum (tomb) that was staged in New York by the Coalition to Free Soviet Jews. The Russian word across the lintel, where Lenin's name should be, is "Freedom." The message: this is where freedom lies buried	181

The photo was taken at a Solidarity Day rally in Dag Hammerskjold Plaza at the UN. My picture is in the lower right corner of the font group.	183
"English Bishop Supports Imprisoned Soviet Jew," by Judy Siegel, Jerusalem Post, July 12, 1984	183
"Prisoner of Zion Steps Up 4-Month Hunger Strike," by Judy Siegel, *Jerusalem Post*, the week of January 13, 1985 (exact date unknown)	187
Letter to the Israeli government from a group of former Prisoners of Zion	190
Press release of the Council of Europe, January 30, 1985	191

Chapter 8

"Kholmyansky Sentenced, Sharansky Ill," *Washington Jewish Week*, February 14, 1985	202
"Crime and Punishment," by Anthony Lewis, *New York Times*, February 14, 1985 (excerpt)	206
Birthday cake baked by residents of Kibbutz Rosh Tzurim (Israel) in honor of my birthday on June 5, 1985. The cake is shaped like a Hebrew-Russian dictionary and reads in Hebrew and Russian: "Next Year in Jerusalem." The picture on the wall is captioned: "Prisoner of Zion in the USSR"	227

Chapter 9

Letter to Mikhail Gorbachev from a group of US Congressmen and UK Members of Parliament, January 25, 1986	243
Back from imprisonment—the family reunion at the Moscow railway station February 2, 1986. My mother is on my right, Anya is on my left, Oksana is next to her	248
My brother Misha (left) and myself, my face still swollen	248

Chapter 10

Finally . . . our hopes had come to pass! Ephraim and Anna Kholmyansky's wedding ceremony	253
A lobbying group of former Prisoners of Zion and Jewish activists. From left to right: Boris Chernobylsky, Alexander Yakir, Vladimir Slepak, Vladimir Kislik, Michael Kholmyansky, Lev Ovsisher, and Victor Brailovsky	255
A lobbying group of former Prisoners of Zion. From left to right: Boris Chernobylsky, Ephraim Kholmyansky (holding the red folder), Lev Elbert, Joseph Begun, and Vladimir Slepak (partially seen)	256
The group "Jewish Women against Refusal." From left to right: top row: Ada Lvovsky, Mara Abramovich, Yelena Dubyansky, Rimma Yakir, Zhenya Lukatsky. Bottom row: Naomi Leibler (a visitor from Australia), Victoria Lifshits, Inna Yoffe-Uspensky, Rosa Yoffe, Yelena Krichevsky, Yulia Lurye, Victoria Khasin	257
Holocaust remembrance rally. I'm holding a sheet of paper, next to me is Colonel Ovsisher; below me, wearing a kippah, is Joseph Begun. Other Jewish activists are holding a video camera and a tape recorder, making a record of the meeting (at significant personal risk)	260
Grigory Kholmyansky with baby Dora	261
Benjamin Netanyahu's letter to Dorrit Hoffer. Translation: "Dear Ms. Hoffer, thank you for your letter. I am very familiar with Alexander Kholmyansky's case, and I have even brought it up in a discussion on human rights at the UN. Of course I will do everything I can to help, including the steps you suggested. Yours truly, Binyamin Netanyahu, Israeli Ambassador to the UN"	262
A parallel solidarity demonstration in Tel Aviv. From left to right: S. Schneerman, C. Chesler, M. Kholmyansky, J. Mendelevich, Y. Edelstein, T. Edelstein, A. Landa, an unknown protester	263
Soviet Ministry of Foreign Affairs	264

At Babi Yar. I'm at the center with a sheet of paper; Mom is next to me, Alexey Lorentson is holding a candle. A KGB man biting his lip can be seen in the background	267
At Babiy Yar. With the local residents	268
A letter from US Senator Edward Kennedy to Mikhail Kholmyansky, October 26, 1987	270
Arrival at Ben-Gurion Airport, January 28, 1988 (2 a.m.)	272
A triumphal ride	273
A victory banquet. The sign displays a quote from the book of Isaiah: "And the redeemed of the Lord shall return, and they shall come singing to Zion"	274
At the Kotel	275

Index

A
Abayev, Rashi, 99-100
Afghanistan, 48-49, 62
Ähijärve, 122
Akhiyezer, Golda, 64-65, 70, 74-75, 91-92, 95, 97, 99
Albrekht, Vladimir, 53, 113
Aleichem, Sholom, 17
aliyah, 22, 24, 27-28, 31, 41, 43, 45, 69, 73, 79-81, 107, 116-18, 140, 182, 197, 260, 263, 271, 273
Alupka, Crimea, 91, 96, 99
America, 23-24, 27, 29, 43-44, 190, 211. See also United States
Andropov, Yuri, 101, 144
Arnett, Peter, 256

B
Babi Yar, 258, 266-68
Baku, Azerbaijan, 66, 100
Baltic states, 14n3, 27, 68
Barzilai, Rivka, 63, 272-73
Bayevsky, Alexander, 68, 196
Begun, Joseph, 102, 120, 255-56, 260
Belarus (Belorussia), 14n3, 48, 68
Belenky, Yakov, 107
Bellman, Jim, 43, 50-52
Ben-Shalom, Reuven, 64-65, 82-84, 103
Ben-Yehuda, Eliezer, 31
Berenstein, Chaya, 92, 123
Berenstein, Joseph, 69, 101, 171, 216, 256
Bessarabia, 14n3
Black Sea, 68, 91
Brailovsky, Victor, 255

Brezhnev, Leonid, 101
Britain, 15
Bukharan Jews, 54

C
Caucasus, 48, 99
Central Asia, 48, 79, 216
Chernenko, Konstantin, 101
Chernobylsky, Boris, 59, 255-56
Civil War, 12-13
Communist Party, 16, 72, 101, 144, 156, 163, 170, 192, 210
Communist revolution of 1917, 175

D
Danovich, Grigory, 83, 119
Dashevsky, Ze'ev, 107
dibbur, 39-40, 43, 46, 48-49, 102
Dhombres, Dominique, 256
Druckman, Haim, Rabbi, 272
Dubrovsky, Boris, 99
Dubyansky, Yelena, 257
Dushanbe, Tajikistan, 54
Dziuba, Ivan, 266

E
Edelstein, Yuli, 48-49, 66-68, 72, 78, 102, 171, 196, 216, 232, 256, 263
Egypt, 25, 178
Eker, Rita, 257
Elbert, Lev, 69, 255-56
Essas, Ilya, 107
Estonia, 14n3, 121, 123, 156, 169, 179

F
Farber, Michael, 100
February Revolution, 12
Feuchtwanger, Leon, 17
France, 23, 25, 40, 197n18, 234
Franco, General, 27
Fulmakht, Victor, 83, 232
Futoriansky, Esther, 92

G
Gaza, 25
Geyzel, Ze'ev, 102-3, 108, 111, 119, 216, 250, 258, 271
Georgia, 27, 49, 68, 75, 99
Gilbert, Martin, 261
Gisser, Shay, 55, 60, 103
Goldstein, Shannie, 117
Gorbachev, Mikhail, 18, 211, 243, 258-59
Gorodetsky, Lev, 102
Green, Polina, 92
Gurevich, Eugene, 68, 85

H
Hammel, Sarah, 272
Hebrew language, 12, 14, 43, 62-64, 110
Hitler, 14, 98, 231
Hoffer, Dorrit, 79, 262, 272

I
Iron Curtain, 17, 23-24, 79

J
Jerusalem, 25, 220, 274

K
Kaminka, Emanuel, 17

Kara-Ivanov, Michael, 107
Kedmi, Yakov, 272
Kemerovo, 92
Kennedy, Edward, 262
Kharkov, 48, 66-68, 268
Khasin, Gennady, 53, 60
Khasin, Natasha, 53, 60, 92, 112-13
Khasin, Victoria, 257
Kholmyansky, Misha, 20, 22, 28, 48-49, 66-68, 72, 84, 103-4, 112, 114, 116, 134, 151, 158, 160, 162, 165, 170, 173, 180, 190, 195, 197, 201, 203, 232, 240-41, 248-49, 255, 263, 270, 272
Khrushchev, Nikita, 16, 32, 62
kibbutz, 22n5, 63-64, 182, 227, 273
Kiev, 66, 69, 92, 101, 103, 216, 266-67
Kipling, Rudyard, 175
Kishinev, 69-70, 92, 160, 165
Kogan, Alex, 92, 98, 160
Koktebel, Crimea, 56, 61, 64, 71
Kontorer, Dov, 107, 116, 118, 216, 250, 258, 269, 271
Kosharovsky, Yuli, 39, 46-48, 56, 61, 68, 73-74, 102
Kuibyshev, 103
Kushnir, Felix, 73-74, 85, 91, 93-99, 116

L
Landa, Ari, 263, 272-73
Latin America, 23
Latvia, 14n3
Leningrad, 29, 45-48, 63, 66, 99, 212, 268
Levitsky, Grisha, 119
Lidsky, Valentin (Benny), 119, 218, 271
Lifshitz, Nechama, 17
Lithuania, 14n3
Livshits, Vladimir, 255
Lorenzon, Alexey, 267

M

Magarik, Alexey, 256
Meir, Golda, 15
Mesh, Yan, 60, 92
Mikhoels, Solomon, 16
Minsk, 48, 68
Mirovich, Igor, 119
Moldova, 27, 48, 69-70, 73, 91-92

N

Natura, Frieda, 103
Nekrasov, Victor, 266
Nepomnyashchy, Chana, 103
Nepomnyashchy, Edda (Yehudit), 55, 60
Nepomnyashchy, Mark, 114
New York, 38, 51, 181
Novosibirsk, 66, 92, 268
Noudler, Michael, 57
Nudel, Ida, 256

O

Odessa, 48, 55-56, 59-61, 65, 72, 92, 103, 114-16
Ovrazhki, 56-59, 66

P

Palchan, Moshe, 31
Pale of Settlement, 12-13
Palestine, 12, 31
Paritsky, Alexander, 67
pogroms, 12, 31
Poland, 14n3
Polonsky, Pinchas, 107
Prestin, Vladimir, 41, 62
purimspiels, 34, 39, 66-67, 83, 102

R

Rabinovich, Bella, 62, 72, 90, 99

Red Army, 15
refusenik, 40-41, 44, 56, 60, 78-79, 83, 105-6, 112, 141, 257, 261, 271
Reuven, 64-65, 82-84, 103. *See also* Reuven Ben-Shalom
Rosenhaus, Nehemiah, 55, 62
Russian empire, 12-13
Bolshevik Revolution (1917), 12, 163. *See also* Communist revolution of 1917.
Rutenberg, Aryeh, 272
Rutenberg, Ora, 272

S

Samarkand, Uzbekistan, 54
samizdat, 16, 42-43, 47, 53, 62-63, 66, 75, 83
Schwartzman, Anatoly, 57
Schwartzman, Clara, 69-70, 92, 165
Shakhnovsky, Ze'ev, 31, 33, 70
Sharansky, Anatoly, 41, 52, 60, 202
Shevardnadze, Eduard, 262-63, 265
Shmulik, 92, 95, 98
Shtern, Yuri, 272
Shultz, George, 185, 262, 265
Silberstein, Michael, 100
Six-Day War, 17, 24, 26, 33
Slepak, Vladimir, 255-56
Soviet Jewry, 17, 25, 41, 45, 117, 147, 181, 197, 254, 262
Soviet Jews, 12, 15, 17-18, 25, 27, 34, 44-45, 48, 65, 79, 117, 178, 181, 206, 211, 249
Soviet Union, 12, 14-15, 23, 27, 31-32, 34, 44-45, 48, 50, 55-56, 105, 108, 116, 185, 211-12, 244, 257, 270. *See also* USSR
Stalin, 14-17, 32, 101, 228, 265
Stratiyevsky, Valery, 92
Sukhumi, Georgia, 68, 70-71, 91

Sverdlovsk, 66, 212-13, 215, 249
Syria, 25

T
Tallinn, 128-29, 151, 161, 163, 168, 170, 184, 196, 203, 212-13
Tashkent, Uzbekistan, 55, 62
Tukachinsky, Lev, 194, 197, 202

U
Ufa, 62, 90
Ukraine, 12, 14n3, 27, 31, 48, 55, 66, 70, 92, 103, 106, 111, 266
Ulanovsky, Lev, 29, 33, 39, 68,
United States, 18, 41, 44, 48-49, 52, 117, 195, 213, 262. *See also* America.
USSR, 14, 17-18, 27, 31-33, 36, 41, 45-46, 48, 54, 75, 78-80, 106, 110, 118, 131, 147, 151-52, 163, 170, 178, 183, 187, 190, 192, 195, 200, 211, 216, 227. *See also* Soviet Union

V
Voinovich, Vladimir, 266
Volkov, Michael, 119, 218, 271
Volvovsky, Ari, 57, 256
Võru, 121, 123-24, 128, 132, 135-36, 193, 197, 206

W
Wiesel, Elie, 17, 178
World War II, 15, 32, 123, 139, 258

Y
Yakir, Alexander, 255
Yalta, 95-98
Yantovsky, Simon, 107
Yerukhimovich, Anya, 70, 118, 158, 164-65, 179, 192, 196-97, 202, 224-27, 244, 248-49, 252, 255, 260, 263-265, 269
Yiddish 13-14, 16-17, 32, 34, 43, 99

Z
Zakharin, Max, 119
Zelichenok, Roald, 255
Zionism, 13-14, 24, 31
Zionists, 13, 94

www.ingramcontent.com/pod-product-compliance
Lightning Source LLC
Chambersburg PA
CBHW071111160426
43196CB00013B/2533